ST.VINCENT MAIN
13.15N·61,12 W   39,7

CARRIACOU
12,30N·61,27 W 10,9MI

MUSTIQUE
12.86N·61,18W 25,7M

SEA SIDE INTERNE

BEQ
13.00N·61,21 31

GRENADA
12,05N·61,75 W 48,3MI

MIAMI-1521 MILES
25.77'N,80,20'W

ITALY
41.8   25 4817MI
NEW YORK 2085 MILES
40,71'N,74,00'W

PROSPER
NORTH DAKOTA
3245 MILES·46.903 N·97.021 W

Footprint Handbook

Grenada, St V   nt
& the Gr

D0878735

LIZZIE WILLIAMS

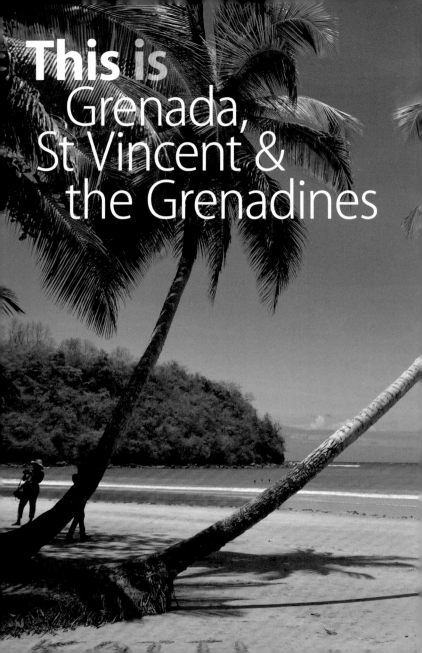

This is
Grenada,
St Vincent &
the Grenadines

Grenada, St Vincent and the Grenadines are part of the Windward group of Caribbean islands, which also include Dominica, St Lucia, Guadeloupe and Martinique, which are *départements* of France. All the islands were at one time colonized by the French and even those which eventually became British still retain French names for many of the towns and villages. French influences can be seen in some old colonial buildings, with gingerbread fretwork and jalousie shutters.

The islands are a series of green volcanic peaks jutting out of the sea and forming a barrier between the Atlantic Ocean and the Caribbean Sea. Sulphur fumaroles and hot springs can be found on the biggest islands where the volcanoes are dormant but not dead, and even under the sea. There are large areas of lush rainforest with national parks protecting places of biodiversity or natural beauty on land or underwater. Hikers and birdwatchers are spoilt for choice on the larger islands. The sea is teeming with fish and other marine life including turtles and manta rays, offering excellent snorkelling and diving.

Yachtsmen are similarly blessed when navigating among the smaller Grenadines, one of the world's most popular sailing destinations, where super yachts and sailboats bob alongside traditional fishing boats in the palm-lined bays. Ringing the shores are outstanding beautiful white-sand beaches. There are peaceful and unpretentious corners of these islands that still bestow a dose of classic Caribbean charm and lifestyle, away from the busy yacht marinas and cruise ship crowds found in the busier ports. After either an action-packed or relaxing day, the rum flows. Sunset cocktails are followed by delicious local dishes featuring freshly caught seafood and delicious tropical fruits and vegetables, enhanced by home-grown organic cocoa, nutmeg, cinnamon and other spices.

Lizzie Williams

Best of
Grenada, St Vincent & the Grenadines

top things to do and see

❶ St George's, Grenada

Explore the narrow streets, historic waterfront and imposing fort of Grenada's tiny capital, one of the prettiest port towns in the Caribbean. With a vibrant esplanade it curves around a horseshoe-shaped harbour backed by volcanic hills. Page 31.

❷ Grand Anse, Grenada

Relax on Grenada's most famous beach, a broad arc of golden sand and calm, clear turquoise shallows fringed by sea grapes and coconut palms. It's perfect for swimming and sunbathing and is lined with many of the island's best resorts and restaurants. Page 39.

❸ Belmont Estate, Grenada

Learn about Grenada's nutmeg and cocoa history on a tour of this 300-year-old plantation. See how these spices are processed, wander through the gardens and museum, and sample some traditional island food in the restaurant. Page 46.

❹ Grand Etang National Park, Grenada

Hike through beautiful scenery and to cascading waterfalls in the mountainous interior of the island. The lush emerald-green landscape features a rich diversity of birds, orchids, and towering rainforest trees. Page 55.

⑥

Richmond ○ *La Soufrière* ▲
ST VINCENT Georgetown ○
  Vermont Nature Trail
Barrouallie ○ ◆ *Montreal Gardens*

Kingstown ○ □
  ⑥ ✝

THE GRENADINES

  ⑦
Port Elizabeth ○ **BEQUIA**

  Isle à Quatre *Baliceaux*
  The Pillories
  Lovell Village ✈ **MUSTIQUE**

  Petit Mustique

  Savan

CANOUAN
  ✈ ○ Charlestown

MAYREAU ⑧
  Tobago Cays *Tobago Basin*
UNION ISLAND ⑨
  Clifton

  ⑤ **PETITE MARTINIQUE**
Paradise Beach ○ Hillsborough ✈
  CARRIACOU

Caribbean Sea

N
⑤

10 km
10 miles

⑤

Sauteurs ○
  ③ □ **Belmont Estate**
Gouyave ○ ▲ *Mt St Catherine*
GRENADA ④
  Grand Etang National Park ○ Grenville

St George's ○ ① □
Grand Anse ○ ②
  ✈

⑦

❺ Paradise Beach, Carriacou

Kick back on this stunning beach that lives up to its name with soft sands, cobalt water and rustic beach bars, while offshore idyllic Sandy Island offers a Robinson Crusoe experience and excellent snorkelling. Page 60.

❻ Ferry-hopping from Kingstown, St Vincent

Jump aboard and travel as Vincentians do on the numerous ferries that make their way southwards through the Grenadines; the views are tremendous and each enchanting island has a unique and infectious character. Page 89.

❼ Belmont Walkway, Bequia

Stroll along this charming waterside walkway to enjoy the restaurants and cafés while admiring the yachts and fishing boats bobbing about in the bay. Then follow it over the headland to the gorgeous and near-deserted Princess Margaret Beach. Page 114.

❽ Tobago Cays

Bask on the sun-bleached beaches and snorkel or dive in the brilliantly blue waters of this beautiful cluster of tiny islets and coral reefs. Make time for a full day by exploring on a traditional schooner, smart yacht or simple water taxi. Page 122.

❾ Clifton, Union Island

Enjoy this informal and jaunty yachting centre and springboard for sailing trips. It has good restaurants and bars, as well as an exceptionally friendly village atmosphere and an animated ferry and fishing harbour. Page 125.

Carriacou Island

Route
planner

In many ways, this region is hard to beat for a Caribbean holiday. How you explore depends on where you arrive and whether you want a one-island holiday or a broader experience of this region that lies in two dependencies; Grenada, and Carriacou and Petit Martinique, and St Vincent and the Grenadines. Grenada is good for staying in one hotel or resort, relaxing on the beach and going on interesting day trips, but is still far less developed for tourism than many other Caribbean islands such as Barbados or Jamaica. St Vincent has less appeal for a long holiday due to its small tourism industry. It's also overshadowed by the more attractive Grenadines to the south. Nevertheless it's a good place to start if you are going to the islands by air or ferry, and has enough attractions for a short stay, including coastal scenery, hiking and a more local flavour. How to approach the Grenadines largely depends on budget; these enchanting islands are popular with the super-wealthy arriving by private jet or small charter flights, but can also be explored by yacht and budget travellers will enjoy the characterful local ferries that meander between the little harbours.

One to two weeks
lazy days, beaches and island tours

Assuming you arrive at Grenada's Maurice Bishop International Airport, the main focus for tourism is on the island's southwest corner, with the best beaches – most notably Grand Anse – as well as hotels, restaurants and bars. With an easy-going atmosphere, it is an ideal place to relax for a few days. Few journeys to nearby attractions take more than 15 minutes, which include Grenada's elegant little capital, St George's, a strong contender for the prettiest harbour in the region. It is well worth wandering around the waterfront Carenage and Esplanade before lunch at a waterfront seafood restaurant with views of the pastel-coloured houses trickling down the lush surrounding hills. Other inviting, and often empty, beaches lie along the indented south coast, and you should also find time to make forays in to the interior to explore the rainforest and waterfalls. A day's island tour up to the slow-paced north usually includes a visit to a nutmeg processing factory, a cocoa plantation and a rum distillery.

With more time, a visit to exceptionally friendly Carriacou is highly recommended, reached from Grenada by a short flight or an enjoyable ferry. At least a couple of days are needed, to experience charming Hillsborough with its cafés, little shops and friendly residents. Paradise Beach lives up to its name and Tyrell Bay is a lively yachting centre. You can go snorkelling and picnicking on one of the offshore sandy islets and party with the locals at the beach bars.

Two weeks or more

black-sand beaches, volcano hiking, and yachts

Arriving on St Vincent opens up access to the Grenadines. A couple of days in the low-key hotels along the island's south coast gives you time to explore vibrant Kingstown, with its markets, street vendors and busy wharfs, or to journey up the windward or leeward coasts to admire their dramatic landscapes of coves with black-sand beaches, rocky headlands and remote traditional fishing villages. Hikers should take a day for the climb of La Soufrière volcano. There are numerous flights and ferries southwards to the islands, or you could travel on a yacht; the journey by sea between these islands is extraordinarily beautiful.

Bequia deserves at least a couple of days and, like Carriacou, has a friendly atmosphere and divine uncrowded beaches unspoilt by mass tourism, but still with excellent restaurants and places to stay. Mustique is the playground of the rich and famous, but is not accessible on a day visit unless you are on a yacht. Similarly, Canouan offers the very wealthy the almost perfect Caribbean retreat, although there is one mid-range option to stay and it can be visited on day trips by sea. Tiny Mayreau with its characterful fishing village has hardly any facilities but can be visited en route to the Tobago Cays, a day trip organized from a number of places.

One of the easiest islands to visit for independent travellers is from Union Island, which has a laid-back charm, is popular with yachties, and has affordable accommodation and a lively atmosphere in its bars and restaurants.

When
to go

Climate

The climate is tropical. Grenada, St Vincent and the Grenadines are volcanic, mountainous and forested islands, attracting more rain than some other, more low-lying islands in the Caribbean. The driest and least humid time of year is usually December-April, coinciding with the winter peak in tourism as tourists escape to the sun from cooler climates in the north and in Europe. During this time temperatures are tempered by cooling trade winds and the climate is very pleasant without being unbearably hot. At other times of the year the greater humidity can make it feel hotter if you are away from the coast.

Although there are sporadic short showers throughout the year, the main rainy season runs from June to November, with hurricane season September and October. However, although Hurricane Ivan devastated Grenada in September 2004, you'd be very unlucky to coincide with an actual hurricane, and even Ivan was an unprecedented and rare occurrence. At this time there is more likely to be tropical storms that can cause flooding and mudslides.

Weather Grenada

January	February	March	April	May	June
28°C	28°C	28°C	29°C	29°C	29°C
23°C	23°C	23°C	24°C	25°C	24°C
117mm	72mm	63mm	62mm	114mm	218mm

July	August	September	October	November	December
29°C	29°C	29°C	29°C	29°C	28°C
24°C	24°C	24°C	24°C	24°C	23°C
223mm	221mm	114mm	217mm	225mm	180mm

See also Festivals in Listings for individual islands and Public holidays, page 156.

Grenada

Late January **Grenada Sailing Festival**, www.grenadasailingfestival.com, is held over four days, based at Port Louis Marina, with international yacht racing around to Prickly Bay Marina, followed the next weekend by the Westerhall White Jack Work Boat Regatta from Grand Anse Beach. The latter attracts sailors from communities with a strong fishing or boat-building heritage, such as Grand Mal, Gouyave, Sauteurs, Woburn, Carriacou and Petite Martinique.

Also at the end of January is the **Budget Marine Spice Island Billfish Tournament**, www.sibtgrenada.com, at Grenada Yacht Club, a three-day sport fishing event that attracts anglers from numerous countries.

7 February **Independence Day**. A public holiday, Grenadians celebrate the anniversary of their independence with ceremonies and parades featuring the Royal Grenada Police Force, Boy Scouts, Girl Guides and various schools, and lots of beach parties.

Early April **Grenada International Triathlon**, or **Tri de Spice**, usually the first Sunday of April, www.tridespice.com, hosted at Port Louis Marina, with the bike and road race course along Kirani James Boulevard (named after Grenada's 400-m Olympic champion).

Mid May **Grenada Chocolate Fest**, www.grenadachocolatefest.com, celebrating Grenada's cocoa heritage with a week's programme of events from chocolate-tasting and cooking demos to rum and chocolate cocktails and music, at various venues including the **House of Chocolate** and **Dodgy Dock** at the True Blue Bay Boutique Resort.

Late June The **Fisherman's Birthday** (the feast of saints Peter and Paul) is celebrated throughout the island, but especially at Gouyave. It involves the blessing of nets and boats by the local Roman Catholic priest, followed by dancing, feasting, street parties and boat races.

Mid-August **Spice Mas Festival**, www.spicemasgrenada.com, Grenada's **Carnival**, is held in the second weekend of August (although some preliminary events and competitions are held from the last week in July), with calypsos, steel bands, dancing, competitions, shows and plenty of drinking. The Sunday night celebrations, Dimanche Gras, continue into Mon, J'Ouvert; Djab Djab Molassi, who represent devils, smear themselves and anyone else (especially the smartly dressed) with black grease. On Monday a carnival pageant is held on the stage at Queen's Park and on Tuesday the bands parade through the streets of St George's to the Market Square and a giant party ensues. During Carnival it is difficult to find anywhere to stay and impossible to hire a car unless booked well in advance.

Carriacou

February-May (variable) **Carriacou and Petit Martinique Carnival**, see Facebook. Carriacou celebrates its carnival at the traditional Lenten time on the Monday and Tuesday before Ash Wednesday every year, unlike Grenada. It is not spectacular but it is fun and there is a good atmosphere, with parades, street dances and calypso competitions. An interesting feature is the **Shakespeare Mas**, when participants, or 'pierrots' (*paywos*) dress up and recite from Shakespeare's plays. If they forget their lines or get something wrong, they are thumped by the others with a bull whip, so their costumes require a lot of padding and they wear a special cape which covers the back of the head. It is very competitive and carnival has traditionally been very violent, with battles between villages or between north and south of the island, led by their carnival 'kings'. The police have in the past frequently had to restore peace.

Last weekend of April Maroon and String Band Music Festival, www.carriacoumaroon.com, a three-day revival of traditional customs held in the historic Belair Park, Hillsborough and Paradise Beach. You can see a display of the Big Drum Nation Dance, string band music and quadrille dancing, as well as Shakespeare Mas and more modern entertainment, such as reggae. There are also stalls demonstrating and selling local smoked food, cultural and art exhibitions.

First weekend of August Carriacou Regatta, see Facebook. A four-day event first established in 1965 with races for work boats, yachts, model boats, donkeys and rowing boats, as well as the greasy pole, tug-o-war and cultural shows.

Mid-December Parang Festival, www.carriacouparangfestival.com, runs over three evenings (Friday-Sunday) the weekend before Christmas. It is a musical celebration: local groups perform Christmas carols on Friday at Silver Beach, Hillsborough. Saturday is the most lively night with visiting Calypsonians and performers from Grenada and other islands at Belair Park judged by visiting dignitaries, and Sunday is the competition between the Parang string bands.

Petite Martinique

May Whitsuntide Regatta Festival, see Facebook, has lots of boat races and land-based fun and games such as the greasy pole, tug-of-war and even a crying competition.

St Vincent

June-July St Vincent's Carnival, called **Vincy Mas**, www.carnivalsvg.com, is held in the last week of June and the first week of July for 10 days. Mas is short for masquerade, and the three main elements of the carnival are the costume parade, the steel pan bands and the calypso competitions. During the day there is J'Ouverte, ole mas, children's carnival and steel pan bands through Kingstown's streets. At night Calypsonians perform in 'tents', there is the King and Queen of the bands show and Miss Carnival, a beauty competition with contestants from other Caribbean countries (a talent contest, a beauty contest and local historical dress). Thousands of visitors come to take part, many from Trinidad.

October 27 Independence. A public holiday, with celebrations similar to Grenada with ceremonies and parades and lots of beach parties.

16-24 December Nine Mornings Festival, see Facebook, during which, for nine mornings from 0400, people parade through Kingstown, and there are creole dances, harmonious carolling, and early morning sea baths among other traditions. It has its roots from the Catholic Novena early morning church services leading up to Christmas, when afterwards worshippers walked the streets or went to bathe in the ocean.

Grenadines

January Bequia Mount Gay Music Fest, www.bequiatourism.com/bequiamusicfest, usually at the end of the month, a four-day music festival featuring performers from across the Caribbean in genres ranging from soca and calypso to reggae and jazz. Venues include the hotels and stages set up on the beaches. It coincides with the **Mustique Blues Festival**, also at the end of January at the famous **Basil's Bar** on Mustique, www.basilsbar.com/blues-festival, which is a week of performances from international guest musicians, and moves across to Bequia on one of the nights during the Bequia Mount Gay Music Fest.

April/May (Easter) Bequia Easter Regatta, www.bequiaregatta.com. This four-day event over the Easter weekend has been going for more than 30 years and the centre of activities is Admiralty Bay in front of the hotels along the Belmont Walkway. Lay Day Sunday is for liming (see box, page 25) with barbecues and parties held on the beaches, and also the main event of the regatta which is the round-the-island single-handed race.

April Mayreau Regatta, usually the last weekend or around 1 May, is a four-day event for fishermen in the southern Grenadines including sailing races, a lionfish fishing competition, a traditional cooking competition, maypole dancing, games and kite-flying, and after-parties. The similar **Canouan Regatta** takes place in mid-May.

What to do

Diving and snorkelling

The reefs around Grenada and Carriacou provide excellent diving and snorkelling for all skill levels, from lazy drifts over coral gardens to challenging exploration of wrecks. Between them they have more than 50 sites from shallow near-shore reefs to deep walls off the remoter uninhabited islets, where visibility ranges from 30 to 90 ft. Grenada is well known for its wreck dives and the unique and extraordinary Grenada Underwater Sculpture Park. There are plenty of diving operators at the resorts in Grand Anse and the southwest, while Carriacou has several dive shops. On St Vincent there are dive shops in the southern hotel area, and the reefs are fairly deep, at 55-100 ft, so scuba diving is more rewarding than snorkelling. The currents moving through the channels in the Grenadines provide the best conditions for sighting pelagics, while the stunning islets and sandbars protected by a huge horseshoe-shaped reef in the Tobago Cays offer shallow diving and snorkelling to see corals and colourful schooling reef fish.

Fishing

The Atlantic side of the islands have some of the world's most exciting game fish, including blue and white marlin, sailfish, wahoo and dorado, and deep-sea fishing charters can be organized with a knowledgeable captain and capable crew who know the best fishing grounds. There's also the option of negotiating to go out with a friendly local fisherman in order to catch barracuda, kingfish, groupers, jacks and snappers; the cost of which can be not much more than sharing your catch with the boat crew. There are a number of tournaments which attract international fishermen including Grenada's Spice Island Billfish Tournament, the biggest event of its kind in the southern Caribbean, while at a more local level some of the regattas on the islands include fishing contests and entertaining fishing boat races.

Hiking

Hiking is rewarding on all the islands, whether through the interior mountains of Grenada and St Vincent accompanied by birdsong and forest sounds or in the hills of the Grenadines with gorgeous views out to sea where yachts bob about between the scattered islands. There are guides and organized tours to take you hiking in the rainforest and to waterfalls in and around Grenada's Grand Etang National Park, while on St Vincent a popular trek is to the volcanic summit of La Soufrière. Less strenuous is a short stroll along a magnificent beach lined with coconut palms where you can paddle as you go, or to just walk on any of the pretty coastal roads away from the urban areas and see where you get to (and get public transport back). It's always a good idea to start early to avoid the midday heat and carry plenty of water. A hat and sunscreen are also essential.

Sailing

Sailing is synonymous with the Caribbean and it is one of the best ways to see these islands. The constant trade winds and warm sun is a draw for both experienced and novice sailors. The Caribbean Sea is generally calm, shallow if you stay near the coasts, distances are short between the islands, and there are some beautiful anchorages and moorings in turquoise bays.

If you don't have your own boat, there are a number of options to explore this part of the Caribbean afloat for a week or more. Boats vary from monohulls to catamarans, and from skippered day charters (easily arranged through hotels) to bareboat or crewed charters and learn-to-sail holidays. Where you start and finish depends on where the yacht charter company is based, but could be St Vincent or Grenada, and there's the possibility of a one-way charter between the two.

On Grenada popular day trips go for a sail up the Caribbean coast with snorkelling and a barbecue lunch on a remote beach. In the Grenadines the day excursion by boat to the Tobago Cays with perhaps a stop at Mayreau and one of the smaller islands is simply not to be missed.

There are plentiful options to explore on longer yachting or learn to sail holidays, or you can simply charter a boat from either Grenada or St Vincent with a skipper and crew and head off. The beautiful sheltered bays and pretty coves make a fine alternative to hotels on land. Rates vary enormously depending on the size of the vessel, its facilities, how many people it caters for and how many members of crew there are. But it is sometimes not as pricey as you may imagine; get a group/family together to the maximum size permitted on the boat and work out the cost per head (and compare it to hotel prices). For a day charter in mid-season (roughly May-July) it's US$315-580, and for a week US$2200-4200; less for low season (August-November) and considerably more for high season (December-April). Additional extra costs could be food and tips for the crew and a drop-off fee if you want to disembark somewhere else other than where the yacht is based. If you're a qualified skipper, you can hire one without crew.

The Caribbean is one of the best places in the world to learn to sail and some of the companies also offer tuition on 'Learn and Cruise' packages. Explore the possibilities with the following yacht charter companies:

Barefoot Yacht Charters, Blue Lagoon Marina, St Vincent, T784-456 9526, www.barefootyachts.com.
Blue Water Sailing, T473-420 1696, St George's, Grenada, www.bluewater-sailing.net.

Footloose Yacht Charters, St George's, Grenada, T473-405 9531, www.grenada-sailing-charters.com.

Horizon Yacht Charters, True Blue Bay Marina, Grenada, T473-439 1002; Blue Lagoon Marina, St Vincent, T473-439 1000, www.horizonyachtcharters.com.

Jambalaya Charters, St George's, Grenada, T473-417 0773, www.windwardschooner.com.

Sail Grenadines, Union Island, T784-533 2909, www.sailgrenadines.com.

Sunsail, Port Louis Marina, Grenada, T784-458 4308, www.sunsail.com.

The Moorings, Port Louis Marina, Grenada, T784-482 0655/0653, www.moorings.com.

Watersports

There are numerous options of playing in the gorgeous warm waters of the Caribbean; from wind- and kitesurfing to hobie cat sailing and stand-up paddle boarding. All-inclusive places, top luxury resorts and private islands include watersports in their packages, but there are also plenty of places to rent equipment for an hour or two. In Grenada, the popular beaches in the southwest have watersports centres, and catamaran sailing, and diving and snorkelling up the coast can be arranged.

Sea kayaking is also popular in the bays and coves of southern Grenada and a trip with **Conservation Kayak** in Woburn is a particularly good opportunity to explore the mangroves and shallows full of marine life.

Union Island in the Grenadines has become a top kitesurfing centre thanks to the establishment of the professional **JT Pro Center Kitesurfing School** and a beach so perfect for the sport, it's now called Kite Beach.

Swimming is always better in the Caribbean; some of the rough Atlantic waters can be dangerous because of strong currents and waves.

Improve your travel photography

Taking pictures is a highlight for many travellers, yet too often the results turn out to be disappointing. Steve Davey, author of Footprint's *Travel Photography*, sets out his top rules for coming home with pictures you can be proud of.

Before you go

Don't waste precious travelling time and do your research before you leave. Find out what festivals or events might be happening or which day the weekly market takes place, and search online image sites such as Flickr to see whether places are best shot at the beginning or end of the day, and what vantage points you should consider.

Get up early

The quality of the light will be better in the few hours after sunrise and again before sunset – especially in the tropics when the sun will be harsh and unforgiving in the middle of the day. Sometimes seeing the sunrise is a part of the whole travel experience: sleep in and you will miss more than just photographs.

Stop and think

Don't just click away without any thought. Pause for a few seconds before raising the camera and ask yourself what you are trying to show with your photograph. Think about what things you need to include in the frame to convey this meaning. Be prepared to move around your subject to get the best angle. Knowing the point of your picture is the first step to making sure that the person looking at the picture will know it too.

Compose your picture

Avoid simply dumping your subject in the centre of the frame every time you take a picture. If you compose with it to one side, then your picture can look more balanced. This will also allow you to show a significant background and make the picture more meaningful. A good rule of thumb is to place your subject or any significant detail a third of the way into the frame; facing into the frame not out of it.

This rule also works for landscapes. Compose with the horizon two-thirds of the way up the frame if the foreground is the most interesting part of the picture; one-third of the way up if the sky is more striking.

Don't get hung up with this so-called Rule of Thirds, though. Exaggerate it by pushing your subject out to the edge of the frame if it makes a more interesting picture; or if the sky is dull in a landscape, try cropping with the horizon near the very top of the frame.

Fill the frame

If you are going to focus on a detail or even a person's face in a close-up portrait, then be bold and make sure that you fill the frame. This is often a case of physically getting in close. You can use a telephoto setting on a zoom lens but this can lead to pictures looking quite flat; moving in close is a lot more fun!

Interact with people

If you want to shoot evocative portraits then it is vital to approach people and seek permission in some way, even if it is just by smiling at someone. Spend a little time with them and they are likely to relax and look less stiff and formal. Action portraits where people are doing something, or environmental portraits, where they are set against a significant background, are a good way to achieve relaxed portraits. Interacting is a good way to find out more about people and their lives, creating memories as well as photographs.

Focus carefully

Your camera can focus quicker than you, but it doesn't know which part of the picture you want to be in focus. If your camera is using the centre focus sensor then move the camera so it is over the subject and half press the button, then, holding it down, recompose the picture. This will lock the focus. Take the now correctly focused picture when you are ready.

Another technique for accurate focusing is to move the active sensor over your subject. Some cameras with touch-sensitive screens allow you to do this by simply clicking on the subject.

Leave light in the sky

Most good night photography is actually taken at dusk when there is some light and colour left in the sky; any lit portions of the picture will balance with the sky and any ambient lighting. There is only a very small window when this will happen, so get into position early, be prepared and keep shooting and reviewing the results. You can take pictures after this time, but avoid shots of tall towers in an inky black sky; crop in close on lit areas to fill the frame.

Bring it home safely

Digital images are inherently ephemeral: they can be deleted or corrupted in a heartbeat. The good news though is they can be copied just as easily. Wherever you travel, you should have a backup strategy. Cloud backups are popular, but make sure that you will have access to fast enough Wi-Fi. If you use RAW format, then you will need some sort of physical back-up. If you don't travel with a laptop or tablet, then you can buy a backup drive that will copy directly from memory cards.

Recently updated and available in both digital and print formats, Footprint's Travel Photography by Steve Davey covers everything you need to know about travelling with a camera, including simple post-processing. More information is available at www.footprinttravelguides.com

Where to stay

Places to stay on the islands include large and small hotels, guesthouses, B&Bs and self-catering apartments or cottages. The islands are notable for having a large number of independent, privately owned hotels, with very few international chains represented; the **Rex**, **Radisson** and **Sandals** all-inclusive resorts on Grenada are the exceptions rather than the rule. High season is mid-December to mid-April, July and August, when hotel prices are at their highest. There are often steep discounts in low season, when prices can be 30% lower. September to November is generally regarded as hurricane season (very few yachts are around at this time), and hotel rates can drop as low as 50%, but this is also the worst time for rainy and windy weather and some hotels may take the opportunity to close for refurbishment or a break.

Hotel rooms vary from US$75 for a double/twin in the cheapest guesthouse to US$200-300 in a mid-range resort, to over US$800 per person per night in the top-end luxury retreats. Unless you're staying in all-inclusive resort, or have opted for a full meal package at a hotel, very few places include breakfast in room rates. The cost of breakfast (when available) can be the equivalent of US$5 for a simple local breakfast like saltfish and up to US$20-30 for a full buffet. The best option for budget travellers – especially a group or family – is to book an apartment. Most have at least two double beds and/or pull out sofa beds, and costs can be brought down further by cooking. Eating in local cafeterias, drinking in rum shops and travelling on buses can also save money.

Price codes

Where to stay

$$$$ over US$300

$$$ US$150-300

$$ US$75-150

$ under US$75

Price codes refer to a standard double/twin room in high season.

Restaurants

$$$ over US$30

$$ US$15-30

$ under US$15

Price codes refer to the cost of a two-course meal, excluding drinks or service charge.

Quality of accommodation varies considerably across the budget range and some have been criticized for lack of maintenance and being in need of renovation. The tourist industry on some of these islands dates back to the 1960s, and so do some of the properties so you may find some of the resort-style places stuck in a time warp in terms of furnishings and decor. But there are also good modern and stylish properties, and the Caribbean is well-known as a retreat for the wealthy. Cleanliness and standard of comfort is rarely an issue, and almost all rooms have air conditioning, cable TV and Wi-Fi (even at the budget end).

Tip...
Good resources for hotels are on the websites of the tourist authorities; see Tourist information in Listings throughout this book. Almost all places have websites to book direct, which gives the opportunity to ask questions and get further information from the proprietors/ reservations teams, and the islands are well-represented on accommodation websites like **Expedia**, www.expedia.com, and **Booking.com**, www.booking.com.

Grenada is particularly well served with good hotels and resorts, and most are in the southwest in the Grand Anse area, close to the airport and the best beaches, but still small enough to be comfortable and friendly, catering for individual travellers, package tours and luxury getaways. There is a clutch of delightful places to stay around the island in some pleasant locations. In St George's there are more guesthouses than hotels, mostly catering for the local business market, and the little capital is only a 10-minute drive from Grand Anse. Other options of accommodation on Grenada are renting a room in someone's home or an entire unit; try **Air BnB** ① *www.airbnb.com*, or **Homestays Grenada** ① *www.homestaysgrenada.com*. Alternatively, you can rent a villa or apartment; look at **Spice Isle Villas** ① *www.spiceislevillas.com*, **HomeAway** ① *www.homeaway.co.uk*, and **Villa Caribella Grenada** ① *www.grenadavilla-caribella.com*.

On **Carriacou**, most accommodation is also in small hotels or guesthouses, or you can rent a villa or apartment; try **Down Island Villa Rental** ① *www.islandvillas.com*, and **Simply Carriacou** ① *www.simplycarriacou.com*.

St Vincent and the Grenadines have accommodation from the height of luxury on Mustique and Canouan, or exclusivity on the private islands of Petit St Vincent or Palm Island, to a simple guesthouse on St Vincent or Union Island. St Vincent itself is not known as a holiday destination, although there is a string of small mid-range hotels along the south coast around Villa to the southeast of Kingstown, which are decent and good for accommodation near the airport. But there are better options (and better beaches) for a longer Caribbean escape in the Grenadines. Villa rental is popular, especially on Bequia; the website of the **Bequia Tourism Association** ① *www.bequiatourism.com*, lists private properties. **Grenadine Escape** ⓘ *www.grenadine-escape.com*, **Bequia Net** ⓘ *www.bequia.net*, and **Grenadine Island Villas** ⓘ *www.grenadinevillas.com*, act as agents for property owners. Mustique and Canouan are firmly in the super-expensive luxurious bracket with their glitzy hotels and resorts and palatial villa rentals. Mayreau is so tiny it only has a couple of basic options, but Union Island, like Bequia, is low-key and casual, frequented by the yachting fraternity and has a good choice of accommodation in the mid-range to lower budgets.

Food
& drink

from conch and callaloo to saltfish and oildown stew

Food

As you might expect of islands, there is a wide variety of seafood on offer. Locally caught fish varies according to the season, but you can find flying fish, tuna, bonito, mahi mahi, snapper and kingfish on the menu as well as lambi (conch), lobster, squid and octopus. Smoked herring and salt cod (called saltfish locally) are often eaten with a fried bake (a pan-fried bread), especially for breakfast. Because of the small nature of the islands, they don't support large herds of cattle, so beef is often imported from the USA, as are dairy products. Goat, pork, chicken and some lamb are produced locally.

There is a riot of tropical fruit and vegetables. The best bananas in the world are grown in the Windward Islands on small farms either organically or using minimal chemicals. They are cheap and incredibly sweet. Don't miss the rich flavours of the *soursop* (*chirimoya* or *guanábana*), the guava, tamarind or the *sapodilla* (zapote). Breakfast buffets are usually groaning under the weight of pineapples, melons, oranges, grapefruits and mangoes, of which there are dozens of varieties, as well as papaya/pawpaw, *carambola* (star fruit) and sugar apple (custard apple or sweetsop). Caribbean oranges are often green when ripe, as there is no cold season to bring out the orange colour, and are meant for juicing not peeling. Portugals are like tangerines.

Avocados have been around since the days of the Arawaks, who also cultivated cassava and cocoa, but many vegetables have their origins from the slave trade, when they were introduced to provide a starchy diet for the slaves. The breadfruit, a common staple, rich in carbohydrates and vitamins A, B and C, was brought from the South Seas in 1793 by Captain Bligh, perhaps more famous for the mutiny on the *Bounty*. A large, round fruit, usually eaten fried or boiled, it grows on huge trees with enormous leaves. A popular dish is oildown, a stew of salt meat, breadfruit, onion, carrot, celery, dasheen and dumplings, cooked slowly in coconut milk. Christophene is another local vegetable, which is delicious baked in a cheese sauce. Dasheen is a root vegetable with green leaves, rather like spinach, which are used to make the tasty and nutritious callaloo soup. Plantains are eaten boiled or fried as a savoury vegetable, while green bananas, known as figs, can be cooked.

The term 'provisions' on a menu refers to root or starchy vegetables: dasheen, yams, sweet potatoes, tannia, pumpkins, etc. The style of cooking is known as Creole and is a mixture of influences of the islands' immigrants over the centuries. The movement of people along the chain of Caribbean islands means that you can also find *rotis* (pancake-like parcel of curried chicken and veg) from Trinidad and spicy jerk meats from Jamaica.

Drink

For non-alcoholic drinks, there is a range of refreshing fruit juices. Sorrel is made from sepals of a plant from the hibiscus family, and mauby, slightly bitter and made from the bark of a tree, is also very popular. Other local soft drinks include tamarind, a bitter sweet drink made from the pods of the tamarind tree. Teas are made from a variety of herbs, often for medicinal purposes. Cocoa tea, however, is drunk at breakfast as is hot chocolate, usually flavoured with spices.

Rum is excellent, and produced in distilleries in both Grenada and St Vincent, and in Grenada rum punches are often flavoured with a sprinkle of ground nutmeg. Most local people have a strong tolerance for rum; the uninitiated should take it easy, especially with the more potent local brews with a high alcohol percentage such as **Jack Iron** rum in Carriacou. The term 'grog', for rum, is supposed to originate in Grenada: taking the first letters of 'Georgius Rex Old Grenada', which was stamped on the casks of rum sent back to England.

In Grenada, the most popular beer is **Carib** lager, produced in Trinidad, while the local beer brewed on St Vincent is **Hairoun**. Wine (imported from Argentina, California and Europe) is generally not cheap but widely available.

Tip...
Look out for coconut water; the clear liquid inside young green coconuts is refreshing and often served by using a machete to cut open the nut. Look for barrows and stalls piled high with coconuts.

Restaurants

There is a wide range of places to eat on Grenada, from snack bars and fast food places to fine dining. Most restaurants are in St George's and the southern part of the island. Outside these areas, there are a few formal restaurants, often in scenic locations, and plenty of roadside places.

There are fewer restaurants on Carriacou, particularly at the upper end of the scale, but bars and family-run cafeterias serve good, filling and delicious meals.

ON THE ROAD
Limin'

A 'lime' is not just something to garnish a rum and Coke, it is also the expression for any (impromptu or pre-arranged) 'hanging out' session. In fact, for hanging out to be considered 'liming', the activity cannot have a larger purpose than doing nothing while sharing food, drink, conversation and laughter with others, be it a family group enjoying a liming picnic on a beach at the weekend, or a group of friends sharing the after-work lime on a step outside a rum shop. Liming is an important part of the Caribbean culture, and everybody goes out of their way to make time for it. No visit to the islands would be complete without a 'lil' lime'.

Kingstown on St Vincent, like St George's, has several restaurants serving local food or fast food; around the bus station and dock you can buy cheap snacks such as salt cod rolls with hot pepper sauce, freshly grilled chicken, and fried breadfruit balls. The rest of St Vincent is limited to snackettes (small takeaway kiosks) and rum shops that may also serve a hot plate of food. The better restaurants on the island are in the Villa Beach area to the east of Kingstown where most of the island's hotels are located.

Local specialities can be found in the villages on the Grenadines, which also have a good scattering of restaurants catering for the yacht and hotel market, especially on Bequia and Union Island with restaurants clustered along the main waterside thoroughfares. Beach bars too, often provide meals, especially fish and lobster.

Opening hours listed for restaurants are liable to change at short notice, and many places close on Sundays, public holidays and sometimes another day of the week in low season. In rural areas and on the islands, smaller local places, kiosks and beach bars are often open daily, but more like when the vendor feels like it, especially where only one person does all the cooking; 'any day, any time'.

Street food snacks start at less than US$4, and portions of local stew, fried chicken, a simple burger or fish and fries will be about US$10-15. Beyond that menu prices steadily get higher to US$60 for a two- to three-course dinner with cocktails or rum in a smart restaurant, and even US$100 per head if you opt for lobster and fine wines.

Tip...
In restaurants, look at the menu or ask the waiting staff what the extra charges are; VAT (15%) is nearly always included but service charge (10%) is usually added to the final bill. There is therefore no need to tip extra unless you want to.

Grenada

Grenada

Known as the spice island because of the nutmeg, mace and other spices it produces, Grenada (pronounced 'Grenayda'), is the most southerly of the Windward Islands. The southern coast, with its beautiful sandy beaches, bays and rocky promontories, is where the main tourist development is, as well as the airport. Here the water is so blue and clear that coral formations can be spotted from the air. There are numerous places to stay, from the last word in luxury to good-value self-catering apartments. The excellent restaurants and fun little beach bars make it everything you would want for a sun, sand and sea holiday.

Striking into the north, the island has a beautiful mountainous interior and is well endowed with lush forests and cascading rivers. Hikers and nature lovers will enjoy the many different ecosystems, from mangroves on the coast, through lush rainforest on the hillsides, to elfin woodland on the peaks.

St George's, the capital, is widely acknowledged as the prettiest harbour city in the West Indies, blending the architectural styles of the French and English with a picturesque setting on steep hills overlooking the bay.

Essential Grenada

Finding your feet

Maurice Bishop International Airport (Maurice Bishop Memorial Highway, T473-444 4555, www.mbiagrenada.com) is just under 7 miles southwest of St George's at the southwestern tip of the island. The only airport transport is taxi; public transport only goes as far as Grand Anse. Taxis are operated by the Grenada Airport Taxi Union and you'll find them outside Arrivals gathered around the little snack bar. As elsewhere on the island, taxi rates are set by the government and taxi associations; expect to pay US$10 to hotels immediately around the airport, US$16 to Grand Anse and to Lance Aux Epines, US$20 to St George's, and US$65 to the northern end of the island at Sauteurs. There are only a couple of car hire kiosks at the airport, but all others will arrange to meet you there – in fact, car hire companies will organize a vehicle at any hotel (see Transport, page 83). You could pre-arrange an airport pick up with your hotel, but these will be taxis so the cost will be the same.

Cruise ships come in to the dedicated Cruise Ship Terminal on the Esplanade on the western side of St George's, while the **Osprey Lines** ferry to and from Carriacou docks in St George's Carenage (the inner harbour) on Wharf Road. Yachts come into The Lagoon south of the working port which has both the Grenada Yacht Club and Port Louis Marina at its entrance (both with customs and immigration facilities).

Best restaurants

BB's Crabback Caribbean Restaurant, page 69
Coconut Beach, page 70
Beach House, page 71
Rhodes at Calabash, page 71
Petite Anse Hotel, page 72

Best beaches

Grand Anse, page 39
Morne Rouge, page 39
Pink Gin, page 41
La Sagesse, page 43
Bathway, page 47

Getting around

The centre of St George's is small enough to walk around but it can be hot work negotiating the hills. The main tourist area around Grand Anse Beach can also be easily navigated on foot, and the 2-mile-long beach itself is a lovely walk. Taxis are expensive but plentiful, and gather at the airport, the Cruise Ship Terminal and **Osprey Lines** ferry in St George's, and at the Spiceland Mall in Grand Anse. Otherwise any hotel/restaurant can phone one, or if you find one you like, get the driver's card/phone number. Apart from a single trip you can hire them per hour, and for the day, say for an around-the-island tour.

Buses (all privately owned minibuses) run along the main roads around the island and are cheap, although they run very infrequently on Sundays. They all start and finish at St George's Bus Terminus on Melville Street north of the Esplanade.

Roads around the island are generally good, though a little narrow and windy in places and renting a car is a good option and gives the best flexibility to see some of the sights that don't lie on the direct bus routes. It is possible to do an island tour in a day taking in the main sights like Belmont Estate and Grand Etang National Park (cruise ships passengers do it), but if you have the time at least one night staying up in the northern part of the island is recommended. See also Transport, page 83.

① Grenada

Grenada maps
1. Grenada, page 30
2. St George's, page 32
3. Grand Anse & Point Salines, page 40

To Carriacou & Petit Martinique

SUGAR LOAF IS
GREEN IS
SANDY IS

Laurant Pt
David Bay
Irvins Bay
Sauteurs Bay
Sauteurs
Levera Beach
Bedford Pt
Prospect
Leaper's Hill
Levera Pond
Levera National Park
Bathway Beach
Duquesne Bay
Duquesne
Morne Fendue
Rose Hill
River Sallee
High Cliff Pt
Crayfish Bay
Industry
Elie Hall
Mt Rose
Lake Antoine
Antoine Bay
River Antoine Rum Distillery
St Mark Bay
Union Estate
Belmont Estate
Artiste Pt
Victoria
Diamond Jouvay Chocolate Factory
Hermitage
Tivoli
Nettle Pt
Tufton Hall Waterfall
Mt St Catherine (2757ft)
Mt Hope
Gros Pt
Maran Bay
Maran
Paraclete
Mt Horne
Pearls
Great River Bay
Gouyave, Nutmeg Processing Station
Clozier
Dunfermline
Paradise
Pearls Airport
Dougaldston Estate
Bylands
Palmiste Pt
Dothan Bay
Mt Granby (2240ft)
Fédon's Camp
Lower Capitol
Telescope Pt
Grenville
Marigot
Grand Roy
Concord Falls
St Margaret
Birch Grove
Brandon Hall
Grenville Bay
Soubise
MARQUIS IS
Black Bay Pt
Halifax Harbour
Concord
Mt Qua Qua
Grand Etang Lake
Seven Sisters & Honeymoon Falls
Mt Carmel
Battle Hill
Marquis Falls
Marquis
Mt Fann
St Andrews Bay
Beauséjour Bay
Beauséjour Estate
Annandale Falls
Grand Etang National Park
Visitors Centre
South East Mt (2348ft)
Mt Lebanon
Munich
Gt Bacolet Bay
Flamingo Bay
Jessamine Eden
Happy Hill
Vendôme
Mt Sinai (2306ft)
Petit Etang
Mt Maitland (1712ft)
Pomme Rose
Thebaide
Crochu
Crochu Bay
Grenada Underwater Sculpture Park
Molinière Pt
Grand Mal Bay
Fontenoy
Richmond Hill
St Paul's
Providence
Bellevue
St David's
Grenada National Stadium
St George's Bay
Mt Airy
De La Grenade Industries
Mardigras
Perdmontemps
Laura Spice & Herb Garden
Requin Bay
Le Petit Trou
St George's
Martins Bay
Port Luis Marina
Hyde Park Tropical Garden
Morne Gazo Nature Trail
B Bacolet
Clarkes Court Rum Distillery
The Cliff
Red Gate
La Sagesse Bay
Grand Anse Bay
Quarantine Pt
Grand Anse
Calivigny
St David's Harbour
Caribbean Sea
Petit Cabrits Pt
Morne Rouge
Woburn
Whisper Cove Marina
Westerhall Point
Prickly Bay Marina
Clark's Court Bay
Chemin Bay
Port Jeudy
Point Salines
Hardy Bay
Lance aux Epines
HOG IS
Woburn Bay
Egmont Harbour
Prickly Pt
True Blue Bay
CALIVIGNY IS
Mt Hartman Bay

N

2 km
2 miles

Where to stay
Almost Paradise Cottages **1**
Cabier Ocean Lodge **2**
Caribbean Cottage Club **3**
Casabella B&B **12**
Coral Cove Cottages & Apartments **4**
Crayfish Bay Estate **5**

La Sagesse **10**
Le Phare Bleu Boutique Hotel & Marina **9**
Mount Hartman Bay Estate **14**
Petite Anse **11**
Rumboat Retreat **6**
Treetops Villa Guest House **7**

Twelve Degrees North **13**
Valley Breeze Guest House **8**

Restaurants
Aggie's Restaurant & Bar **1**
Boots Cuisine **2**
By the Sea **3**

The Deck restaurant & Bar **4**
Tiki Bar **7**

Bars & clubs
Nimrod's Rum Shop **8**
Roger's Barefoot Beach Bar **6**

a charming Caribbean historic harbour with pretty hillsides and a commanding fort

Located on the southwestern coast of the island, St George's is one of the Caribbean's most beautiful harbour towns. Unlike many Caribbean ports, which are built around bays on coastal plains, St George's straddles a promontory, and stands on an almost landlocked sparkling blue harbour against a background of green and hazy blue hills.

It was established in 1705 by French settlers, and much of its charm comes from the blend of two colonial cultures: typical 18th-century French provincial houses intermingle with fine examples of English Georgian architecture. With a population today of about 7500, much of Grenada's capital remains unchanged from those colonial days, with narrow streets lined with shops winding up and down, brick warehouses clinging to the waterfront, and terraces of pale colour-washed houses with cheerful red roofs rising up the steep hills. It's a small, neat place to explore, with long flights of steps and sharp bends, where police on point duty try to prevent chaos at the blind junctions, and at every turn is a different view or angle of the town, the harbour or the coast.

The Carenage

The Carenage is an almost perfect horseshoe-shaped inner harbour, which is believed once to have been part of a much bigger sunken crater of an old volcano, and also includes most of the outer harbour and what is known as **The Lagoon**, a yacht anchorage on the southeast side. Between the Carenage and The Lagoon is the Port of St George, the point of arrival for cargo ships. The **Osprey** ferry to Carriacou departs from opposite the fire station on the eastern side of the Carenage, not far from the tourist office. Cruise ships used to dock here too, but now arrive at the Cruise Ship Terminal, built on the Esplanade in 2005 (see below). Wharf Road runs around the entire Carenage and connects with both Young Street, which climbs over the hill to the centre of town, and the **Sendall Tunnel** to the Esplanade.

There is always plenty of dockside activity on the Carenage, which is full of fishing boats moored right up to the narrow walkway that sits just above the water, and in this part of town are many brick and stone warehouses, roofed with red, fishtail tiles brought from Europe as ballast. Many of these today serve as offices, supermarkets or hardware stores, and the Carenage also has a number of lively bars and restaurants. There's great liming here (see box, page 25) on Friday and Saturday nights when another layer of street food stalls emerge alongside the moored fishing boats. Day time too is a pleasant walk around from town and you can sit at the couple of terrace cafés and watch what's going on.

Fact...

The 340-ft-long car and pedestrian Sendall Tunnel was built in 1895 and named after British governor Sir Walter Sendall. It provides a flat shortcut between the Carenage and the Esplanade underneath Fort George Point. It was originally constructed when horse and donkey carts were the main mode of transport, and coming down the mountainous inclines, the tunnel prevented these carts from hurtling into the sea when carrying heavy loads downhill. Still an adventure in itself for pedestrians, be very careful when walking through as there's not much room when cars are coming through.

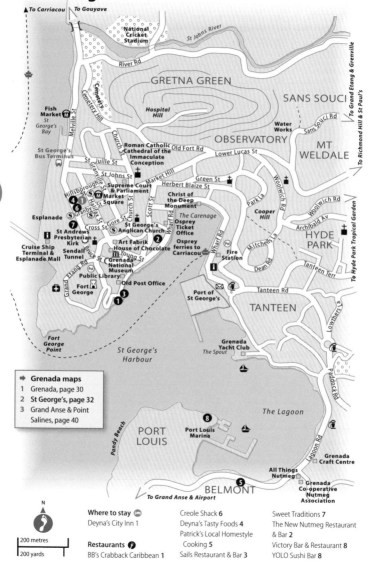

To Carriacou **To Gouyave**

St Johns River

National Cricket Stadium

River Rd

GRETNA GREEN

SANS SOUCI

Cemetery Hill

Hospital Hill

Water Works

Sans Souci Rd

To Grand Etang & Grenville

To Richmond Hill & St Paul's

Fish Market
St George's Bay

Melville St

OBSERVATORY

MT WELDALE

Church St

Old Fort Rd

St George's Bus Terminus

St Juille St

Roman Catholic Cathedral of the Immaculate Conception

Lower Lucas St

Granville St

St Johns St

Market Hill

Green St

Woolwich Rd

Woolwich Rd

Herbert Blaize St

Hillsborough St

Supreme Court & Parliament

Market Square

Scott St

Christ of the Deep Monument

Park La

Cooper Hill

Archibald Av

HYDE PARK

To Hyde Park Tropical Garden

Esplanade

Cross St

Gore St

Church St

St George's Anglican Church

The Carenage

Wharf Rd

Osprey Ticket Office

Mitchell's St

St Andrews Presbyterian Kirk

Art Fabrik
House of Chocolate

Osprey ferries to Carriacou

Fire Station

Dean Rd

Tanteen Terr

To Hyde Park Tropical Garden

Cruise Ship Terminal & Esplanade Mall

Sendall Tunnel

Bruce St

Young St

Grenada National Museum

Public Library

Old Post Office

Port of St George's

Tanteen Rd

TANTEEN

Lowther's La

Grand Etang Rd

Fort George

Fort George Point

St George's Harbour

Grenada Yacht Club
The Spout

Paddock Rd

Grenada maps
1 Grenada, page 30
2 St George's, page 32
3 Grand Anse & Point Salines, page 40

The Lagoon

Lagoon Rd

PORT LOUIS

Port Louis Marina

BELMONT

To Grand Anse & Airport

Pandy Beach

All Things Nutmeg

Grenada Craft Centre

Grenada Co-operative Nutmeg Association

N

200 metres
200 yards

Where to stay 🛏
Deyna's City Inn 1

Restaurants 🍴
BB's Crabback Caribbean 1

Creole Shack 6
Deyna's Tasty Foods 4
Patrick's Local Homestyle Cooking 5
Sails Restaurant & Bar 3

Sweet Traditions 7
The New Nutmeg Restaurant & Bar 2
Victory Bar & Restaurant 8
YOLO Sushi Bar 8

Look out for the **Christ of the Deep (Christi Degli Abbissi) Monument**, which stands on the walkway in the 'inner' middle of Wharf Road. It commemorates "the hospitality extended to the crew and passengers of the ill-fated liner, Bianca C", an Italian cruise liner that accidentally caught fire and sank in the harbour in 1961.

Young Street

From the Carenage head up Young Street, with its number of tall warehouses and colonial houses. It's one of the oldest streets in St George's and is named after William Young, the Commissioner of Land Sales for the island from 1762. The small **Grenada National Museum** ① *corner of Young and Monckton streets, T473-440 3725, www. grenadamuseum.gd, Mon-Fri 0900-1630, Sat 1000-1330, also on Sun when there are cruise ships in town, US$0.90, under 12s US$0.40,* is housed in the former French barracks built in 1704, which was used as a prison by the British for female inmates from 1767-1880. It later became two different hotels under different owners and at one point was used as a merchant's warehouse. Note the cast iron balcony, not many of which are left in St George's. Displays cover a wide range of historical topics, pre-Columbian, natural history, colonial, military, Independence, the Cuban crisis, some items from West Africa, exhibits from the sugar and spice industries and of local shells and fauna. It isn't the grandest museum in the world but it is very informative, staff are helpful and knowledgeable and remarkably it celebrated its 40th anniversary in 2016. There is also a small café at the back and on occasional Friday evenings there are cultural events such as art exhibitions and jazz and gospel music concerts.

Next door to the museum is the **House of Chocolate** ① *10 Young St, T473-440 2310, www.houseofchocolategnd.com, Mon-Sat 1000-1800, Sun 1000-1400,* which is a combination of museum, craft shop and café. It is an outlet for the **Grenada Chocolate Company** (www.grenadachocolate.com), which produces organic, Fairtrade and even carbon-neutral chocolate and who source their cocoa beans as part of a wider co-operative on the island (also see Belmont Estate, page 46). Here is a mini-museum documenting the history of cocoa on Grenada, a small café serving handmade chocolates, ice cream, delicious chocolate brownies and cakes, and drinks including (naturally) hot chocolate and mocaccinos. You can smell the delicious aromas anywhere along Young Street. Not surprisingly, this is one of the main venues for events during the **Grenada Chocolate Fest** organized in May (www.grenadachocolatefest.com).

> **Tip...**
> Drop into **Art Fabrik**, almost opposite the House of Chocolate on Young Street, a lovely shop selling handmade batiks where you can watch the artists at work in the studio upstairs; see Shopping, page 77.

Church Street and around

On the brow of the hill on Young Street is the junction with Grand Etang Road, which leads up to Fort George (see below), and Church Street, where there are a number of important buildings: **St George's Anglican Church** (1825); the **Roman Catholic Cathedral of the Immaculate Conception** ① *Sun Mass 0800-1000,* with a tower dating from 1818, the building from 1884; and the **Supreme Court and Parliament buildings** (late 18th, early 19th century). On the way up to the fort on Grand Etang Road is **St Andrew's Presbyterian Kirk** (1833), so called because it was built by Scotsmen who had come to, or had been sent to, Grenada as masons and workmen.

Many of these buildings lost their roofs and sustained other damage from wind and rain during Hurricane Ivan in September 2004 and are still today in various states of repair. The

BACKGROUND

Grenada

The island's first known inhabitants were Arawak Indians, who canoed from the nearby South American continent all the way up the Caribbean island chain. They were followed by another, fiercer group, the Caribs (also known as the Kalinago) who supplanted them. In 1498 the island was spotted and named Concepción by Christopher Columbus. Reminding Spanish sailors of Andalucía, the island was then called Granada. The name stuck as the island subsequently changed hands, and it was the British who gave it the current spelling and pronunciation (Grenada, Gre-nay-da).

Aggressive defence of the island by the Caribs prevented settlement by Europeans until the 17th century. In 1609 some Englishmen tried and failed, followed by a group of Frenchmen in 1638, but it was not until 1650 that a French expedition from Martinique landed and made initial friendly contact with the inhabitants. When relations soured, the French brought reinforcements and exterminated the last of the Carib population. Sauteurs on the north coast is named after the last 40 Caribs jumped to their death in the sea rather than surrender to the French.

The French and British battled for possession of Grenada for the next 90 years, leaving a legacy of forts, cannons and French place names. Overlooking St George's Harbour are enduring relics of that struggle: Fort Frederick, Fort Matthew and Fort George. From the early 1700s was a period of economic expansion and population growth, as colonists and slaves arrived to grow tobacco and sugar at first, followed by cotton, cocoa and coffee.

It was during the Seven Years' War in the 18th century that Grenada fell into British hands and was ceded by France to Britain as part of a land settlement in the 1763 Treaty of Paris. The new administration renamed it St George's Town, after the patron saint of England. Although the French regained control in 1779, their occupation was brief and the island was returned to Britain in 1783 under the Treaty of Versailles. The British introduced nutmeg in the 1780s, after natural disasters wiped out the sugar industry. A major slave revolt took place in 1795, led by a free coloured Grenadian called Julien Fédon (see box, page 56), but slavery was not abolished until 1834, as in the rest of the British Empire. In 1833, Grenada was incorporated into the British Windward Islands and, following Britain's withdrawal from Bridgetown, Barbados, in the mid-1880s, St George's became the replacement capital of the colony.

Cathedral has been painstakingly restored, keeping the tower and the sanctuary, which were structurally sound, but demolishing the rest and replacing it with a steel structure and new roof. It took over a decade to raise enough funds to restore St George's Anglican Church, which at the time of writing was underway. Meanwhile St Andrew's – one of the worst damaged – still remains an imposing shell on the hillside. However, to date the cliff wall it sits on has been reinforced to protect the entrance to the Sendall Tunnel below, and also the bell tower, or steeple, has been repaired enough to allow visitors to climb to the top. Drop in at the office in Knox House on Grand Etang Road or contact them (T473-440 2436, www.presbyterianchurchgrenada.com).

The British Windward Islands survived until 1958 when it was dissolved and Grenada joined the Federation of the West Indies. The Federation collapsed in 1962 and in 1967 Grenada became an associated state, with full autonomy over internal affairs, but with Britain retaining responsibility for defence and foreign relations. Grenada was the first of the associated states to seek full Independence, which was granted in 1974.

Political leadership after the 1950s alternated between Eric Gairy's Grenada United Labour Party (GULP) and Herbert Blaize's Grenada National Party (GNP). At the time of Independence, Gairy was Prime Minister, but his style of government was widely viewed as authoritarian and corrupt, becoming increasingly resented by a large proportion of the population. In 1979 he was ousted in a bloodless coup by the New JEWEL Movement (NJM; Joint Endeavour for Welfare, Education and Liberation), which formed a government headed by Prime Minister Maurice Bishop. It was a socialist/communist government with ties to Cuba and the Soviet Union, who provided aid and technical assistance. In 1983, a power struggle within the government led to Bishop being deposed and he and many of his followers were murdered by a rival faction shortly afterwards.

In the chaos that followed a joint US-Caribbean force invaded the island in a now-famous 'rescue mission' to restore order. They imprisoned Bishop's murderers and expelled Cubans and other socialist nationalities engaged in building the new airport and other development projects. Elections were held in 1984, and were won by the New National Party (NNP), headed by Herbert Blaize. After the intervention, Grenada moved closer to the US, but in 1999 diplomatic relations with Cuba were restored too and embassies were opened in St George's and Havana.

In 1991 the government decided to commute to life imprisonment the death sentences on 14 people convicted of murdering Maurice Bishop. In 2006 the Truth and Reconciliation Commission released its long-awaited report about the events of October 1983, but it still left some questions unanswered. Herbert Blaize died in 1989 and Sir Eric Gairy in 1997.

Grenada is now an independent state within the Commonwealth, with the British monarch as head of state represented by a governor general. There are two legislative houses, the House of Representatives with 15 members, and the Senate with 13 members.

Fort George
Grand Etang Rd, ww.forts.org, daily 0700-1700, US$1.85 per person.

Dominating the town from its hilltop position 175 feet above the harbour, Fort George was built between 1705 and 1710 on an earlier battery erected by the French in the 1600s. Originally named Fort Royale, it was renamed Fort George in 1763 in honour of King George III when the British took possession of the island. It is basically a small bastion tracer fort, which means that each level can give covering fire for the other level. It is currently home to the Royal Grenada Police, but has sections which are open to the public, although it is a very steep hike up the hill from town. Only the exterior walls are intact, and there is limited historical evidence except some dungeons, guard rooms and underground passages where bats now roost. Some old cannons are still in their positions, and there is a plaque in the parade ground marking the execution of Maurice Bishop and his supporters; killed by the more Marxist wing of their party on 19 October 1983. But the real reason to climb up here is the tremendous views of the coast and harbour. From the walls on the southern section of the fort, you can look towards Grand Anse Beach, from the north directly down into the heart of the town, and on the western side, the Cruise Ship Terminal; the sight of perhaps four huge vessels berthed at once is simply quite extraordinary.

The Esplanade and around

The Esplanade is a fancier name for Melville Street, which runs along the western seaward side of St George's. The **Grenada Port Authority Cruise Ship Terminal** ⓘ *www. grenadaports.com*, here was developed in 2005 to take pressure off the Carenage and to accommodate the ever-bigger cruise ships in deeper waters, and now up to four ships can be docked at once. Between October and May, some 225 cruise ships pull in to Grenada in a busy season, which can amount to a staggering 225,000 plus passengers. After passing through immigration, cruise passengers exit past a tourist information kiosk and spill into the terminal's **Esplanade Mall** ⓘ *Mon-Sat 0900-1700, Sun when a cruise ship is in but in reality many of the touristy shops only open when ships are docked*, which sells expensive tax-free jewellery and souvenirs. If you're here on a 'dry day', as the shop owners like to call a day without ships in, you may pick up some bargains as prices can be negotiable.

Outside, there is a landscaped public square, from where it's a short walk north to St George's Bus Terminus and then the fish market, all built on reclaimed land on the seaward side of the road. Across from Esplanade Mall and Melville Street the side roads will take you to **Market Square** (off Halifax Street), which is the heart of St George's commercial centre, and was once used as a place for public executions, trading slaves and for political speeches. On sale in the market is a wide variety of local tropical fruit and vegetables, baskets, brooms, clothing, coconut water, herbs, spices and souvenirs.

> **Tip...**
> The covered market here is always busy on weekday mornings, but the best time to come is on Saturday from 0800 until noon, when extra traders set up rickety stalls shaded by umbrellas. Ask permission before taking photos of people, and take small change so you can pay for tastings.

Hyde Park Tropical Garden

Woolwich Rd, T473-440 8395, www.hydeparkgrenada.com, 1-hr tours by appointment only.

Keen gardeners should book a tour of this garden, situated on the hillside overlooking The Lagoon and Port Louis Marina with views towards the city. Six generations of the Roberts family have lived here and the small estate is now in the hands of Fay Roberts Miller and her husband, John Miller, who between them have transformed former orchards and grazing land into one of the finest gardens in the Caribbean. The display of tropical flowers is so highly regarded that specimens are shipped to the Chelsea Flower Show in London each year to form part of the Grenada display, which invariably wins prizes. If you go in the morning you'll see the waterlilies out and can have a refreshing glass of home-made lemonade. The sunset tour is also delightful and is followed by a glass of wine on the veranda with the owners to take in the view and the colours.

ON THE ROAD
Grenada flourishing at the Chelsea Flower Show

In 2016, Grenada exhibited for the 18th consecutive year at the UK's prestigious Royal Horticultural Society's annual Chelsea Flower Show. The island has won a prize at the show every year so far, including 11 gold awards, and it triumphed once again in May 2016 winning its 12th gold for a display called 'Three Enchanting Islands – Pure Grenada' with flowers from Grenada, Carriacou and Petite Martinique. A good part of any success at Chelsea comes from mastering the art of transporting flowers and foliage, and each year team Grenada individually wraps every petal, leaf and stem before boxing them up and dispatching them across the Atlantic to London with British Airways. Keen garden-lovers can book a four-hour trip with the local tour operators (see page 82) to see several local gardens, both public and private, where some of these flowers are grown; around US$60 per person.

Richmond Hill

Richmond Hill is 1¼ steep winding miles east of town on the road to St Paul's, where there is Fort Matthew and Fort Frederick, and the remains of the prison in which were held those convicted of murdering Maurice Bishop before Hurricane Ivan blew the roof off in 2004.

When the French defeated the British in 1779, they attacked from high ground inland rather than from the sea, which is what the British had expected. Fearing that the same might happen to them, the French built these forts with their cannon facing east, or inland, gaining them the nickname 'backwards facing forts'. However, a few years later, the island was returned to the British under the 1783 Treaty of Versailles, and the French never had time to finish their fortress building. Realizing their strategic importance, the British finished the job. Fort Frederick and Fort Adolphus were named after two sons of King George III, on the throne at the time; Fort Matthew was named after the island's governor, Edward Matthew, and a fourth, Fort Lucas, was named after the man from whom the French had acquired the land, William Lucas. **Fort Matthew** is the largest on the island and, although not open to the public, it is sometimes used for weddings and other functions and there are occasional guided tours when you can see the 18th-century kitchen, bathrooms, cells used to restrain the insane and underground tunnels. At **Fort Frederick** ⓘ entry US$1.85 per person, daily 0800-sunset, the massive walls and some grand arches remain and there are some passages you can explore, and there are excellent views onto St George's and the Carenage and southwest down the peninsula to Grand Anse Beach and the airport.

East of St George's

Eastern Main Road heads east from Richmond Hill twisting and turning through numerous villages. About 3½ miles east of the St George's in St Paul's is **De La Grenade Industries** ⓘ Morne Delice Estate, T473-440 3241, www.delagrenade.com, Mon-Fri 0830-1700, Sat 0900-1230, US$1.85 per person to visit the garden, the business of la Grenade family, set up in the 1960s as a cottage industry by Sybil la Grenade and now run by her daughter, Cécile. The company is famous for its nutmeg jelly, nutmeg syrup and sauces, beverages and preserves using local ingredients. As well as the good shop, it also has a delightful Nutmeg Garden, covering 2 acres beside the factory. Here you can wander along paths of nutmeg shells among aromatic spices, herbs and fruit trees as well as flowering plants, all well-labelled, although there are also tour guides to explain plants' uses and pick fruit for you to try (see also box, page 51).

Off Eastern Main Road after St Paul's and on the way to St David's, on your right is the car park for the **Morne Gazo Nature Trail** ① *Mon-Sat 0900-1600, Sun 1000-1500, closed public holidays, US$1.85 per person.* The conical Morne Gazo (or Delice Hill as it's also known) rises to 1140 ft. Here the Forestry Department has created a short 1-mile trail, covered with nutmeg shells in the lush forest, that climbs 250 ft to the summit (there are hand rails on the steeper parts) where a lookout platform has been built around a large tree. It has panoramic view of the island, down to the airport in the south, across to La Sagesse and up to the hills around Grand Etang.

Further along Eastern Main Road near Perdmontemps is the turning for **Laura's Spice and Herb Garden** ① *T473-443 2604, Mon-Fri 0830-1600, US$1.85 per person,* where you can see nutmeg, cloves, cinnamon, pimento, bay trees, and all the other spices and herbs grown on the island. A guide will give you a short 30-minute tour of the property, explaining all the uses of the plants, and there is a small gift shop where you can buy spices. It is not well signposted; ask for Laura Road.

Southwest Grenada

rocky bays, long beaches and sunset views over the Caribbean

The southwest tip (or 'toe') of the island is the most popular destination for holidaymakers and is where Grenada's main tourist facilities are concentrated: smart hotels, sprawling all-inclusive resorts, restaurants, shopping malls and nightlife. And for good reason: Grand Anse Beach is a stunning long swathe of sand, packed with roasting cruise ships passengers when a ship is docked in St George's, but is refreshingly quiet at other times. Beyond on the southwest peninsula, are a string of sheltered coves and beaches, where some good accommodation options have made the most of their settings on the calm brilliantly blue Caribbean Sea.

Additionally, on the south coast are a series of sheltered bays, separated by long rocky peninsulas and tiny islets, which have moorings and marinas for the yacht community. Among the tourist hotspots, most of this southwestern peninsula is dotted with residential suburbs, so is well served by buses from St George's.

The Lagoon

In the early days, the area that is now Lagoon Road was at the far reaches of St George's and was called the 'Mang' because of the mangroves here, but is now a busy commercial area leading down the coast to Grand Anse Main Road. Just after the stacked container ships in Port of St George's, on the right you come to the boomed entrance gate to the **Grenada Yacht Club** ①*Lagoon Rd, T473-440 6826, www.grenadayachtclub.com, bar open daily 0900-late,* which has been serving yachts since the 1950s. It occupies what is called The Spout, which guards the entrance to The Lagoon from the main harbour. The broad wooden deck at the bar is a fine place to have a drink and admire its marina and yachts, and at weekends you may see tiny sail-training dinghies on the water; the yacht club has a programme that teaches school children how to sail for free.

On the other side of The Lagoon is the **Port Louis Marina** ① *Lagoon Rd, T473-439 0000 www.portlouisgrenada.com,* a development of mixed-use for the maritime community and a world-class marina with British entrepreneur and former America's Cup yachtsman Peter de Savary at the helm. It has 160 berths for yachts, including super-yachts up to 300 ft in length. Ashore, the marina village with its colonnaded buildings copying the architecture of St George's has a sail-maker, boat maintenance and provisioning services, a clutch of luxury apartments and villas (available to rent), and for landlubbers, a couple of very good restaurants (see page 70). **Pandy Beach** on the leeward side is a little scrappy, but has great views back into the harbour and Fort George.

Grand Anse See map, page 40.

Just over 2 miles south of Port Louis you come to Grand Anse, Grenada's most famous beach, fringed by sea grapes, a gleaming 2-mile semicircle of white sand, lapped by gentle clear turquoise surf. It is popular with resort guests, cruise ship passengers and locals but there's plenty of room for everyone. Along its length are many resorts, but by law, no development may be taller than a coconut palm. Some have restaurants, and there are watersports centres where you can hire snorkelling gear. Public access with toilets, changing facilities

Essential Grand Anse

Access

Grand Anse can be reached from St George's in 10 minutes by taxi (US$16), or bus (US$0.90). The buses end at (and turn around) near the car park of Spiceland Mall on Morne Rouge Rd; they do not go on to Morne Rouge so you'll have to walk over the hill from here. There's also a taxi stand at Spiceland Mall (T473-439 9070). You can also catch a water taxi from St George's Cruise Ship Terminal, but they only operate in high season and when there are cruise ships in port; these are small colourful boats with an outboard motor, which leave when full, take about 15 minutes, and cost around US$3.70-4.40. It's a fun way to get to/from town, but expect to get a little damp. The boats are restricted to one section of the beach, and arrive/depart from a jetty on a floating pontoon near the Grand Anse Craft and Spice Market.

and parking is at Camerhogue Park by the **Spiceland Mall** (see Shopping, page 78). You can also get to the beach through the **Grand Anse Craft and Spice Market** ⓘ *Grand Anse Main Rd, daily 0900-1700, 1900 in high season,* a touristy complex selling crafts, spices, jewellery and clothing.

Morne Rouge

One bay south of Grand Anse, and over the hill past **Mount Cinnamon** and **Flamboyant Hotel & Villas** (see pages 62 and 63), Morne Rouge Beach is quieter, has good snorkelling and fewer vendors. It is quite lovely with soft white sands, in a U-shaped bay where the wooded hillsides haven't been completely covered with development yet. It faces due west for perfect sunsets and is a popular venue for liming families (see box, page 25) on a Sunday.

The two resorts here are the co-owned **Kalinago Beach Resort** and **Gem Holiday Beach Resort** (see page 64). These are on the site of Grenada's first beach club – **Blanco's Beach Club** – which was opened in the 1960s, and Morne Rouge Beach is often called BBC Beach (you may have to tell a taxi driver you want to go to BBC instead of Morne Rouge). The lush foliage fringing the beach provides plenty of shade. If you have small children, this beach is probably one of the best choices as Morne Rouge Bay is the water is calm and shallow.

Other beaches and bays on the southwest peninsula

Grand Anse Main Road heads inland near the Spiceland Mall to the middle of the peninsula and Sugar Mill Roundabout (probably the busiest and most important intersection on the whole of Grenada). It connects Maurice Bishop Memorial Highway to the airport and university to the southwest, Grand Anse Valley Road towards the southeast of the island, and Lanse aux Epines Main Road south to the Lance aux Épines headland. From the roundabout it's 2½ miles to the airport along Maurice Bishop Memorial Highway, off which are a number of side roads to the beaches and bays along the northern side of the southwest peninsula.

Portici and **Parc à Boeuf** beaches are both good for swimming and Portici in particular has excellent snorkelling around Petit Cabrits Point at its northeast end. The next road to the right leads to **Magazine** and **Pingouin** beaches and it is at this point you are very

③ Grand Anse & Point Salines

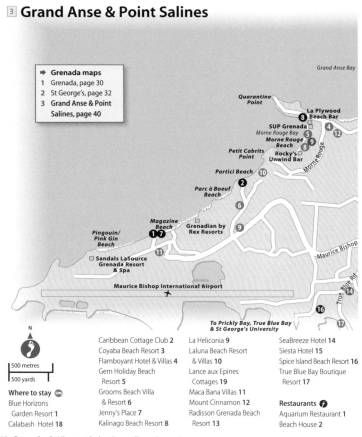

➡ **Grenada maps**
1 Grenada, page 30
2 St George's, page 32
3 **Grand Anse & Point Salines, page 40**

Grand Anse Bay

Quarantine Point

La Plywood Beach Bar
❽ ④
SUP Grenada ☐ ⑫
Morne Rouge Bay
Morne Rouge Beach ❾ ❽
Petit Cabrits Point Rocky's ☐
Unwind Bar
Morne Rouge

Portici Beach ❿
❷

Parc à Boeuf Beach
❻

Magazine Beach ☐
Pingouin/ Pink Gin Beach ❶❼ **Grenadian by Rex Resorts** ❾

☐ **Sandals LaSource Grenada Resort & Spa** ⑪

Maurice Bishop

Maurice Bishop International Airport ✈

⑯

True Blue Rd
⑭
⑰

To Prickly Bay, True Blue Bay & St George's University

N ⬆

500 metres
500 yards

Where to stay 🛏
Blue Horizons Garden Resort **1**
Calabash Hotel **18**
Caribbean Cottage Club **2**
Coyaba Beach Resort **3**
Flamboyant Hotel & Villas **4**
Gem Holiday Beach Resort **5**
Grooms Beach Villa & Resort **6**
Jenny's Place **7**
Kalinago Beach Resort **8**
La Heliconia **9**
Laluna Beach Resort & Villas **10**
Lance aux Epines Cottages **19**
Maca Bana Villas **11**
Mount Cinnamon **12**
Radisson Grenada Beach Resort **13**
SeaBreeze Hotel **14**
Siesta Hotel **15**
Spice Island Beach Resort **16**
True Blue Bay Boutique Resort **17**

Restaurants 🍴
Aquarium Restaurant **1**
Beach House **2**

close to the airport, which lies on the southern side of the peninsula, while a ridge of hills separates these beaches on the northern side. Magazine Beach is the location of the all-inclusive **Grenadian by Rex Resorts** ⓘ *www.rexresorts.com*, and the **Aquarium Restaurant & La Sirena Beach Bar** (see page 71). **Pingouin Beach** is better known as **Pink Gin Beach**, although the sand is gloriously white, not pink. The clear water here is very calm, with a gently sloping shore. Snorkelling is good around

Tip...

There are two excellent little informal beach bars on BBC Beach: **La Plywood** is at the north end where Nigel offers rum punch and fish tacos, opens 'any day, any time' and is next to **SUP Grenada** for stand-up paddle boarding (see page 83). **Rocky's Unwind Bar** is further down beyond Kalinago, and is only open at the weekends from 1100 (Rocky has a real job during the week) and is a lovely spot for cold drinks on the wooden patio beneath the trees.

the rocks, and you can rent kayaks from **La Sirena Beach Bar** and paddle round. At the western end of Pink Gin Beach almost at Point Salines is the all-inclusive couples-only **Sandals LaSource Grenada Resort & Spa**. Day passes are available to use all the facilities and eat/drink as much as you like in the 10 restaurants/bars (US$150, 1000-1800; US$180, 1800-0200; and US$300, 1000-0200); not good value unless you drink a lot of cocktails.

Back on Maurice Bishop Memorial Highway, and about half a mile after the Sugar Mill Roundabout, True Blue Road leads to the southern side of the southwest peninsula. **True Blue Bay** has no real beach, but **Dodgy Dock** bar (page 75) has great views and is a popular mooring for yachts. Occupying a peninsula jutting into True Blue Bay is **St George's University** with its popular School of Medicine that attracts many North Americans; you'll see their buses ferrying students all over the Grand Anse area where most live, and in the supermarket at Spiceland Mall trainee doctors and nurses are often still in their scrubs.

Tip...

Buses don't go beyond Grand Anse, so the options of visiting the southwest peninsula and to get to the airport are taxis or a hire car.

Carib Sushi **3**
Coconut Beach **4**
La Boulangerie **6**
La Sirena Beach Bar **7**
Mocha Spoke **16**
Red Crab **11**
Sangria Restaurant Bar
& Lounge **8**
The Edge **5**

Bars & clubs 🎵
Bananas **14**
Club Fantazia Grenada **9**
Esther's Beach Bar **10**
Junction Bar & Grill **15**
Umbrellas **12**
Venus Restaurant
& Sports Lounge **13**

Lance aux Épines

From Sugar Mill Roundabout, Lance aux Epines Main Road heads south to the Lance aux Épines headland. This peninsula forms the most southerly tip of Grenada and is primarily an upmarket residential community. Luxury homes take up much of the eastern Lance aux Épines side of Prickly Bay down to Prickly Point. **Prickly Bay Marina** ① *www. pricklybaymarina.com*, is one of the most popular yachting centres on Grenada in a lovely location overlooking the mangrove-lined shores. Its Tiki Bar (see page 72) is a good place for a cooked breakfast or late-night drink with the yachties. **Lance aux Épines Beach** is small and fairly secluded where the lawns of the **Calabash Hotel** (see page 65) run down to the white sands.

On the eastern side of the peninsula are a number of hotels and cottages overlooking Mount Hartman Bay.

On Lance aux Épines Main Road is the **West Indies Beer Co** ① *T473-232 2337, www. westindiesbeer.com, Mon-Thu 1300-0100, Fri-Sat 1300-0200, Sun 1300-2300,* which produces hand-crafted beers including blond ales and English-style bitters as well as dry and cloudy ciders. There's a beer garden, **The Brewery**, where they are sold on tap and you can pop in during the day to have a look at the brewing process at the back.

Woburn and around

From Sugar Mill Roundabout you can head east along Grand Anse Valley Road to the top of Woburn Bay, which you can also reach by following Springs Main Road from St George's. On the way to Woburn in Woodlands, is the **Clarkes Court Rum Distillery** ① *Woodlands Main Rd, T473-444 5363, www.clarkescourtrum.com, Mon-Fri 0800-1600, may open weekends if there's a cruise ship in, US$1.85,* where a 15-minute tour at the Sugar Factory Museum goes over the basics of the rum producing process. At the end you can try some of the rums they produce in their sampling bar and purchase a bottle or two at the shop. It is a steam-driven operation, unlike the waterwheel system at the River Antoine Rum Distillery (see page 45), and old steam engines can be seen, the oldest dating from 1886. There has been a sugar mill on the estate since the 18th century and this factory dates from 1937, although no sugar has been crushed here since 2003 and molasses are now imported.

> **Tip...**
> If you want to sample a few rums and don't want to drive, the distillery is an easy 10- to 15-minute bus ride from St George's (on routes going to Woburn or Grenville) and buses will drop off on Woodlands Main Road right in front.

Once in Woburn, **Whisper Cove Marina** ① *off Lower Woburn Rd, T473-444 5296, www. whispercovemarina.com,* is at Clarke's Court Bay, a smaller inlet on the eastern side of Woburn Bay, and has yacht berths and the **Steakhouse Restaurant & Bar** (see page 72), where colourful iguanas come up to the drinking pools right below the restaurant deck. The **Meat & Meet' Butcher Shop** ① *open Mon 0800-1300, Tue-Sat 0800-1900, Sun 1000-1300,* sells meat but also has a small deli and grocery section. Also from Whisper Cove Marina you can go kayaking with **Conservation Kayak** (see page 81) around Woburn Bay and out to Hog Island checking out mangroves, coral reefs and the good birdlife.

> **Tip...**
> From St George's get the No 2 orange bus to Woburn, and ask to be dropped off at **Nimrod's Rum Shop**, a great little rum shop (see page 76) next to the bus stop. It's a fine place to wait for a bus back to town.

The uninhabited Hog Island is a favourite anchorage spot for sailors who often moor their yachts in the bay and have barbecues on the beach and a drink at the thatched **Roger's Barefoot Beach Bar** ① *T473-404 5265, see Facebook, open Sat-Sun*, and is also reachable by water taxi from the jetty at Lower Woburn. There is also a causeway across to the island; by foot only and you need a 4WD to get to it on the rough track from Mount Hartman Bay.

East coast Grenada
a coconut palm-lined Atlantic coast, rum, nutmeg and Grenada's northern tip

The journey up the Atlantic east coast is a popular route and many tours start a day trip of the island by following the east coast road along the wild Atlantic bays. The principal sightseeing attractions are Belmont Estate, where the island's nutmeg and cocoa heritage can be explored, and the historical River Antoine Rum Distillery, the best place to see how the Caribbean's famous rum has been produced over the centuries. Those with more time can explore Grenada's lesser-known beaches like beautiful La Sagesse or delightful Bathway, and visit the isolated northern tip of the island.

Woburn to Grenville
Heading east along the main road from Woburn any number of dirt roads and paths go down to interesting and isolated bays or run along the *rias* and headlands along the southern coast of Grenada such as Calivigny, Fort Jeudy and Westerhall Point. While most of these small peninsulas have houses and villas, many are accessible only by jeep or on foot. The options of exploring without a car are to get the No 2 orange bus between St George's and Grenville and get off somewhere at the start of a track, or get a taxi to drop you off and pick you up later.

At Red Gate is the junction with the Eastern Main Road that comes across inland from St George's, and beyond here is perhaps the best bay on this stretch of southeast coast, which is about 3 miles south of St David's. **La Sagesse Bay** is a peaceful refuge sheltered by cliffs and fringed with coastal woodland full of bougainvillea, purple and red hibiscus and crimson anthurium. Coconut palms bend into the wind on the beach, and it has **La Sagesse Beach**, a perfect half-mile-long crescent of golden sand, a mangrove estuary

Tip...
To get to La Sagesse, turn off south opposite an old sugar mill on a dirt road through a banana plantation. The No 2 orange bus between St George's and Grenville drops off on the main road from where it's a just over a 1-mile flat and pleasant walk. If you are driving directly from Grand Anse, it takes about 30-40 minutes.

and a salt pond. The snorkelling and swimming is good and there is a reef just offshore, and birdwatchers will enjoy the nature trails that lead off through the undeveloped, surrounding forest. Apart from the stunning beach, the main attraction here is **La Sagesse**, a hotel, restaurant and beach bar (see page 66); you don't have to be staying to enjoy the facilities. You will have the beach almost virtually to yourself.

Beyond the turn-off to Sagesse, the Eastern Main Road cuts inland some way in from the Atlantic coast and its wild and empty peninsulas and bays and winds its way north through the parishes of St David and St Andrew. You'll notice numerous Janet houses perched on the hillsides (see box, page 44) and a number of tracks (mostly 4WD) go down to the points on the coast; one of which is at Crochu to **Cabier Ocean Lodge** (see

ON THE ROAD
Janet houses

Around Grenada you will see small wooden shacks clinging to their existence, perched on concrete pillars at each corner. These prefabricated homes made of timber and corrugated iron roofs were so named as many were put up after the passage of the devastating Hurricane Janet in 1955, which swept through Grenada and the Grenadines before making landfall in Mexico.

Designed as homes for the poor and homeless after the storm, Janet Houses were originally meant as temporary housing, and while they were very strong, if you broke them down and re-erected them somewhere else, they never fitted together quite the same and there would be gaps in the walls. But over the years since Hurricane Janet, owners customized, extended and reinforced them into proper homes. There are few of the original ones left today (Hurricane Ivan in 2004 took care of that) but the style of building has been copied for newer houses and the basic structure remains the same. Building on tall concrete plinths has many advantages; they can be constructed on steep hillsides, the space beneath can be very useful for storage and hanging out washing, storm water and drains run downhill underneath, and the accommodation on the top floors has the best views.

page 66). Two miles south of Grenville are the **Marquis Falls** ① *an entrance fee (US$1.85) is charged by the owners of the property, guides are available at the small bar/shop by the sign for the falls on the road, there have been complaints of hassling but there's no compulsion to hire a guide*, also called Royal Mount Carmel Falls. The 230 ft combined height of the two cascading drops makes the waterfall among the highest in Grenada. It's an easy 10- to 15-minute walk from the road unless it has been raining, when it becomes muddy and slippery on the trail and a guide can be helpful for the less able. You can take a dip in the pool downstream and a power shower in the waterfalls.

Grenville

Grenville was named for British Prime Minister George Grenville (1763-65), but is also known by its old French name, La Baye, and is the main town on the east coast and capital of St Andrew's Parish, the largest parish in Grenada. It is a collection point for bananas, nutmeg and cocoa, and also a fishing port. There are some well-preserved old buildings, including the Court House, Anglican Church, police station and post office. Good local food can be found here along the two parallel main streets – Victoria Road and Ben Jones Street – and numerous 'snackettes' sell rotis, curry mutton, stewfish, and rice and peas. If heading to the top of the island, it's also a good place to fill up with both fuel from the petrol stations and cash from the ATMs as these facilities in Sauteurs cannot always be relied upon. As well as heading north, from Grenville you can also cut across the island to Gouyave or head beck to St George's on the interior road via Grand Etang.

Pearls Airport

Opened in 1943, Grenada's first international airport was built on an ancient Amerindian site, and this unlikely tourist attraction is worth a quick detour off the main road (it's 2 miles north of Grenville). On 25 October 1983, US marines from the 8th Marine Regiment landed in helicopters and captured Pearls Airport during the invasion of Grenada, meeting only light resistance. A major impetus for this incursion was a dispute about the construction of Grenada's current airport – then Point Salines International Airport, now Maurice Bishop International Airport – which was being funded with aid provided by Cuba and the Soviet Union, which opened in 1984.

Today you can see two old planes lying on the grass beside the airstrip at Pearls Airport; one is Cuban, a **Cubana Airlines** passenger aircraft, and the other is Russian, a crop-duster. Both planes were damaged in the invasion, and have sat here rusting ever since. You can also see the old terminal building and duty-free shops, now a ghost town. The abandoned airport today has got some other uses. It's a grazing area for cows and goats, and the runway is used for driving lessons, cricket, biking and drag-racing. Nearby is the excellent **By the Sea** restaurant/bar (see page 73).

River Antoine Rum Distillery
T473-442 7109, Mon-Fri 0800-1700, Sat 0900-1500, Sun when cruise ships are in, US$3.70, tip the guide for the tour.

Almost on the boundary between the parishes of St Andrew and St Patrick, the road splits at the village of Tivoli. Turn left to go to the Belmont Estate and Sauteurs, turn right and it's a short drive to the River Antoine Rum Distillery. This historical distillery driven by a water mill is by far the most interesting place on Grenada to learn all about the process of rum production, and the best thing about it is the method at the still working operation has seen little change since the paddle wheel was installed in 1785. It is the oldest functioning water-propelled distillery in the Caribbean. Under the label Rivers Royale Grenadian Rum, it produces *rhum agricole*, the French term for cane juice rum, a style of rum originally distilled in the French Caribbean islands from freshly squeezed sugar cane juice rather than molasses.

Fascinating guided tours (the guides are really proud of this facility and its heritage) will lead you through the real day-to-day rum-making process, from the harvesting of sugar cane that comes from adjacent fields, the giant press powered by the waterwheel where the cane is crushed (the discarded husks are then used as fuel to fire the boilers to boil the juice), and then on to the fermentation process in huge (and smelly) pits and the distilling in copper vats.

> **Tip...**
> Rivers Royale Grenadian Rum is 75% alcohol. After sampling a tot, you might be tempted to take a bottle home as a souvenir. However, all civil aviation authorities ban the transport of alcohol where the percentage of alcohol by volume is greater than 70%. The distillery produces a special 69% version for that reason.

You can also stroll along River Antoine to see the dam where the water is channelled from to power the waterwheel. After the tour, you'll be treated to a free sample in the shop, a breathtaking firewater. A restaurant next door serves local food.

About 1 mile north of the distillery, the coastal road runs past **Lake Antoine**, a shallow volcanic crater lake similar to size and character to the one at Grand Etang (page 55) but it lies at the bottom of a deeper crater. Well signposted from the road, there's a short easily drivable track up to a viewpoint at the top of the lake. You can park here and walk down and around the path that circles the lake where you can see whistling ducks and other birds peacefully resting on the water. From here, or the distillery, the options are to back track and go to Belmont Estate, or continue north and on to Bathway Beach. If you want to go to all of them then a little bit of driving around in circles is required – just check the opening times of places and choose where you might like to be for lunch.

ON THE ROAD

Ivan the Terrible

Hurricane Ivan was a large, long-lived, hurricane that caused widespread damage in the Caribbean and US. It formed on 2 September 2004, from a large tropical wave southwest of Cape Verde on the West African coast, and as the system moved west over the Atlantic it intensified rapidly. About 1000 miles to the east of Tobago, it reached hurricane strength with winds of 125 mph. As it moved east and north, the storm passed over Grenada and some of the other Windward Islands on 7 September, causing catastrophic damage.

September 2004 was the month no Grenadian will ever forget. Hurricane Ivan passed directly over the island with furious winds peaking at 133 mph, killing 39 people, injuring about 700, destroying 30% and damaging 90% of homes and leaving 18,000 homeless. The winds downed 80% of the nutmeg trees on the island, with other crop losses varying between 60–90 %. Water, electricity and phone services were cut off, looting was rife and a dawn to dusk curfew was imposed with the help of regional security services, who were also drafted to help guard prisoners after the prison had its roof blown off. It took several weeks for power to be restored, but shortages of food and building supplies continued for months, with many homes unrepaired for lack of materials. Tourism was adversely affected; an estimated 60% of hotel rooms were damaged, although most hotels were soon open for business, even if some rooms were still out of action, and some took the opportunity for an extended closure to carry out improvements and upgrading. By the winter season, cruise ships were calling again and the airport was back to normal.

Today you will still notice some evidence of the hurricane's passing; church roofs are still missing, many tree stumps are still evident in the forests, and houses are more visible on the hillsides without the trees which used to obscure them.

Belmont Estate

At Tivoli turn towards Sauteurs, at the next junction turn left and Belmont is on your right after a minute or so, T473-442 9524, www.belmontestate.net, Sun-Fri 0800-1600, standard tour US$4.80, lunch 1200-1430 US$4.80 (inclusive of taxes), Bean to Bar tour of estate, and The Grenada Chocolate Company and lunch US$65.

This 400-acre estate dates from the 17th century and was a nutmeg producer before Hurricane Ivan (see box, above) destroyed most of its trees. Cocoa has now replaced nutmeg as the main crop, helped by the establishment of the **Grenada Chocolate Company** ⓘ *www.grenadachocolate.com*, a mile away at Hermitage. Producers here and on other farms were encouraged to go organic and offered a guaranteed price for their beans. **The Grenada Chocolate Company** and a tourism collaboration with Belmont flourished. Now Belmont is one of the major tourist attractions on the island.

There are interesting and well-guided tours of the fully functioning farm, goat dairy, gardens, Heritage Museum and cocoa and nutmeg processes. The standard tour lasts about 30-45 minutes and begins at the boucan, where you see the cocoa being fermented, the cleaning of mace, and cocoa beans drying in large wooden racks that are mounted on rails and can easily be slid away under cover when it rains.

In the Heritage Museum you can see some items retrieved from the Great House that was flattened by Hurricane Ivan, like furniture, paintings and old ledgers from the estate, and taste nutmeg products like syrup and jams, and chocolate. Longer tours of the Grenada Chocolate Company factory can be done as part of the 'bean to bar' tour (organized by Belmont, reservations required). Using certified organic cocoa beans from local growers and organic sugar imported from a cooperative in Paraguay, this tiny factory roasts and grinds all its own beans and produces some of the world's finest chocolate. The whole operation is solar powered and the shells and dust are recycled as fertilizer around the cocoa bushes. Staff will explain and show you the manufacturing process.

> **Tip...**
> Also visit the **House of Chocolate** in St George's (page 33), another outlet for **The Grenada Chocolate Company**. The pure chocolate will not melt in the car and survives island-hopping or transatlantic flights.

The **BonBon Shop** sells **The Grenada Chocolate Company**'s dark chocolate bars and delicious truffles flavoured with local spices. A buffet lunch at the restaurant uses all local ingredients, including goats' cheese, cocoa, fruit and vegetables as well as serving local specialities such as callaloo and pepperpot.

Bathway Beach

The coast road from the River Antoine Rum Distillery, or an inland route from Belmont Estate, leads via River Sallee to the northeast corner of Grenada at Levera. On the way Bathway Beach is a broad strip of dark golden sand, with cliffs at either end, trees for shade, changing rooms/toilets, a good beach bar and picnic tables. A ridge of rocks just offshore, parallel with the beach, provides protection from the rough Atlantic surf, almost like a swimming pool, but you must not swim beyond the rocks as the currents beyond are dangerous. Pronounced 'Bat-way' locally, it is a magnet for folk at weekends and public holidays, but is almost deserted at other times. There is a raised wooden green corrugated-iron building that is home to a number of kiosks for snacks and drinks; some of the women here will also cook up hot plates of food for lunch. Otherwise **Aggie's Restaurant & Bar** is well-recommended for a good lunch stop on an island tour (see page 73). Also here is the Levera National Park visitor centre and meeting point for turtle-watching trips to Levera Beach further north.

Levera National Park
No admission fee.

Beyond Bathway Beach the road becomes gravel and leads into Levera National Park. This covers 450 acres around Levera Pond, one of the island's largest mangrove swamps, as well as the coastal region of coconut palms, cactus and scrub that provides a habitat for iguanas and land crabs, and the white beaches that are nesting sites for leatherback turtles. Offshore are coral reefs, sea grass beds and the cone-shaped Sugar Loaf Island (privately owned with one house on it), and Green and Sandy islands (uninhabited). The road from Bathway first goes past **Levera Pond**, a 23-acre freshwater pond surrounded by mangroves and an important wetland attracting migratory and resident birds, including herons and waterfowl, and sea birds such as boobies and frigate birds. A short trail over a boardwalk leads from the road to a viewing platform. Once at the beautiful, long, sandy and isolated **Levera Beach,** swimming is good and there is occasional surf, but do not swim far out as there is a current in the narrows between the beach and **Sugar Loaf Island**. Sea birds here include the frigates, boobies and brown pelicans.

ON THE ROAD

Grenada's birds

About 150 species of birds have been recorded in Grenada, although terrestrial birds only number an estimated 35 species; the remainder are migrants, waterfowl and seabirds. There are only two endemics; the Grenada dove (*Leptotila wellsi*), and the Grenada hook-billed kite (a large hawk, *Chondrohierax uncinatus mirus*). Both are rarely seen and critically endangered, and are even on the brink of extinction. The dove is thought to number less than 135 individuals, while the kite perhaps only 50-75. The island's small size, predators like mongooses, cats and rats, and habitat lose has been credited for the demise in the numbers; not just hurricanes destroying forests but construction development too. However, birdwatchers may be lucky at Grand Etang which is home to the emerald-throated hummingbird, yellow-billed cuckoo, red-necked pigeon, ruddy quail-dove, cocoa thrush, lesser Antillean swift and Antillean crested hummingbird among other forest birds. The few lakes on the island attract herons, ducks, and grebes, and shore and seabirds can be spotted at Levera National Park and on the west and southwest Atlantic coasts. These include the roseate, bridled and sooty tern, frigatebirds, boobies and brown pelicans, and some of the unpopulated islets between Grenada and Carriacou are important areas for breeding seabirds, particularly the red-footed and brown booby.

The leatherback turtle nesting season is 1 April to 31 August, when the beach is closed 1800-0600 and security guards ensure no one strays on the sand unless they are on an organized turtle-watching trip. The leatherbacks and the turtle-watching trips are monitored by the turtle conservation organization **Ocean Spirits** ① *T473-534 4324, www.oceanspirits.org*, but they do not run the tours. Each turtle season, the **Ocean Spirits** research teams on Levera Beach will decide (depending on how many turtles they encounter) when guided trips can come up from the Levera National Park visitor centre at Bathway Beach to see the nesting turtles, and in most cases there is an excellent chance of seeing them, especially between April and July. See also box, opposite.

The guides themselves are part of **St Patrick's Environmental and Community Tourism Organization** ① *SPECTO; T473-405 8395/442 2721, see Facebook*. You need to be at the visitor centre at 1900; drive, or book with a tour operator/taxi. The important thing is you need transport and there is a maximum number each night of 13 people, so it's always best to phone or send a message on Facebook and book first. Permits cost US$20, and tours start at 1930 with a short presentation about leatherbacks, conservation efforts in Grenada and essential rules (no flash photography or torches), before the drive up to Levera Beach. Ensure you tip the guide.

Sauteurs

Pronounced 'Sau-tez', this is the largest town in the north of Grenada and the capital of St Patrick's Parish, and while not particularly attractive, does sit in a marvellous hilly position on the north coast overlooking Sauteurs Bay to the west and Irvins Bay to the east. Sauteurs is roughly 23 miles from St George's on both the west and east coast routes; because of the windy roads, it's about 1½ hours' drive without stops.

Driving through Sauteurs is similar to Gouyave and Victoria on the west coast in that the heart of the town is on one street and the mainstay of the economy is fishing. The beach

ON THE ROAD
Leatherback turtles

Levera Beach attracts Grenada's largest population of nesting leatherback turtles (*Dermochelys coriacea*). This turtle gets its name from its unique soft shell, and is the largest of the sea turtle family weighing up to 2000 lbs and expanding up to 6 ft long. Instead of a bony shell (like the green and hawksbill turtle) the carapace of the leatherback is covered by skin and oily flesh, which is an inky-blue colour and somewhat flexible and almost rubbery to the touch – hence the name – and ridges help give it a more hydrodynamic structure. They dive to depths of 4000 ft – far deeper than any other turtle – and can stay down for up to 85 minutes.

Leatherbacks have the widest global distribution of all reptile species, and possibly of any vertebrate. They can be found in the tropic and temperate waters of the Atlantic, Pacific, and Indian Oceans, as well as the Mediterranean Sea, and, given that they can retain body heat to survive in cold water, adults have been seen as far north as Canada and Norway and as far south as New Zealand and the bottom of South America. Leatherbacks undertake the longest migrations between breeding and feeding areas of any sea turtle, averaging 3700 miles each way; a turtle seen in the Caribbean may have come from as far away as Madagascar.

After mating at sea, females come ashore during the breeding season to nest. The night-time ritual involves hauling herself up on to the beach through the surf, excavating a hole in the sand with her back flippers, depositing eggs, re-filling the nest, leaving a large, disturbed area of sand that makes detection by predators difficult, and finally returning to the sea. They visit up to nine times per season, laying 75 to 120 eggs in one 'clutch', each time about 10 days apart. Incubation time is 60 days, so about two months later, the eggs hatch, and the baby turtles ('hatchlings') dig themselves out of their nests and hustle – awkwardly and adorably – to the open sea. The temperature inside the nest determines the sex of the hatchlings. A mix of male and female hatchlings occurs when the nest temperature is approximately 29°C, while higher temperatures produce females and cooler temperatures produce males. Female hatchlings that make it to the sea will roam the oceans until they reach sexual maturity. Astonishingly, they then return to the very same beach where they themselves hatched to produce their own offspring. Males spend the rest of their lives at sea.

However, only about one egg in a thousand produces a hatchling that actually survives and makes it back to the sea; the eggs either do not incubate, or the eggs or the hatchlings get taken by crabs, birds or dogs. There are other dangers too and leatherbacks are classed as critically endangered; in 1980 there was an estimated global population of nesting females of around 120,000, but in 2016 figures were put at around 40,000. The population of males is unknown as they never come out of the sea and are rarely seen. Hazards to them are sharks, many get caught up in fishing nets or are struck by boats, and leatherbacks can also die if they ingest floating plastic debris mistaken for their favourite food: jellyfish. Other threats include poachers – turtle meat is known as the 'beef of the sea' in some communities – disconcerting man-made light (they only follow the light of the moon), beach erosion and pollution like oils spills.

on Sauteurs Bay has leaning palm trees and is easily accessible with no rocks or reefs. The area has historic importance; after subduing the Arawak population, the Carib Indians (Kalinago) claimed Grenada as their own and aggressively defended it from settlement by the Europeans. However, French colonizers were eventually successful in breaching the island and the town is renowned as the site of the mass suicide of Grenada's last 40 Caribs who jumped off a cliff in 1651 rather than face domination by the conquering French. Thus the town was named Sauteurs, which is French for 'jumpers'. The cliff itself, **Leapers' Hill** or **Carib's Leap**, is located just north of the town and descends vertically into the sea for more than 100 feet. It is well-signposted and there is a monument celebrating the courage of the Caribs and their story. There are views from here upwards to Carriacou and on a clear day some of the other Grenadines; a board shows all the islands you can see looking out to the north.

On the opposite hill, the French established **St Patrick's Catholic Church** in 1721, which in 1784 the British government handed over to the Anglicans. The church was destroyed by fire but a new St Patrick's Anglican Church was built in 1840, and today is the oldest church in the parish. Accessed from the eastern end of the main street in town, it also offers incredible views of the Caribbean Sea and islands. In March Sauteurs celebrates **St Patrick's Day** with a mini street festival.

West coast Grenada
a winding journey through quiet fishing villages and gorgeous Caribbean views

The journey heading north out of St George's on Western Main Road first goes past the Grenada National Stadium and the ugly oil and petrol depots along Grand Mal Bay, but then it opens up to a beautiful road that hugs the shore all the way to Duquesne Bay with lovely views of the ocean and numerous West Coast bays. The largest town on this coast is Gouyave, famous for its Fish Friday and old nutmeg processing plant, where there is the option of turning inland and across towards Grenville on the east coast, or continue up through the sleepy fishing community of Victoria to the north tip of the island.

St George's to Gouyave
For the most part the shoreline on the west coast is rocky, but the first option after leaving St George's is about 4½ miles north where the road runs adjacent to the small beach at Beauséjour Bay where there are toilets and parking. Just before this beach is the turn-off inland on to the Beauséjour Road from where you can see the ruins of the sugar mill and distillery of Beauséjour Estate, once the island's largest sugar estate. Continuing along Beauséjour Road through rural countryside is **Jessamine Eden** ① *Grenville Vale Rd, T473-231 1501, www.jessamine-eden.com, Mon-Sat 0900-1700 by appointment only, US$10.* Much of this private 60-acre organic farm and estate in the southern hills of Grand Etang is a botanical garden through which flow rivers and streams. It's also known as the Grenville Vale Tropical Botanical Garden. The onsite apiary houses nearly 100 hives of bees that create honey from the gardens to produce a variety of honeys (for sale in the shop) and there are several trails through the gardens. It takes an hour to go around and it's pretty, but, as few plants are labelled, the experience can be unedifying (especially for the entry fee). Jessamine is a milkwood flowering plant that is a native to the Caribbean, and five species are grown here.

ON THE ROAD

Nutmeg

One of Grenada's most important historical dates is 1843, the year that nutmeg was introduced (clandestinely taken from Dutch-occupied Indonesia). In those days the commodity was nearly as precious as gold and the plantation system dominated the early colonial days, and led Grenada to become known as the 'Island of Spice'. Before 2004, it was the world's second largest producer of nutmeg after Indonesia, before Hurricane Ivan destroyed 80% of the nutmeg trees (and 60-70% of cocoa bushes). The nutmeg industry on Grenada cannot be resurrected quickly as it takes at least 10 years for a nutmeg tree to grow big enough to produce fruit. Nevertheless, nutmeg is still an important crop, even though export output has diminished greatly, and today the **Grenada Co-operative Nutmeg Association** (www.gcnanutmeg.com) is encouraging a number of rejuvenation projects to restore some of the plantations and helping local people to plant trees on their properties.

The reason that nutmeg does so well on Grenada is that the densely foliaged evergreen tree, *Myristica Fragrans*, thrives at an elevation of 1500-2500 ft in the rich volcanic soil found in the sheltered valleys of the island. It produces a yellowish egg-shaped pericarp, or fleshy fruit, from which two distinct spices, nutmeg and mace is derived. When ripe, the pericarp splits open, exposing the brilliant scarlet, web-like membrane: the mace, which encircles a dark brown brittle shell. Inside is a single glossy brown, oily seed: the nutmeg.

Nutmeg and mace are similar in aroma and taste but mace is mellower and is often preferred for the bright orange, saffron-like hue it gives to food, while nutmeg is sweeter and more highly aromatic. Culinary uses of both include savoury and sweet dishes. In Grenada, they are added to meat stews, vegetable sauces, egg dishes, fruit salads and pie fillings and are sprinkled liberally in rum punch and other cocktails. Commercially, nutmeg is utilised in the manufacture of perfumes, soaps and shampoos, and is also an ingredient in inhalants and liniments which are used to relieve congestion caused by flu and colds.

Back on the coast road beyond Beauséjour is **Halifax Bay**, the remains of a volcanic crater which erupted some 15,000 years ago and one of Grenada's most protected natural harbours. It was settled first by Amerindians before being taken over by colonial planters and was also popular with smugglers. Sadly today it is marred by the presence of overhead electricity pylons and an unsightly municipal landfill rubbish dump close to its south shore. If it wasn't for these it would undoubtedly be popular as a protected yacht mooring; instead boats anchor in the north of the outer bay right under Black Bay Point.

North of Halifax Bay, and about 8 miles north of St George's, at the village of Concord, a turn-off on to Concord Mountain Road runs up the valley through guava and clove trees to the **Concord Falls** ⓘ *daily 0900-1700, use of toilets/changing rooms US$1.85.* They are actually a series of three waterfalls on the Concord River, and the first and most accessible is at the end of the road; a 1½-mile drive or a 45-minute hot walk from the coast road. The car park and the first falls can be very busy when cruise passenger tour buses are in, which also attract vendors selling spices and other souvenirs, but are fairly quiet otherwise. You can bathe in the small cascade (access is via steps with hand rails), and the water is crystal clear, but it is also ice cold and there isn't much of it in the dry season.

The second Concord Falls (**Au Coin**) are bigger and higher, a 30- to 45-minute walk (each way) from the first falls, with a river to cross four times (the bridges were never replaced after Hurricane Ivan washed them away, so be prepared to get wet feet). The trail goes through a nutmeg plantation and is marked so there is no need for a guide.

The third falls (**Fontainebleu**) are the hardest to get to, at least one hour from the first falls, and although the trail is still easily recognizable, there are slippery rocks to navigate so you may want to take a guide (organized at the car park). It has a 65-ft cascade down the cliff face into a pool. Swimming is not allowed above the first falls as the water is part of the island's domestic water supply and you will see a small dam which diverts the flow.

North of Concord, just before Gouyave, is a turn-off to **Dougaldston Estate** ⓘ *Mon-Fri 0900-1600, free but tips for a demonstration necessary.* Turn right just before a wide bridge, opposite a playing field. When the road bends to the right, go straight on and look for a gate on your left. Up until the 1980s, more than 200 people were employed here, cultivating spices and other crops. Today it's almost derelict and only a handful of family members continue to dry spices in the traditional way on racks which are wheeled under the building if it rains. Their income comes from tips from visitors for demonstrating the process and explaining all the uses of the various layers of the nutmeg (see box, page 51), and selling small bags of cinnamon, cloves or nutmeg for around US$1.85. It's a bit like entering a forgotten world with its tumbledown walls, ramshackle buildings and prolific vegetation growing over everything. But you can walk around and see the old processing sheds, drying racks and a few examples of 19th-century machinery and imagine how it used to be.

Gouyave

Gouyave (pronounced 'Gwarve') was founded by the French in 1734, when it was first named 'Bourg de L'Ance Gouyave' and, although the British changed the name to Charlotte Town (after the wife of King George III), the French name prevails today. It is the largest town on the West Coast, capital of the Parish of St John and a thriving fishing port and the bay is dotted with gaily coloured boats. It is well worth stopping to have a wander around here, the narrow main street (**Depradine Street**; upper, lower and central) is lively with plenty of little local shops and 'snackette' kiosks, and you may be able to get some coconut water from a vendor with a barrow piled with green nuts. You can also pop your head into the newly built **Gouyave Fish Market** (funded by the Japanese) and walk to the end of the jetty to see the fishing boats.

There are a few interesting old buildings (in various states of repair) including the gothic **Anglican Church** which was built in 1834, and the **Roman Catholic Church** in 1899. But the most interesting is the **Nutmeg Processing Station** ⓘ *Central Depradine St (close to the fuel station), T473-440 2217, Mon-Fri 0800-1600, weekends when cruise ships are in, 30-min tour US$1,* a great old wooden building by the sea built in the 1940s, with a very powerful smell, which is locally called the 'Nutmeg Pool'. The tour here is highly recommended to see all the stages of drying, grading and packing; notice the hessian sacks are printed with names of countries they are destined to with handmade stencils. A group of women sit in a group on the ground floor sorting and separating the nutmeg and mace (no photos without permission first)

On the top floor mace is dried for four months in Canadian pine boxes before being graded. There are three grades, used for culinary spice, corned beef or cosmetics, and only Grenada produces grade one mace for cooking. On the first floor, nutmeg is dried on racks for two months, turned occasionally with a rake. The lighter ones are then used in medicine and the heavier ones for culinary spices. The husks are used for fuel or mulch

ON THE ROAD
Kirani James

Kirani James, from Gouyave, is the first Grenadian to win an Olympic medal in any sport, having won gold at the 2012 London Olympics in the 400 m. A prodigious runner from a young age, he burst onto the headlines when, aged 14, he ran the fastest time ever by a boy of his age: 46.96 secs over 400 m at the 2007 World Youth Championship. He then went on to be the first boy to win the double 200 m/400 m at the 2009 World Youth Championships, smashing records in his wake. At least 10 colleges in the USA competed to offer him places, but he accepted a scholarship at Alabama, where he improved on his personal best times and set new college records.

He continued to impress once he moved into adult competition, winning the 400 m at the 2011 World Championships in South Korea with a personal best of 44.60 secs, aged 18, making him the youngest ever 400-m world champion and the first Grenadian to bring home a medal from a World Championship games. Shortly afterwards he improved his personal best with a time of 44.36 secs at the 2011 IAAF Diamond League in Zurich, winning gold again. His triumph at the 2012 London Olympics was achieved with a time of 43.94, making him the first non-US runner to break the 44-sec barrier.

On his return home his reception in Grenada proved to be a euphoric one. Thousands lined the streets in preparation of his return, and he was showered with plaudits; the government issued a commemorative stamp in his honour, named the new stadium after him, appointed him a tourism ambassador and awarded him bonds valued at US$185,000.

Since then he has continued to improve. At the IAAF Diamond League Lausanne 2014 he clocked up a winning time of 43.74 secs in the 400 m, at the time the fastest time by a non-US athlete. At the Commonwealth Games held in Glasgow in 2014, James set a new Commonwealth record of 44.24 secs and won Grenada's first ever Commonwealth Gold Medal.

At the 2015 World Championships in Beijing, James won the Bronze Medal for the 400 m – Gold went to South African Wayde van Niekerk (43.48 secs) and Silver to US LaShawn Merritt (43.65), followed by James with a time of 43.78 secs. This race was the first time ever that the top three athletes broke the 44 second barrier for the 400 m.

and the fruit is made into nutmeg jelly (a good alternative to breakfast marmalade), syrup or liquor. A little shop sells nutmeg products.

Managed by the **Grenada Co-operative Nutmeg Association**, the **Gouyave Nutmeg Processing Plant** is one of only three remaining nutmeg stations on the island since Hurricane Ivan destroyed most of the trees (see box, page 46). The other two are at Victoria and Grenville, but they no longer process the nutmegs and simply collect them and send them to Gouyave for processing and export.

Gouyave is also locally dubbed the 'the town that never sleeps'. Derived partly from the fact that along the north end of the main street beyond the fish market (called Palmiste Lane at this end), there is a particularly rough string of loud rum shops, but also because Gouyave has some lively events such as Fish Friday (see box, page 73). It is also the principal place to go to for the **Fisherman's Birthday Festival**, see page 12.

Victoria

A 10-minute drive north of Gouyave, Victoria is another fishing village strung along the coastal road and is the main centre of St Mark's, the smallest parish on the island. It was called Grand Pauvre by the French and renamed after their Queen by the British, although some of the place names in the parish retained their French names, such as La Resource, Bonjour, Bonair and Belair. Fishing boats line the black-sand beach along St Mark Bay in Victoria. There is an annual festival here, **St Mark's Day**, in mid-April (see Festivals, page 77)

A worthwhile stop in Victoria is the **Diamond Jouvay Chocolate Factory** ① *Diamond Estates, turn off at the fuel station in Victoria and follow Diamond St for just under 1 mile into the residential area in the hills above the village, T473-437 1839/537 2398, www.jouvay chocolate.com, Mon-Thu 0800-1600, Fri-Sat 0800-1700,* where there's a delightful shop and café housed in a converted former rum distillery built by French monks in 1774. Later it was used for cocoa production and outside you can see the old drying trays. This is a relaxing spot to enjoy a coffee, cocoa tea, hot chocolate or Carib beer and the gift shop sells some good crafts and chocolate from a small chilled room. Jouvert chocolate bars are 60-75% pure cocoa. Tours of the factory and a stroll through the 3-acre cocoa and spice farm are by appointment although sometimes someone is available if you just turn up.

Victoria is the starting point for one of the toughest hikes on the island up to the tallest waterfall on Grenada at 80 ft: **Tufton Hall Waterfall**, which lies in the foothills of the tallest mountain on the island, **Mount St Catherine** (2757 ft). In 2004 Hurricane Ivan (see box, page 46) destroyed the historical Tufton Hall Estate House near the falls, after which they are named. For the fit, the hike will take up to three hours each way, so it is an all-day adventure. Along the way you will see other waterfalls, pools, sulphur springs and dense undergrowth as you get deeper into the beautiful countryside. Wear sturdy shoes that you don't mind getting wet as much of the hike is in the St Mark's River or alongside it clambering over boulders. It is possible to just follow the river from Queen Street in town (for experienced hikers and always hike in a group) or you can ask around town for a guide.

From Victoria, the road continues along the west coast and turns inland at **Duquesne** (pronounced 'Duquaine'). Here is a beautiful grey sand beach, although it's not particularly clean because of the fishing, but at the southern end are some petroglyphs carved into large stones believed to have been etched by the Caribs (or Kalinago). They are not easy to see among the rocks and the sea covers them at high tide, but a fisherman will point you in the right direction. The road then cuts inland before returning to the sea at **Sauteurs**, the capital of St Patrick's Parish, on the north coast (see page 48).

The interior

a road rising up to the rainforest, often entering the clouds

In the middle of the island, the road from Grenville on the east coast and the one from Gouyave on the west coast converge at the tiny settlement of Castaigne and join a road that runs over the central mountain range to/from St George's, passing right through Grand Etang National Park as it does so. It is well surfaced, but twisty and narrow, and the climb up and down goes through some lovely forest where epiphytes and mosses cling to the tree trunks and many species of fern and grasses provide thick undergrowth. Even if you're not a hiker, a stop at the visitor centre at the very top is well worthwhile, even for just refreshments and to enjoy the cool air and flowering gardens, before swinging down the hillside into St George's.

Seven Sisters Falls

About 1¼ miles before reaching the visitor centre at Grand Etang is the well-signposted trail to Seven Sisters Falls on the left. There is a tiny car park, shaded picnic area and a small shop that sells cold drinks; you need to pay a trail fee at the shop (US$1.85). The two falls at the end of the trail are very beautiful and you can have a refreshing swim in the pool at the base. They are only a 45-minute walk from the main road, but you begin from one of the highest points on the island (about 1900 ft) and descend 900 ft to the waterfalls, and the same to climb up out again (which takes much longer). There are also muddy steps and boulders to negotiate, so coming with a hiking guide can be useful here if you are likely to need assistance; Seven Sisters is a popular cruise ship trip and many do come on organized tours (see Tour operators, page 82).

As the first part of the hike goes through a private plantation of nutmeg and banana trees, before narrowing and plunging into the lush green rainforest, guides can also explain how these are grown, as well as point out the natural plants and trees on the way. For the energetic, about 20 minutes further upstream are the delightful **Honeymoon Falls**, a wet and tricky scramble over boulders and through cascades.

Grand Etang National Park

Daily 0800-1600, US$2, visitor centre has exhibitions and leaflets about the trails, restaurant/ bar, shop, toilets.

Established in 1992 from a former forest reserve, the focal point of Grenada's nature tourism lies 7 miles from the capital up in the clouds of the central mountain range. The National Park is named after Grand Etang ('large pond' in French), one of the two volcanic crater lakes on the island (the other being Lake Antoine, page 45). Grand Etang lies at 1800 ft above sea level, is approximately 20 ft deep and covers 3½ acres. It's peaceful and green and is surrounded by lush tropical forest. The visitor centre lies on the brow of the hill in lovely gardens where you pay the entrance fee at the boom gate, from where the Morne Labaye nature trail, which is only 15 minutes long, goes to a wooden lookout tower that you can climb for glorious views over the top of the tree canopy. The lake is accessed on the opposite side of the road a little down the hill towards Grenville, where there's a car park, picnic shelters and a shoreline trail around the lake, which takes about 1½ hours and is moderately easy.

Grand Etang's flora includes towering mahogany, teak and gommier trees, as well as a multitude of ferns and tropical flowers such as orchids. These provide shelter for birds including the broad-winged hawk (known here as the gree-gree), lesser Antillean swift and Antillean-crested hummingbird. There are plenty of frogs and lizards, but rarely seen are opossums and armadillos. Mona monkeys are believed to have originally arrived on the island from West Africa aboard slave ships, and they used to be spotted quite regularly in the car parks (thanks to cruise ship tour groups feeding them fruit). But since Hurricane Ivan felled many trees and the monas suffered from partial habitat loss, the population has diminished and there may only be around 500 on the whole of Grenada.

Also within the park are the peaks of **Mount Qua Qua**, **Mount Granby** and **Morne Fédon** (also known as Fédon's

> **Tip...**
> If hiking in Grand Etang, come prepared; with 160 inches of annual rainfall, it's a good idea to wear sturdy footwear and have waterproofs. Long trousers are also recommended because of razor grass and mosquitoes, walking sticks are a help, and take food and water.

BACKGROUND
Julien Fédon, revolutionary and folk hero

Julien Fédon was the first revolutionary on Grenada and has become something of a folk hero, influencing nationalist leaders and later revolutionaries. He was the leader of a slave revolt in Grenada between 2 March 1795 and 19 June 1796, around the time that other rebellions were flaring up in other Caribbean islands such as Cuba and Jamaica.

He was born on Martinique, the son of a French jeweller and a freed black slave, but the family moved to Grenada in the 1750s when the island was under French control. Fédon was influenced by ideology surrounding the French and Haitian Revolutions and his aim in the 1790s was to abolish slavery, to get rid of British rule and make Grenada a black republic. He set out with a force of about 100 freed slaves, attacking and killing British settlers in Gouyave and Grenville, looting and burning their houses. He then retreated to the mountains of Belvedere where the rebels were joined by runaway slaves who had escaped from their plantations and they established several fortifications against the British retaliation. It is believed that about half the 28,000 slaves on Grenada at the time were allied to the revolutionary forces, together with many resident French citizens who wanted to get the island back to French control. On 8 April 1796, Fédon's brother was killed in action. To avenge his death, Fédon executed 48 prisoners, including Governor Ninian Home. The British regrouped with reinforcements and attacked the rebels on the steep slopes of Mount Qua Qua, many of whom threw themselves down the mountain rather than risk capture. Fédon was never found. However, the demanding path leading up to the cave-like recess of Fedon's Camp is today a popular destination for hikers.

Camp). Around 25 miles of hiking trails have been marked, which are well worth the effort for the beautiful forest and views, but can be muddy and slippery after rain. The Mount Qua Qua hike takes around 1½ hours from Grand Etang Lake to the top, which reaches just over 2300 ft above sea level and from which you get expansive and beautiful views. But the path is steep and can get muddy and messy after rain. The trail then leads down through the rainforest canopy and over hilltops for another arduous three hours to the triple cascades of **Concord Falls** (see page 51). An extra 30-minute spur on this route goes to **Fédon's Camp** (see box, above), and takes you deep into the very heart of Grand Etang through shady groves of mahoganies, teaks and giant ferns. Once at Concord Falls you don't have to return the same way and instead can follow the trail down to the west coast road to get a bus to St George's.

After Grand Etang, there is a **viewpoint** at 1910 ft overlooking St George's. A bit further down the hill is a detour to the pretty **Annandale Falls** ⓘ *Mon-Fri 0800-1700, Sat-Sun 0900-1700, US$1.85,* which plunge about 40 ft into a pool where the locals dive and swim. Foreigners can too, but most people just walk to the viewing platform and don't stop long. Tourists are pestered for money here; it is on the cruise ship tour circuit and suffers as a result. If coming from St George's on Grenville Road, fork left at the Methodist Church about half way to Grand Etang.

Carriacou (pronounced 'Carry-a-coo'), named Kayryouacou by the Caribs, which means 'island of reefs', is an attractive island of gentle green hills descending to both white and black sandy beaches. It is 14 miles long, 2 miles wide and is one of the least developed Caribbean islands. The friendly population of around 7000 Carricouians, or Kyaks as they are known locally, are happy to share their island with you. Carriacou is less mountainous than Grenada, which means that any cloudy or rainy weather clears much quicker, and you can walk just about anywhere, while coral reefs lie offshore for great diving and snorkelling. The island also offers the yachting fraternity some peaceful bays for anchorages.

Located 20 miles north of Grenada, and along with Petit Martinique, part of the same territory, it is in fact the most southerly and largest island of the Grenadines, and lies just to the south of Union Island in St Vincent territory. The main settlements on the island are Hillsborough, L'Esterre, Harvey Vale and Windward.

Carriacou offers visitors a pleasing taste of the old Caribbean, with a number of small villages where subsistence farming, livestock rearing and fishing are traditionally the mainstay of life. Boat building is part of the culture, being celebrated in festivals and regattas throughout the year.

Essential Carriacou

Finding your feet

Carriacou's Lauriston Airport is on the coast just over 1 mile west of Hillsborough. The airport is so small that a fire engine drives out from Hillsborough to meet incoming flights, taking the immigration officer with it. Taxis meet the flights and it costs US$7.40 into town.

The jetty for all boat services is on Main Street in the middle of tiny Hillsborough. If you are coming by sea from St Vincent and the Grenadines, Carriacou's customs and immigration offices are at the police station on Main Street in Hillsborough (Monday-Friday 0800-1200, 1300-1700, Saturday-Sunday and public holidays 0900-1200, 1300-1500; if you arrive outside these hours, a phone call will bring the officers but a service fee of US$7.50 will be charged). Yacht arrivals can also go to another immigration and customs facility at Carriacou Marine in Tyrell Bay. See also Transport, page 84.

Best coffees or cocktails
Callaloo, page 74
Gallery Café, page 74
Kayak Kafe & Juice Bar, page 74
La Playa Beach Bar & Bistro, page 74
Off the Hook Bar & Grill, page 74

Getting around

Car hire is available, but is hardly necessary if you don't mind taking the cheap public transport or taxis over the short distances. Minibuses run to most parts of the island and will convert to a taxi to take you off route. Note on Sundays there are no buses and even most taxi drivers take the day off. Walking is rewarding and some beaches can only be reached on foot or by boat, but the heat may be a problem so avoid setting off on foot in the middle of the day. There are also water taxis between Hillsborough, Paradise Beach and Tyrell Bay, which you can also commandeer for Sandy Island or one of the remoter beaches.

Hillsborough

Carriacou's tiny and quite charming capital dates from a colonial settlement towards the late 18th century and was used by Admiral Ralph Abercrombie who came with 150 ships to launch an attack on the Spanish in 1796 and capture Trinidad. **Main Street** runs parallel to the sea and the hub of activity is the town jetty area with the tourist office (see page 62), behind which is the police station and the customs and immigration offices. One street back is the little minibus terminal and fruit and vegetable stalls. Also along Main Street there are guesthouses, a few restaurants, bars, a couple of supermarkets (the biggest and best is underneath Ade's Dream), shops, banks with ATMs and the dive shop **Deefer Diving**. The town is also blessed with a lovely beach, a huge curve of white sand with good sunset views and excellent swimming, despite the presence of the jetty and large cargo ships.

The people from Carriacou are referred to as Kajaks, and they maintain a strong adherence to their African origins. The Big Drum Dances that take place at Maroons

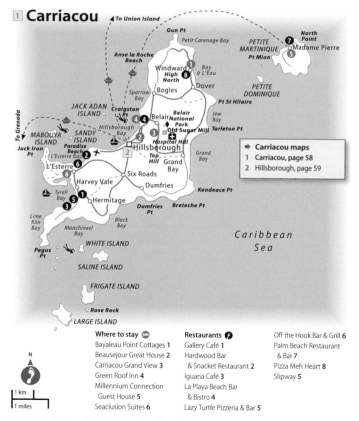

1 Carriacou ◄ To Union Island

Gun Pt

North Point

Petit Carenage Bay

PETITE MARTINIQUE ⑦ Madame Pierre
Pt Mion ⑤

Anse la Roche Beach

Windward High North ①
Bay à L'Eau ⑧
Bogles
Sparrow Bay
Dover

PETITE DOMINIQUE

JACK ADAN ISLAND
Craigston Pt ④
Belair
Belair National Park
Pt St Hilaire
Jew Bay
Tarleton Pt

To Grenada
Hillsborough Bay
③ Old Sugar Mill
② Hillsborough
Hospital Hill

MABOUYA ISLAND
SANDY ISLAND
Paradise Beach
Jack Iron Pt
L'Esterre Bay ⑥
Top Hill
Grand Bay

Grand Bay

➡ Carriacou maps
1 Carriacou, page 58
2 Hillsborough, page 59

L'Esterre ⑥
Six Roads
Harvey Vale
Dumfries

Tyrell Bay
⑤ ①
③ Hermitage

Kendeace Pt

Lime Kiln Bay
Manchineel Bay
Black Bay
Dumfries Pt
Breteche Pt

Caribbean Sea

Pegus Pt
WHITE ISLAND

SALINE ISLAND

FRIGATE ISLAND

Rose Rock
LARGE ISLAND

N

1 km
1 miles

Where to stay 🛏
Bayaleau Point Cottages 1
Beausejour Great House 2
Carriacou Grand View 3
Green Roof Inn 4
Millennium Connection Guest House 5
Seaclusion Suites 6

Restaurants 🍴
Gallery Café 1
Hardwood Bar & Snacket Restaurant 2
Iguana Café 3
La Playa Beach Bar & Bistro 4
Lazy Turtle Pizzeria & Bar 5

Off the Hook Bar & Grill 6
Palm Beach Restaurant & Bar 7
Pizza Meh Heart 8
Slipway 5

(community gatherings most usually held in spring to cry out to the gods for rain) and also performed at weddings, wakes, tombstone feasts and boat launches, are almost purely West African. The best time to see such an event is at the three-day **Carriacou Maroon Music Festival** held in late April (see Festivals, page 77).

Carriacou Historical Society Museum ⓘ *Patterson St, T473-443 8288, www.carriacou museum.org, Mon-Fri 1000-1600, Sat 1100-1500, US$5.55, under 16s US$0.90*, housed in an old cotton ginnery, has exhibits from Amerindian settlements in the island and from later periods in its history, including African artefacts, documents, furniture, household items and pottery (there's a small shop for gifts, cards, books and local music). The manager is happy to explain the exhibits in a short guided tour.

North of Hillsborough

The **Anglican Rectory** at Sea View was formerly the Beausejour Great House which dates to a 1669 sugar estate established under the French occupation. It's on a slight hill so that the master could watch his slaves in the fields below. The house is now single storey, having lost the second floor in Hurricane Janet in 1955, but the remains of the sugar boiling house and the aqueduct that brought the water from the sea can still be seen.

At **Belair National Park** ⓘ *no entry fee*, is a small and hilly forest reserve containing teak and mahogany, and the ruins of the old government house. The house was stripped bare during the US invasion of Grenada but the park is now used to hold the annual **Carriacou Maroon Music Festival** (see Festivals, page 77) and there are good trails for a pleasant walk.

On **Hospital Hill**, Belair, northeast of Hillsborough, there is an old sugar mill with stunning views. The tower is well preserved, but not much else is left. The slaves had to

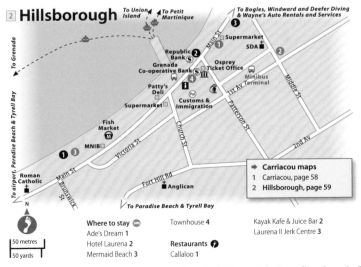

2 **Hillsborough**

Where to stay
Ade's Dream 1
Hotel Laurena 2
Mermaid Beach 3
Townhouse 4

Restaurants
Callaloo 1
Kayak Kafe & Juice Bar 2
Laurena II Jerk Centre 3

➡ Carriacou maps
1 Carriacou, page 58
2 Hillsborough, page 59

Tip...
The Caribbean coast is spectacular in places and a walk from Windward to Dover, and then following the coast road until it becomes a dirt road leading to Dumfries, is very pleasant and secluded.

carry the sugar cane all the way up the hill. The best views, however, are from the **Princess Royal Hospital** itself, built on top of the hill in 1907-1909 because of an outbreak of malaria. The wind up on the hill is too strong for mosquitoes and it was also considered a pleasant, quiet spot for patients to recuperate. From here you get a fabulous view of Hillsborough, and most of the southern part of the island. A few old cannons were put here in 1948.

Bogles is the most northerly village on the west side of the island and the end of the concrete road. From here a 4WD or at at least high-clearance vehicle is necessary in the wet season. A beautiful beach is **Anse La Roche**, which faces west and has a spectacular view across the strait to the mountains of rugged Union Island. Snorkelling is good, particularly among the rocks at the side. Take food and drink and no valuables of any sort; there are no facilities and few people. It is very easy to get lost walking to Anse La Roche Beach as you have to hike down through the woods from the road, and it is easier to take a water taxi there, although if you do walk, you're advised to take insect repellent. It's very peaceful watching the yachts rounding the headland on their way to anchorage.

You can walk all round the northern tip of the island from the west or east side from Windward. **Gun Point** is named after the cannon erected by the British in 1780, and from here a path leads down to the beach at **Petit Carenage Bay**, known locally as 'L'islet Beach' and also as Turtle Beach because turtles often go to nest at night. It has coarse, coral sand, good swimming and modest surf in some conditions.

Windward is a delightful old fishing and boat building village strung along its main road with a few shops and local bars (reached by No 11 bus from Hillsborough). Scottish boat builders settled here in the 19th century, and both Scottish names (and fair-skinned people) survive, as do the boatbuilding skills and traditional sailing fishing vessels known as Carriacou sloops are still made here; the sturdy vessels are built and repaired without the use of power tools in the shade of the mangroves on the beach (look out for the sign board explaining the practice). To show the qualities of these local boats, the **Carriacou Regatta** was initiated in 1965, see page 13.

South of Hillsborough

The coast road goes through Coconut Grove to the airport at Lauriston Point; it used to (alarmingly) cross the runway but now ends at a gate to the runway, and the route south goes from Hillsborough inland to Six Roads and back to the coast at Paradise Beach and on to L'Esterre. The long swathe of **Paradise Beach** lines L'Esterre Bay and is one of the loveliest beaches on the island (reached by No 10 bus). It's aptly named with pristine white sand, and clear, blue, shallow water with a wonderful view across to Sandy Island. There are beach bars including **Hardwood Bar & Snacket** and **Off the Hook Bar** (see page 74); perfect places to while away an afternoon. At both you can rent snorkelling gear for around US$11 per day and organize water taxis across to Sandy Island, five minutes each way, US$15 return. You can also get to the island by water taxi from

Tip...
Grab a picnic from **Patty's Deli** (see page 78), find a water taxi and play Robinson Crusoe on Sandy Island, but lather up with sunscreen and take plenty of water.

Hillsborough US$25, 30 minutes each way, or join a dive boat for an excursion with diving or snorkelling. **Sandy Island** is a tiny, low-lying atoll in Hillsborough Bay off Lauriston Point, a sand spit or cay with a few palm trees for shade and a bit of scrub. There is excellent swimming and snorkelling, and a marine protected area prevents cruise ships swamping the sand bank with 200 tourists at a time, damaging the reef with anchor chains. Now people come in small groups on small boats and stay for a few hours; there are moorings for yachts, which have to pay a fee.

Tip...
As an alternative to Sandy Island, get a water taxi across to White Island, a similar islet in Manchineel Bay, 1 mile off the south coast, fringed by beaches except for a steep cliff face at one end. This is one of the favourite Sunday limes (see box, page 25) for locals and is excellent for swimming and snorkelling off powdery white sand.

The local painter, **Canute Calliste** (1914-2005), had his studio at **L'Esterre**. His naïve style captured the scenes of Carriacou. The road then cuts across the peninsula to **Harvey Vale**, at Tyrell Bay. Visitors should see the oyster beds at **Tyrell Bay** where 'tree-oysters' grow on mangrove roots. Tyrell Bay is an anchorage for yachts and the mangroves are a hurricane hole. There are several good restaurants and bars along the bay side, popular with the yachting fraternity, attracted also by **Carriacou Marine** ① *T473-443 6292, www.carriacoumarine.com*, which is a port of entry as well as chandlery and boatyard; there's a small convenience store here for basic groceries and cold drinks, and the **Iguana Café** (see page 74).

Petite Martinique

a tiny island fishing community untouched by extravagant tourist facilities

Reached from Hillsborough by the Osprey ferry in 20 minutes, or water taxis from Windward, Petite Martinique is 2½ miles away from Carriacou and is the only offshore island from Carriacou on which people live. The population is descended from French fishermen, Glaswegian shipwrights, pirates and slaves.

The largest village was named Madame Pierre after the wife of the first French owner who had come from Martinique. It is thought that he figured that the isle was shaped roughly like Martinique so he named it Petite (little) Martinique. As a result of the French settlement, the population is mainly Roman Catholic and the parish priest is always the council chairman. It covers 486 acres, rising to a small, volcanic peak, and only a very small channel separates it from Petit St Vincent, where many people work at the resort. The principal legal occupations are boatbuilding and fishing, but for generations the islanders have been involved in smuggling and they are noticeably more prosperous than their neighbours.

A famous story is when in 1997 there was excitement when the government proposed to build a house for 12 coast guard personnel in the campaign against drug smuggling. Half the population turned out to demonstrate against the arrival of government surveyors and clashed with armed police and the Special Services Unit.

The big event of the year is the **Petite Martinique Whitsuntide Regatta** in May, see page 12.

The island has a church, school, bank, post office, health centre, fuel station, a few grocery stores and basic guesthouses and a good restaurant and bar, popular with charter yachts. If you come in by ferry for lunch (see page 150 for times), it takes about 1½ hours to walk around the whole island with a swim at the beach on the northwest coast.

Tourist information

St George's

Pure Grenada Tourism Information Centre
Wharf Rd, the Carenage, St George's, T473-440 2279/2001, www.puregrenada.com. Mon-Fri 0800-1600. A kiosk opens at the Cruise Ship Terminal when ships are in town.
The staff are very helpful and there are brochures/maps to pick up.

Carriacou

Tourist office
Across from the jetty on Main Street (in front of the police/immigration/customs building, Hillsborough, T473-443 7948, www.puregrenada.com. Mon-Fri 0800-1600.
Very helpful, lots of brochures/maps to pick up and they can tell you everything you need to know about Carriacou. You can leave your luggage here while you find accommodation and the staff will call places for you.

Where to stay

Unless otherwise stated, all hotel rooms have a/c, TV and Wi-Fi. Hotel tax (10%) and service (10%) are charged by all accommodation options, usually as a single charge of 20%. Check if this has been included in quoted rates.

St George's *map page 32.*
There's hardly anywhere to stay in St George's, and as lovely as it is, neither is there any reason to given that the Grand Anse area is only about a 10-min drive away. Rather visit on a day trip or come into town for a meal or liming (see box, page 25) at the weekend.

$$-$ Deyna's City Inn
Melville St, T473-435 7007, www.deynascityinn.co.
If you need to stay in town, this neat budget-priced hotel will do, with 12 small but spotless and comfortable rooms and some attractive decorative touches. There's an excellent local breakfast to set you up for the day. Right on the Esplanade with views of the cruise ships you're at the heart of things; don't expect peace and quiet but there's always something to watch from the balcony. Lunch, snacks and drinks at **Deyna's Tasty Foods** downstairs (see Restaurants, below).

Southwest Grenada
There are a couple of large all-inclusive resorts on the southwest peninsula: the couples-only **Sandals LaSource Grenada Resort & Spa** (www.sandals.com) on Pink Gin Beach, and the family-orientated **Grenadian by Rex Resorts** (www.rexresorts.com) on Magazine Beach. A huge development is currently underway on Grand Anse Main Rd; **Silver Sands Resort** will be a 5-star hotel with more than 50 suites and villas taking up more than 300 yards of frontage on Grand Anse Beach.

Grand Anse *map page 40.*

$$$$ Mount Cinnamon
Morne Rouge Rd, T473-439 4400, www.mountcinnamongrenadahotel.com.
The flagship boutique resort on the island, owned by British entrepreneur and former America's Cup yachtsman Peter de Savary. It's set in tropical gardens at the southwest end of Grand Anse Beach on the hillside leading over to Morne Rouge. The 21 high-end and chic hacienda-style villas and suites, arranged around relaxing central semi-open public areas, have sea-view balconies, 4-poster beds, pull-out sofas and kitchens; the more expensive have plunge pools and 1-3 bedrooms. Fantastic decor throughout with splashes of vibrant colours. All the facilities you could need including **Savvy's at Mount Cinnamon** restaurant, pool, tennis, yoga, spa treatments

and gym, and across the road a path leads down to **Beach Cabana**, a separate beach club on Grand Anse (open to all 0800-1930; US$18.50), which also hosts a great Fri night barbecue with a bonfire and steelpan band (reservations required).

$$$$ Radisson Grenada Beach Resort
Grand Anse Main Rd, T473-444 4371, www.radisson.com.
With good Radisson standards and service this resort is set in lawned gardens along the beach. The 229 spacious rooms have modern, contemporary, bright interiors, balconies/patios and coffeemakers. Facilities including pool with waterfalls, gym, 2 restaurants, beach bar, **Native Spirit Scuba** dive school (see page 79). B&B or all-inclusive rates.

$$$$ Spice Island Beach Resort
Grand Anse Beach, T473-444 4258, www.spiceislandbeachresort.com.
A luxury all-inclusive resort on the beach with 64 very private and romantic suites of varying sizes in cool white buildings with warm colours for interior furnishings, all with terraces and some with plunge pools. Facilities include 2 restaurants, pool, gym, gorgeous spa, the **Nutmeg Pod** children's activity centre and watersports.

$$$ Blue Horizons Garden Resort
Morne Rouge Rd, T473-444 4316, www.grenadabluehorizons.com.
Set back from the beach, but less than a 5-min walk and you can use facilities at Spice Island, the sister hotel (above). 32 tastefully decorated studios and 1-bed units in duplex cottages with kitchenettes and patios, some interconnect, pool, pleasant grounds with mature, tall trees and palms attracting birds, **La Belle Créole** restaurant serves good breakfasts and dinners, and there's a pool bar for light meals and cocktails.

$$$ Flamboyant Hotel & Villas
Morne Rouge Rd, T473-444 4247, www.flamboyant.com.

Next to **Mount Cinnamon** on the way to Morne Rouge, 60 units in rooms and cottages, some with kitchenettes, on the hillside with lovely views, although it's a steep walk down from the highest ones (with the best views). Not luxurious, but more than adequate with friendly staff and gym, pool, beachside restaurant and late-night sports bar. **Dive Grenada** is based here (see page 79).

$$$-$$ Coyaba Beach Resort
Grand Anse Main Rd, T473-444 4129, www.coyaba.com.
Occupying a central position on Grand Anse Beach, decent mid-range option with 70 casual rooms in low blocks, each with wood furnishings and colourful accents, balconies/patios, more expensive are at the front with views, 2 restaurants, 3 bars, including a swim-up one at the pool, gym, spa, tennis court and a dive shop for **Eco-Dive** (page 79). Rates are room-only or all-inclusive.

$$$-$$ Jenny's Place
Grand Anse Main Rd, T473-439 5186, www.jennysplacegrenada.com.
In its own private garden set back from the quiet northeastern end of the beach, this relaxed option has 6 spacious self-catering studios and 1 budget room that sleeps 2-4. Furnishings are a little tired but there are big bathrooms and balconies. Friendly and excellent value for the location. The **Edge** restaurant on the beach (see page 71), buses stop at the top of the road, and other restaurants and shops nearby; everything is handy and convenient.

$$ Siesta Hotel
Morne Rouge Rd, T473-444 4645, www.siestahotel.com.
Budget hotel set in a hillside cluster of whitewashed properties near Spiceland Mall, a 5-min walk to Grand Anse Beach, 37 bright and white, functional studios and 1- to 2-bedroom apartments with basic cooking facilities. **La Deliciosa Restaurant** serves

Creole and international food and you can walk to other places.

$$-$ SeaBreeze Hotel
Grand Anse Main Rd, T473-439 0809, see Facebook.
Opposite Grand Anse Craft and Spice Market and previously the Blue Orchid (if taxi drivers get confused), the idea of new owners Lotten and Robert is to make this like a European backpacker hostel. 16 rooms, some triples and family rooms with bunk beds neatly and colourfully decorated with fridge, microwave and kettle, all have balconies and views across to Grand Anse Beach, outdoor area at back with communal kitchen and lounging area, local breakfast like bakes with saltfish or cheese, bus stop across the road. Can organize all activities and run their own island tours (US$90) and have 2 jeeps for hire (from US$55 per day).

$ Caribbean Cottage Club
Grey Stones, Belmont, T473-420 4213, www.grenadacottages.com.
Off the main road between Port Louis and Grand Anse, this is great value from US$60 for a double out of season. There are 4 pretty wooden cottages set in tropical gardens, with basic kitchen, screened windows, verandas; the larger 2 have outdoor dining tables and couches, each sleeps 2-4 and extra beds can be provided for up to 6. Peaceful, private and a 10-min walk to Grand Anse Beach.

Morne Rouge *map page 40.*
As these 2 properties are co-owned, the option here is to upgrade from the **Gem** to the **Kalinago** if you so choose and there is availability.

$$$ Kalinago Beach Resort
T473-444 5255, www.kalinagobeachresort.com.
Next to the **Gem Holiday Beach Resort** (below) on Morne Rouge Beach, and newer and more upmarket, relaxed and peaceful, with 29 comfortable and cheerful rooms in a neat 3-storey block with balconies, fridge,

kettle and microwave, with only the pool between them and the sea. Restaurant with upper floor terrace serving a mix of international and local food, good breakfasts, swim-up pool bar, and frequent events like beach barbecues.

$$ Gem Holiday Beach Resort
T473-444 4224, www.gembeachresort.com.
A little dated but super friendly with a fun holiday atmosphere, with 20 large 1- and 2-bedroom self-catering apartments with garden or ocean views and balconies, comfortable living room with dining table, old but adequate kitchen units. Excellent value for groups/families. **Sur la Mer** restaurant/beach bar with reasonable food including rotis and a popular Sat night seafood buffet, and the **Fantazia** nightclub attached (see Bars and clubs, page 75).

Other beaches and bays on the southwest peninsula *map page 40.*

$$$$ Laluna Beach Resort and Villas
Portici Beach, T437-439 0001, www.laluna.com.
Always highly rated, this romantic 16-cottage boutique property is known for its beachside yoga pavilion, Asian spa, Italian restaurant (see page 71) and stylish decor that blends Balinese, Caribbean, and Italian influences. It sits on 10 acres of secluded hillside and each cottage is very private with plunge pool, also 2-5 bedroom villas on an adjoining property. Complimentary mountain bikes, snorkelling, hobie cats and kayaks, daily yoga and pilates (US$12 per session for visitors).

$$$$ Maca Bana Villas
Off Maurice Bishop Memorial Hwy above Magazine Beach, T437-439 5355, www.macabana.com.
Perched on top of a hill this small luxury resort has 7 charming 1-, 2- and 3-bedroom villas, spacious and comfortable with state-of-the-art kitchen and open-plan living/dining area leading onto expansive veranda with hot tub and sunbeds. The pretty gardens attract birds and butterflies

although it's a bit of a steep walk down and back from the **Aquarium** restaurant (see page 71) and Magazine Beach. It's worth it though for the views looking all along the coastline to St George's. It's within walking distance from the airport, although there is a shuttle bus.

$$$ True Blue Bay Boutique Resort
Old Mill Rd, True Blue Bay, T473-443 8783, www.truebluebay.com.
Above and overlooking True Blue Bay though not quite on the beach (a long walk or short shuttle ride away), cheerful family-friendly mid-range resort, 49 large rooms and villas, all colourfully painted with kitchenettes, sea view balconies with hammocks, the 2-bedroom villas have plunge pools. Infinity pool with manmade sandy beach, gym and spa, and **Dodgy Dock** restaurant/bar over the water (see page 75).

$$ Grooms Beach Villa & Resort
Dr Grooms Rd, T473-439 7666, www.groomsbeachresort.com.
Newly built in cheerful yellow blocks, 38 units in rooms with fridge and coffeemakers, or 1- and 2-bedroom apartments with kitchens, balconies or terraces, well-priced spacious and clean. A short walk to Portici and Parc à Boeuf beaches and a 15-min walk from the airport, laid-back restaurant/bar and gardens with a pool.

$$-$ La Heliconia
Maurice Bishop Highway, T473-439 8585, www.laheliconia.com.
Simple accommodation in 9 apartments with shared balconies in walking distance (and views of) the airport, and close to Magazine Beach. Reality is a little shabbier than the pretty pictures on the website, but nonetheless it's good value, especially for 3-4 sharing, and adequate airport accommodation if you are arriving late/are delayed before moving on. Small day spa (open to all) on site.

Lance aux Épines *maps pages 30 and 40.*

$$$$ Calabash Hotel
Beach Lane, T473-444 4334, www.calabashhotel.com.
This is one of the oldest and best hotels on the island in one of the loveliest settings, the 30 super-stylish and spacious suites and villas are arranged around an elegant central lawn with palms and flowering bushes leading down to Lance aux Épines Beach; breakfast is served on a large balcony. Notable for its **Rhodes at Calabash restaurant** (see page 71), and also has **The Beach Club** (1130-1800), for lunch, tapas and snacks. Watersports, tennis and gym.

$$$$ Mount Hartman Bay Estate
Reef View Dr, T473-407 4504, www.mounthartmanbay.com.
One of the island's newest luxury boutique hotels and once a private house, 12 suites in beautiful grounds full of flowers, the main sitting room/bar has a vaulted ceiling with an internal waterfall, and there's a stunning infinity pool overlooking Hartman Bay, private beach and jetty for yachts. The **Cave House Restaurant** offers gourmet food and is so called because of its interior of pebbly walls and cool white arches but also has a sunny deck.

$$$ Twelve Degrees North
Lance Aux Épines Main Rd, T473-444 4580, www.twelvedegreesnorth.com.
Apartment resort in a small complex of just 8 units on the waterfront overlooking Prickly Bay in lovely gardens with tennis court, pool, and small private beach and dock, snorkelling gear, kayaks and sunfish sail boats to use. Owner-managed by Joseph Gaylord, an excellent host, with an exceptional team of housekeepers who will shop and cook for you at no extra cost, providing delicious meals on your balcony. No children under 15.

$$$-$$ Coral Cove Cottages and Apartments
Ocean Breeze Dr, T473-444 4422, www.coralcovecottages.com.

Good-value spot, quiet, immaculate gardens, good for kids, with 11 self-catering 1- or 2-bedroom units; either in lovely, breezy cottages or apartments with larger kitchens and balconies. Beautiful view of Mount Hartman Bay, 15 mins' walk to restaurants and minimarket, own beach and jetty with gazebo at the end for snorkelling in shallow water, pool and tennis court.

$$$-$$ Lance aux Épines Cottages
Lance Aux Épines Main Rd, T473-444 4565, www.laecottages.com.
Built in the 1970s and still under the same family ownership, well-priced simple option and great for families, the 11 cottages and apartments are bright and have 1-, 2- or 3-bedrooms, furnishings are a little old-fashioned but the kitchens are well-equipped, and set in 3 acres of gardens right on Lance aux Épines Beach with beach bar (there's no pool though). A 5-min walk to Prickly Bay Marina for restaurant and mini-market.

$$ Casabella Bed & Breakfast
Hummingbird Dr, T473-444 4796, www.casabellagrenada.com.
A deservedly popular B&B in a modern 3-storey house with 7 single, double and family rooms in a smart and quiet suburb. Good breakfasts, nice pool, Lance Aux Épines Beach is nearby and you can walk to Prickly Bay Marina.

East coast Grenada *map page 30.*

$$$$-$$$ Le Phare Bleu Boutique Hotel & Marina
Petite Calivigny Bay, Calivigny, T473-444 2400, www.lepharebleu.com.
This eco-conscious hotel and yacht marina is a lovely small chilled hideaway with 5 1- and 2-bedroom villas and 2 studio apartments, set in tropical gardens close to the beach, each with well-equipped kitchens, and stylish decor. Pool, snorkelling gear and kayaks and hobies can be hired, **The Deck Restaurant & Bar** (see page 73) and the marina is home to **Petite Calivigny Yacht Club**.

$$$$-$$$ Petite Anse Hotel
Prospect Rd, Sauteurs, T473-442 5252, www.petiteanse.com.
A delightful and relaxing pretty boutique hotel at the northern tip of the island on a secluded beach hemmed in by hills, this is a good base for exploring the north and has a stunning view across the sea to the Grenadines. English owners Phillip and Annie Clift are on hand for any requests or information. The 11 chalet rooms all have sea view and some are only steps from the ocean with deck or terrace. Excellent restaurant that's worth coming to on an island tour (see page 72).

$$$ La Sagesse
La Sagesse Bay, T473-444 6458, www.lasagesse.com.
Low-key and understated, in coastal forest on the edge of gorgeous La Sagesse Beach, the most notable building here is the striking pink manor house built in the 1960s for the late Lord Brownlow, a cousin of the Queen. 12 rooms in the house, cottages or a split-level building, it's worth paying extra for a terrace and sea views, plainly furnished but comfortable and mostly spacious, a walkway to the beach is lined with conch shells. The restaurant and beach bar is well worth pulling in to on a drive around this part of the coast (see page 72).

$$$-$$ Cabier Ocean Lodge
Crochu, T473-444 6013, www.cabier-vision.com.
Fairly simple but wonderfully remote on a spit jutting into the Atlantic, with honey-coloured beaches on either side in Crochu and Cabier bays, though a little tricky to get to on the bumpy dirt road and swimming/snorkelling is only doable if it's calm. But friendly German-owned spot, with 10 rooms, some with basic kitchens, and 1 villa with a pool and the best view, which sleeps up to 10 but can be split into 3 units. German-speaking island tours can be arranged from here. Bruno's restaurant (under separate management) serves breakfasts, light lunches and set 3-course

dinners on a terrace, and also has a small collection of animals (mostly rescued) ranging from donkeys and monkeys to piglets and talking parrots.

$$ Almost Paradise Cottages
Prospect Rd, Sauteurs, T473-442 0608, www.almost-paradise-grenada.com.
Run by Kate (Canadian) and Uwe (German) Baumann, peaceful and relaxing with 8 simple, breezy wooden cottages of varying sizes in delightful hillside garden setting, and along with **Petite Anse** next door, the best location to stay on this end of the island with simply breathtaking views up the islands. Each has outdoor shower, balcony with hammock, kitchen and colourful decor. Bar, meals on request, path through forest to the beach, and Sauteurs is a 20-min walk.

$$ Treetops Villa Guest House
Mt Alexander, off Prospect Rd, Sauteurs, T473-442 0984, www.treetopsgrenada.com.
Up the hill from **Almost Paradise** and run by Pam and Chas, this modern house is built in the pretty traditional gingerbread style and has great ocean views, B&B accommodation in 2 spacious rooms with small kitchenettes and shared balcony. Guests can use the jacuzzi.

$ Valley Breeze Guest House
Grand Bras, Grenville, T473-442 5375, www.valleybreezeguesthouse.com.
Not holiday accommodation but suitable for an overnight or handy for hikers, 7 1- and 2-bedroom apartments and mini swimming pool run by Yvette in a newly built block, on a quiet road outside of Grenville, about a 30-min walk or buses stop outside, Grand Bras continues to the junction with the interior road to Grand Etang.

West coast Grenada *map page 30.*

$$ Rumboat Retreat
Mount Nesbit, Gouyave, T473-437 1726, www.rumboatretreat.com.
With great ocean views from its hillside position in the village, this guesthouse has just 4 rooms in a plantation-style house with balconies, modern, spacious and with vibrant decor. Lisette, the owner, and her staff can provide very good seafood and other meals taken on the terrace, and organize rum tasting and walking tours around Gouyave including to the Nutmeg Processing Plant (see page 52).

$ Crayfish Bay Estate
Non Pareil, between Victoria and Duquesne, T473-442 1897, www.crayfishbay.com.
On a working cocoa estate where fruit and vegetables are also grown, the 'Little House' is available for guests and is a simple wooden cabin with 2 bedrooms and a loft area for children. Self-catering – and you can buy local produce and fish – but breakfast with home-made bread and evening meal can be provided on request. Rum shops and buses in walking distance but restaurants are a drive away. Off the beaten track, you experience rustic farm and village life here.

Carriacou *maps pages 58 and 59.*
The accommodation on Carriacou is very affordable, but those wanting something more upmarket might want to rent a villa or apartment on the island, try: www.island villas.com and www.simplycarriacou.com.

$$$-$$ Mermaid Beach Hotel
Main Street, Hillsborough, T473-443 8286, www.mermaidhotelcarriacou.com.
This old property reopened in 2015 and is now neat as a pin, with 22 rooms centred around an attractive, open and airy atrium that leads to the small beach (with sun loungers) and the 4 larger suites have ocean views. A little bare still, and the bathrooms could do with the odd towel rail etc, but easily one of the best positioned hotels and well-managed. Runs **Callaloo** restaurant and bar next door (see Restaurants, below).

$$ Green Roof Inn
10 mins north of Hillsborough, T473-443 6399, www.greenroofinn.com.

On hillside with ocean views, Swedish-owned guesthouse with 5 rooms and a breezy restaurant on the upstairs veranda, plus 2 garden cottages, 1 with kitchenette, extra beds available, breakfast included, airport/jetty transfers, sandy area in front for swimming. Also runs **La Playa Beach Bar & Bistro** (see page 74).

$$ Hotel Laurena
Middle St, Hillsborough, T473-443 8759, www.hotellaurena.com.
The largest hotel on the island but suffers from little character and maintenance and service issues. Nevertheless it's fairly modern, central and a short walk from the ferry, with 26 rooms and 1- and 2-bedroom apartments with kitchenettes, in 4 colonial style buildings with brick façades. Its restaurant/bar, **Laurena II Jerk Centre**, is in town, a short walk away (see below).

$$ Seaclusion Suites
L`Esterre, T473-407 2779, www.seaclusionsuites.com.
Set on a pretty hillside with panoramic views across to Sandy Island, Bob and Marie Jasin have 2 delightful apartments with fully equipped kitchen and patio in gardens where there's an outdoor shower, barbecue and hammocks. All meals can be arranged if you don't want to cook. Paradise Beach is 5-10 min walk away, and Bob is a wealth of local information.

$$-$ Bayaleau Point Cottages
Windward, T473-443 7984, www.carriacoucottages.com.
Set on the panoramic eastern most point of Windward Bay, this simple, laid-back, family-friendly spot has 4 lovely, colourful wooden cottages in chattel house style with kitchen equipment, verandas, hammocks and own little beach. Owner Dave Goldhill is helpful and friendly and will take you on his boat, *Mostly Harmless*, for snorkelling to the offshore reef or to the Tobago Cays for a wonderful day trip (US$135 per person, minimum 4; contact him even if not staying).

$$-$ Carriacou Grand View
Belair Rd, Hillsborough, T473-443 6348, www.carriacougrandview.com.
A family-run hotel located on a hillside overlooking Hillsborough with 12 rooms and self-catering apartments sleeping 4, nothing fancy but comfortable and well-equipped and some have balconies, restaurant/bar for home-style meals and pleasant pool. Easy walk downhill to town and a taxi ride back uphill with shopping.

$ Ade's Dream
Main St, Hillsborough, T473-443 7317, www.adesdream.com.
This popular hotel is right in the middle of things on Main St, close to the ferry and bus terminal, has super-friendly staff and 16 studios with kitchenettes and double/triple rooms with balconies, plus 7 great value budget rooms sleeping up to 4 with a shared communal kitchen and balcony at the back overlooking the bus terminal. Supermarket downstairs, restaurant/bar across the road with sea frontage and tasty breakfasts including saltfish and bake, plus other local food and seafood.

$ Town House
Above Grenada Cooperative Bank, Main St, Hillsborough, T473-409 0346, www.ospreylines.com.
Affiliated with the **Osprey Lines** ferry (the jetty is across the road), manageress Reisha offers 9 basic but spotless tiled rooms with microwave, kettle and modern bathrooms.

Petite Martinique

$$-$ Palm Beach Restaurant & Bar
T473-443 9103.
The main focus on the island for eating and drinking (see below) but also rents out 2 apartments, 1 twin/double, the other family-sized, on a hillside overlooking the bay, a 10-min walk away from the restaurant and beach. Neat and modern with tiled floors and well-equipped kitchens, and lovely views.

$ Millennium Connection Guest House
T473-443 9243, www.petitemartinique.com.
Just past the Petite Martinique Primary
School and a 3-min walk from the jetty,
3 rooms, a communal lounge/dining room,
large covered veranda and guests can use
the kitchen. The simple yellow house is part
of a small business complex which is also
home to Matthew's Supermarket.

Restaurants

VAT on restaurant bills is 15%, but this is
nearly always included in menu prices;
10% service charge is however usually
added to the bill.

St George's *map page 32.*
For hot drinks and divine cakes, pop into
the **House of Chocolate**, or the café next
door at the **Grenada National Museum**
is also very pleasant. Both on Young St
(see page 33). You can also get hot plates
of food at the market. On the Carenage
on Fri and Sat nights, street food vendors
set up stalls selling the likes of fried fish,
chicken and breadfruit.

$$$ BB's Crabback Caribbean Restaurant
*Progress House, on the Carenage, T473-435
7058, www.bbscrabbackrestaurant.com.
Mon-Sat 0800-2130, bar until 2300.*
Overlooking the water with a lovely view of
the harbour, friendly and welcoming and
visitors have expressed their appreciation
by writing on the walls. Tasty seafood dishes
and local meat specialities such as coconut
curried goat/mutton and jerk pork/chicken.
Don't miss the famous crabback: crabmeat
baked with herbs, cheese and wine and
served in the shell with warm bakes. Owned
by charismatic Brian Benjamin, who had a
restaurant of the same name in west London
for many years.

$$$-$$ Sails Restaurant & Bar
*Next to BB's on the Carenage, T473-440 9747,
see Facebook. Mon-Sat 0900-2200.*
Light, breezy place with wonderful views
of the harbour and the entire horseshoe-
shaped Carenage and tables perched
directly over the water with windows that
open wide; perfect too for a morning coffee
or evening drink. Offers lunchtime salads,
wraps and burgers and a more sophisticated
evening menu including seafood platters,
steamed crab, lobster and lambi, and tasty
vegetarian options. Is well known for its
attentive service.

$ Creole Shack
*Melville St, T473-439 9377. Sun-Thu 0700-
2200, Fri-Sat 0700-2400.*
Overlooking the cruise ships, this upstairs
local food cafeteria and bar is popular at
lunchtime with long queues, for the specials
such as curry lambi, stew oxtail and salt fish
souse, oildown and fresh juices; the mac and
cheese has lots of local spices and is very
tasty. Karaoke Sat and Sun from 1800.

$ Deyna's Tasty Foods
*Melville St, T473-435 7007. Mon-Sat 0630-
1900, Sun 0700-1600.*
The colourfully decorated downstairs café
of **Deyna's City Inn** serves tasty local food
at local prices, and lots of it; breakfast will
set you up for the day, the filling rotis are
good at any time, and try the sorrel, mauby
or passionfruit juice. It's always crowded
at lunch and there's a separate queue for
takeaway meals.

$ Sweet Traditions
*At the entrance of Esplanade Mall, Cruise Ship
Terminal, T473-440 1600. Mon-Thu and Sat
0800-1830, Fri 0800-1930.*
A canteen and bakery offering a variety of
food including hot lunches (sit down or in
a box), hot and cold drinks, savoury pies
and pastries, sugary cakes, soft serve ice
cream, very convenient if you're wandering
around town and need a carb/sugar fix and
it's cheap.

$ The New Nutmeg Restaurant & Bar
*On the Carenage, T473-435 9525.
Mon-Sat 0800-2200.*

Although a restaurant has been here since 1962, this newer version is still good for local dishes including lambie and fish and chips, sandwiches, rotis, soups, salads or just a cold beer, sorrel juice or rum punch. Get a table by the wide open windows overlooking the Carenage and the boats in the harbour.

Southwest Grenada *map page 32*
The Lagoon

$$$-$$ Patrick's Local Homestyle Cooking
Lagoon Rd, opposite Port Louis Marina, T473-449 7243, see Facebook. Daily 1200-1400, 1800-2300.
Reservations required for dinner. This simple one-of-a-kind restaurant has a great friendly atmosphere and is the place to try Grenadian cuisine. The fixed price dinner of up to 20 different dishes is served tapas style and costs around US$25 and includes the likes of breadfruit and green papaya salads, stir-fried rabbit, aubergine in beer batter, crayfish broth, tannia cakes with shrimps and oildown with coconut cream. It's a unique and fun experience accompanied by a good rum punch. There's a lighter menu at lunchtime.

$$$-$$ Victory Bar & Restaurant and YOLO Sushi Bar
Port Louis Marina, Lagoon Rd, T473-435 7263, see Facebook. Daily 0730-2300.
A little overpriced but you can't beat the lovely waterside setting at this world-class marina with a view of the lights of St George's twinkling across the harbour and crews prepping up their yachts. Open for English or French-style breakfasts, and has a grill (steaks/ribs/chicken) and pizza menu for lunch and dinner. Happy Hour 1700-2000. Adjoining it is **YOLO** ('You Only Live Once'), a good sushi, wine and cocktail bar (Mon-Sat 1700-2300).

Grand Anse *map page 40.*

$$$-$$ Carib Sushi
Le Marquis Mall, Morne Rouge Rd, 473-439-5640, www.caribsushi.com. Mon-Sat 1100-1400, daily 1800-2100.
Next to **La Boulangerie** (below), rated for its consistently good sushi and long menu of soups, sashimi, ceviche, specials like lobster salad and deep fried ice cream for dessert. The team of Japanese chefs are wonderful to watch and there's a lively outdoor deck, even though it overlooks the road.

$$ Coconut Beach
Just north of Grand Anse Craft and Spice Market, T473-444 4644, www.coconutbeachgrenada.com. Open 1230-2230, closed Tue.
On the beach, this French creole restaurant has colourfully painted picnic tables so you can dine with your feet in the sand or more formal seating indoors with jalousie windows to let in the breeze. Lots of fish and seafood, plenty of lobster, plus steak, chicken and vegetarian dishes, and lunchtime options include sandwiches, omelettes and salads, and local desserts such as delicious coconut pie.

$$ Sangria Restaurant Bar & Lounge
On Morne Rouge Bay but accessed from the top of the hill over from Grand Anse, T473-439 7491, see Facebook. Mon-Sat 1200-2230, Sun 1600-2230.
Pleasant deck high up over Morne Rouge with comfortable couches and lovely views, small but interesting Mediterranean menu including tapas and good seafood like linguine and shrimp or tuna ceviche, and the grilled catch of the day is always tasty, plenty of sangria with a sunset view.

$$-$ La Boulangerie
Le Marquis Mall, Morne Rouge Rd, T473-444 1131. Mon-Sat 0830-2130, Sun 0900-2100.
Not much to look at in a little shopping centre at the back of Grand Anse Beach, but you can eat on the simple terrace or takeaway. Good for breakfast with croissants,

Danish pastries or full American, coffee and freshly squeezed juice, lunch and dinner of really good pizza and pastas, salads, sandwiches, Italian ice cream.

$$-$ The Edge
At Jenny's Place, T473-439 5186, www.jennysplacegrenada.com. Tue-Sat 1600-2200, Sun 1000-1800.
At the very northern point of Grand Anse Beach, this seafront bistro right on the water gets its name from its location. The menu offers a variety of food; soups, pastas, salads, burgers, sandwiches for lunch or chicken curry, steak au poivre, catch of the day, pork tenderloin for supper, or just come for a sunset drink.

Other beaches and bays on the southwest peninsula *map page 40.*

$$$ Laluna
At Laluna Beach Resort and Villas, Portici Beach, T437-439 0001, www.laluna.com. Lunch and dinner to non-guests by reservation only.
This open-air, thatched-roofed, Italian restaurant is a lovely spot, right behind the beach, with a mellow, romantic ambience (no under 12s). Some ingredients such as olives, sun-dried tomatoes and cold meats are imported from Italy, while dishes such as a pumpkin and ginger soup and seafood spaghetti with fish, shrimps, clams and scallops make the most of local produce. Good choice of Italian wines.

$$$-$$ Beach House
Portici Beach, T473-444 4455, www.beach housegrenada.com. Lunch Dec-Mar 1130-1730, dinner all year 1800-2230, reservations preferred, provides a shuttle service from hotels in the southwest.
One of the best restaurants on Grenada not affiliated to a hotel, the open-air Beach House is very pretty, with tables and hammocks in gardens on the beach. Good food, lots of oriental influences with sushi and satay, fish, steak and other meats and yummy desserts, while simpler dishes – burgers, pasta, rotis – are available at lunchtime.

$$ Aquarium Restaurant & La Sirena Beach Bar
Magazine Beach, T473-444 1410, www. aquarium-grenada.com. Tue-Sun 1000-2300.
Under the same ownership as **Maca Bana Villas** up on the hill above, see page 64, this casual beachfront restaurant is tucked into the cliff at one end of Magazine Beach. With sun loungers, showers and snorkelling offshore, it's a great place to hang out during the day. Light lunches include fish sandwiches and seafood salads and a Sun lunch barbecue with reggae band.

$ Mocha Spoke
True Blue Bay, just before St George's University, T473-533 2470, www. mochaspoke.com. Daily 0730-1830.
Great little café made out of old bright yellow shipping containers, popular with students, good range of coffees and smoothies, breakfasts, paninis, salads and amazing waffles (bananas, whipped cream and chocolate syrup). Also hires out bikes (see What to do, page 79).

Lance aux Épines *map page 30.*

$$$ Rhodes at Calabash
At Calabash Hotel, Beach Lane, T473-444 4334, www.calabashhotel.com. Daily 1900-2130.
Reservations required. Gary Rhodes' first restaurant outside the UK (he now has 2 more in Dubai) but always supervised by one of his top chefs to ensure consistent quality, using Rhodes' recipes and local ingredients. Open-air dining on a very elegant terrace, a fine dining international menu with some interesting daily fish and seafood specials, excellent choice of wines, attentive service and complimentary transport is available.

$$$-$$ The Red Crab
Lance Aux Epines Main Rd, T473-444 4424, see Facebook. Mon-Sat 1100-1400, 1800-2300.

A British pub-style bar/restaurant with indoor and outdoor tables, but as it's by the busy road, you're best inside. Excellent steaks and local seafood, and naturally surf 'n turf combos, plus salads, sandwiches, burgers and catch of the day. Live music Mon and Fri, Latin music on Thu and lobsterfest on Sat. Service however can suffer when it's busy.

$$-$ Tiki Bar
Prickly Bay Marina, off Lance Aux Épines Rd, T473-439 5265, www.pricklybaymarina.com. Daily 0700-2400.
Open-air bar/restaurant popular with ex-pats and yachties with a great vibe, the menu features cooked breakfasts, tacos, wraps and sandwiches, and grills in the evening including fish, lobster tail, steak and ribs. The cheese on toast with Branston pickle, bangers and mash and Sunday roast may give a clue to the main nationality this place is popular with. A good sunset spot, quiz night on Tue, bingo on Wed, party night on Fri with live music, free Wi-Fi.

Woburn and around

$$$ Boots Cuisine
Grand Anse Valley Rd, Woodlands, T473-444 215. Lunch and dinner by reservation only.
Ruby and Roland (Boots) McSween run this small, delightful restaurant at their home serving excellent local food; a 4-course set meal that might include melt-in-the-mouth lambi, delicious callaloo, goat, curried chicken, stew rabbit, grill fish, baked provisions and stew peas, and leave room for desserts like bread pudding with nutmeg ice cream. Rustic, open air dining surrounded by plants, when phoning to make a reservation, see if Ruby will come and pick you up in the Grand Anse area and around for a fee that's less than a taxi.

$$$-$ Steakhouse Restaurant & Bar
At Whisper Cove Marina, off Lower Woburn Rd, T473-444 5296, www. whispercovemarina.com. Mon 0800-1700, Tue-Sat 0800-2030, Sun 0800-1500.

The pleasant wooden deck here overlooks Clarke's Court Bay and is well-positioned for the sunset and is popular with yachties and worth a trip out from the Grand Anse area for the Sun brunch buffet (reservations required; US$24 per person). At other times there's a good choice of sandwiches made with delicious home-made baguettes and floury bread, salads, steaks of course, and specials like roast chicken on Thu and pizza on Fri nights.

West coast Grenada *map page 30.*
A popular lunch stop on an island tour is Belmont Estate (see page 46).

$$$-$ La Sagesse
La Sagesse Bay, T473-444 6458, www.la sagesse.com. Daily 0800-2200, reservations required for dinner.
The open-air restaurant and beach bar at this resort is in a peaceful location in tropical gardens right on beautiful La Sagesse Beach. The menu features a combination of local and continental dishes including salads, sandwiches, grilled fish and chicken for lunch and the likes of callaloo soup, lobster tail, seared tuna or beef curry for dinner. You can spend time relaxing on the sand or walking a meal off on a nature trail.

$$$-$ Petite Anse Hotel
Prospect Rd, Sauteurs, T473-442 5252, www.petiteanse.com. Daily 1000-1700, dinner by reservation only.
The restaurant at this lovely hotel is built right at the top of the property and has a stunning view across the sea to the Grenadines. The lunch menu features sandwiches, paninis, omelettes, chicken pie, lasagne and a variety of desserts including home-made ice cream and cake, while dinner is a choice of fish, 2 different meat dishes and a vegetarian option. Much of the fresh produce is from their kitchen garden, and the bar offers English beer and cider.

Gouyave Fish Friday Festival (T473-444 8430, see Facebook) is a weekly event in Gouyave when many tourists come up to visit for the evening. On Fridays from 1800 St Francis and St Dominic streets are closed to traffic, stalls are set up selling delicious seafood such as shrimp kebabs, baked fish in garlic sauce, fried snapper or jack and grilled lobster; walk around and look at everything before you make your choice. There's live entertainment and a fun atmosphere with drinking and dancing until about 2300. It's about a 45-minute drive up from Grand Anse and 35 minutes from St George's; if you don't want to drive take a taxi or organize transfers with a tour operator.

$$ The Deck Restaurant & Bar
At the Le Phare Bleu Boutique Hotel & Marina, Petite Calivigny Bay, Calivigny, T473-444 2400, www.lepharebleu.com. Daily 0800-2200.
Popular with visiting yachties and locals, this offers breakfast, lunch and dinner, from snacks to à la carte meals with specials on the blackboard, pizza night is Tue, and there's live music on Fri evening. Tables overlook the marina and if you eat here you can use the swimming pool. Happy hour is 1600-1800.

$$-$ Aggie's Restaurant & Bar
Bathway Beach, T473-442 2336. Tue-Sun 1100-2000.
Run by delightful and charismatic Aggie who does all the cooking, this is the only restaurant on Bathway Beach and the shady tables are tucked in a little garden compound behind coconut fronds and decorated with colourful Caribbean colours. From her tiny open kitchen Aggie produces delicious seafood including lobster, lambi and shrimps, and be sure to order a portion of her special fried breadfruit balls. If her Austrian husband Peter is around, there might also be schnitzel and crepes with chocolate sauce.

$$-$ By the Sea
Estuary Lane, north of Grenville near Pearls Airport, T473-437 3663, see Facebook. Tue-Sun 1000-2200.
In a lovely garden with tall coconut palms and grassy lawns and with a pleasant terrace 'by the sea', this is enormously better than the limited eating options in Grenville and is Greek/German owned with a menu of burgers, Greek salads, antipasti and grilled fish. Popular with locals and expats on this side of the island for the DJ on Fri and really good bands play on Sun afternoon from 1630.

Carriacou *maps pages 58 and 59.*
Some basic local bar/restaurants often run out of food quite early or close in the evenings, check if they will be open for dinner. The majority of places also close on Sun, the day of rest/family day on Carriacou. Several small bars and restaurants in Tyrell Bay do takeaways and other services for visiting yachts.

$$$-$$ Slipway
Tyrell Bay, T473-443 6500, www.slipway restaurantcarriacou.com. Tue-Sat 1130-1400, 1800-2100, Sun 1130-1400, bar open throughout the day, closed Thu May-Nov.
At the southern end of Tyrell Bay Beach, this restaurant is in a converted old boatyard on the water's edge. Excellent food, very popular with locals and yachties, reservations needed evenings and Sun. The small menu is chalked up on a board and everything is fresh, great tuna carpaccio if available, also good steak, mahi mahi and burgers. Let them know if you're a vegetarian when you make your reservation.

$$ Callaloo

Next to and run by the Mermaid Beach Hotel, Main Street Hillsborough, T473-443 8286, www.mermaidhotelcarriacou.com. Daily 0800-2100.

With a deck that extends out to the beach, this relaxed place is reasonably priced and one of the few places open on Sun. Breakfasts of fresh fruit and wonderful banana bread, mains include tasty ribs and coleslaw and grilled fish, always a vegetarian option like caramelized onion and feta tart, freshly squeezed juices, rum punch and probably the best coffee on Carriacou.

$$-$ La Playa Beach Bar & Bistro

10 mins north of Hillsborough, T473-410 4216, www.greenroofinn.com. Mon-Sat 1100-2200.

Close to and run by the **Green Roof Inn** (see page 67), the bar serves a good selection of cocktails and food is simple and wholesome: La Playa Burger is made with 100% Carriacou beef, fish burgers made from tuna, dorado or mahi mahi, and daily specials such as smoked lobster or barracuda, plus a cake of the day served with fresh fruit and cream. A reggae band plays Sat from 1500.

$$-$ Lazy Turtle Pizzeria & Bar

Tyrell Bay, T473-443 8322, www.lazy turtlewi.com. Daily 1100-2200.

Casual pizzeria on a deck over the beach serving excellent thin-crust pizzas with some inventive and tasty toppings, plus pasta, seafood and meat dishes, usually chalked up on the specials board on the door to the bar, free Wi-Fi, friendly staff, a lovely view over Tyrell Bay, and popular with the yachting crowd.

$$-$ Off the Hook Bar & Grill

Paradise Beach, T473-443 8748, see Facebook. Daily 0900-2400, closed Tue out of season.

This rustic and cheerful wooden beach bar is on a perfect stretch of the beach with stunning views of the islands and offers grilled fish, lobster and chicken, pizza, sandwiches, cold beer, cocktails and coffees. The charismatic owner, Curtis, will take you

in his boat out to Sandy Island, live music at weekends, bonfire on the beach on Wed night, and the sun loungers mean you can make a relaxing day of it.

$ Gallery Café

Tyrell Bay, T473-4437069, see Facebook. Mon-Sat 0800-1600.

Popular with yachties and part gallery selling local paintings and good crafts like jewellery, soaps and candles, offering breakfasts, mid-morning snacks of Italian coffee and home-made cakes, and tasty lunches from seafood salad to great toasted sandwiches and everything is well-presented. Free Wi-Fi, sit indoors or on the pretty veranda.

$ Hardwood Bar & Snacket Restaurant

Paradise Beach, T473-443 6839. Daily 0900-2200.

Simple and fantastically named beach bar run by Joy and her extended family and a hub of the local community. The menu includes grilled catch of the day, chicken or pork, served with rice, breadfruit, salad and local veg. Plus cheap Carib beer and rum punch, and water taxi service to Sandy Island.

$ Iguana Café

At Carriacou Marine, Tyrell Bay, T473-443 6292. Daily 0730-2100.

Good location overlooking the yachts in the bay and in dry dock, serves breakfast and coffees, light lunches and sundowner drinks; also evening barbecues in high season. Popular with yachties for the giant TV and Wed evening film nights.

$ Kayak Kafe & Juice Bar

Main St, Hillsborough, T473-406 2151, see Facebook. Daily except Wed, 0730-1430.

Pleasant eating on a veranda overlooking the jetty, with wooden tables and chairs in a mix of pastel colours for a cool, calm atmosphere. Offers full English breakfast and sandwiches to local delicacies such as lambi fritters and callaloo soup, plus a wide choice of coffees and delicious juices and smoothies. A perfect spot to head to straight off the ferry or to kill time waiting for it while watching all the comings and goings. Steps down to the little beach below.

$ Laurena II Jerk Centre
Main St, Hillsborough, T473-443 8759, www.hotellaurena.com. Mon-Sat 1100 until the food runs out, usually about 1930.
Run by the nearby **Hotel Laurena**, casual, mainly lunchtime venue serves plates or takeout boxes of jerk chicken and pork, and other dishes might be stewed mutton with rice and peas, macaroni pie and salad, or if you're lucky curried lobster – each is not much more than US$5.50-6.50. If you have a microwave in your accommodation, picking up something for supper here is an option.

$ Pizza Meh Heart
Main St, Windward, T473-456 6426, see Facebook. Open 1400-2200 except Wed.
This wonderful spot in a cheerful shack opposite the jetty is an unexpected surprise, and offers amazing pizza, toppings include pepperoni, ham and pineapple, saltfish and garlic, by the slice for US$1.85 or whole from US$13, also cold beer, wine and soft drinks. Get the bus out here for a late lunch or early supper and watch village life go by from the little deck.

Petite Martinique

$$-$ Palm Beach Restaurant & Bar
T473-443 9103. Mon-Sat 0800-2200, Sun 1400-2200.
Located on the only major beach on Petite Martinique, this informal family-run spot offers seafood, ribs and chicken, Caribbean dishes (if you're lucky, creole shrimp or lobster) and rum-based drinks. Dining is in rustic huts on the sand with good views of the neighbouring islands. There's a free water taxi service for those yachts anchored in Petit St Vincent across the water to the north.

Bars and clubs

Grenada *maps pages 30, 32 and 40.*
For the most part, Grenada's nightlife is centred on hotel/resort bars, most of the restaurants are bar orientated too and there are beach bars and regular events like Fish Friday in Gouyave (see box, page 73) or liming (see box, page 25) along the Carenage in St George's at the weekends.

Bananas
True Blue Rd, True Blue Bay, T473-444 4662, www.bananas.gd. Mon-Thu 1200-2400, Fri 1200-0400, Sat 1600-0400, Sun 1600-2400.
Sports bar with events like Bananas BFF lime (Beers, Food & Football), restaurant serving pizzas and burgers and a nightclub with open-air dance floor and regular party nights (see Facebook for what's on), popular with students from the nearby St George's University. Happy hour 1700-1900.

Club Fantazia Grenada
Gem Holiday Beach Resort, Morne Rouge Beach, T473-444 4224, see Facebook. Wed, Fri-Sat 2200-0400.
The most popular nightclub on the island that doesn't get going until after midnight, with circular dance floor with seating along the sides, state-of-the-art sound and lighting, mixed clientele and varied music from golden oldies (on Wed) to R&B, soca, fast calypso and reggae. Also holds a day-long party on the rooftop terrace of the **Gem** on the 3rd Sat of the month.

Dodgy Dock
At True Blue Bay Boutique Resort, Old Mill Rd, True Blue Bay, T437-443 8783, www. dodgydock.com. Daily 0700-2400.
Built in lovely design out over the water under a tent roof, this lively bar/restaurant is popular with yachties (there are moorings) and offers great cocktails, and weekly events including a Grenadian night on Tue with rum tasting, local food and a steelpan band, and a live calypso band on Sat evening, plus DJs on most other nights. Pleasant for a sundowner, after dinner drink, or

ON THE ROAD
'Jack Iron' rum

Originally bottled on Carriacou by the schooner sailors, this local rum (99% proof) is a local hazard – it's so strong that ice sinks in it, and it is said that when Carriacouans run out of oil for their lamps they burn 'Jack Iron'. It is today commercially (and officially) only distilled on Trinidad (though is also bottled on Grenada) at 70% proof, but many of the local bars and shops in Hillsborough bottle their own more potent knock-off version made from fermented molasses in whatever container they can rinse out. It is cheap and is liberally dispensed on all high days and holidays (and fairly liberally on other days too); administer with care.

the popular Fri after-work lime (see box, page 25). Reasonable food from breakfasts, pizzas and pastas, and bar snacks like mozzarella sticks and buffalo wings.

Esther's Beach Bar
Grand Anse Craft and Spice Market.
Open 'any day, any time'.
For a pure Grenadian experience, come to Esther's for a Carib or beer made at the **West Indies Beer Co**, or a mudslide or frozen lime mojito, run by exceedingly friendly Esther and Kimani with views and access to Grand Anse Beach. Measures don't skimp so make sure you have a paracetamol available the next morning.

Junction Bar & Grill
L'Anse aux Épines Main Rd, L'Anse aux Épines, T473-420 1086, see Facebook. Wed-Sat 1700-0100.
Close to the **Red Crab** restaurant and next door to the **West Indies Beer Co** (also a good place for a drink, see page 42), always something going on here including DJs, karaoke, Latin nights and live music, popular with the university crowd and for the after-work Fri lime, a fun place with friendly staff, good service and food, the burgers are particularly good, and the attached café (Mon-Sat 0700-1500) serves coffee and cakes.

Nimrod's Rum Shop
Lower Woburn Rd, next to the bus stop, T473-458 8686, see Facebook. Daily 0900-2400.
This long-standing spot is popular with yachties anchored in Woburn Bay, and is often referred to as 'Sep's'; the name of the owner. What began as a little rum shop has grown into a full-fledged bar and restaurant with a menu including great home-made burgers and fries and chicken and beef rotis with hot sauce. There's often a music 'jamming session' on Thu night.

Umbrellas
Grand Anse Beach, T473-439 9149, see Facebook. Tue-Thu 1100-2200, Fri-Sat 1000-2300, Sun 1000-2100.
Hugely popular beach bar, always lively with holidaymakers, in a shuttered building, with attractive, vaulted and fan-cooled interior and picnic tables out front and on the roof deck, in a great location on Grand Anse only a few steps from the ocean. Ideal for a cold Carib beer or cocktail, but also does good food like fish sandwiches, burgers, steaks and lambi fritters.

Venus Restaurant & Sports Lounge
Upstairs from the Republic Bank, Grand Anse Main Rd, Grand Anse, T473-439 1800, www.venusgrenada.com. Mon-Sat 1100-0200, Sun 1700-2400.
Right in the tourist belt this popular late-night neon-lit bar offers TVs for watching sport, pool tables, live bands Sat and Sun nights, and a snack menu of burgers and nachos and the like.

Entertainment

Grenada
Cinemas
Movie Palace, *Excel Plaza, Grand Anse Main Rd, near Sugar Mill Roundabout, T473-444 6688, www.moviepalace.gd.* 8-screen movie theatre with shows Tue-Sun 1630-2100; US$9.25, under 12s US$7.40, family of 4 ticket US$28.

Festivals

West coast Grenada
Gouyave
29 Jun Fisherman's Birthday Festival. This honours St Peter, the patron saint of fishermen. The event sees fishermen coming from all over Grenada for competitive boat racing, a mini-carnival of soca music and fireworks, and the most important element: the blessing of the local fishing fleet by the town's Roman Catholic priest.

Victoria
Mid-Apr St Mark's Day. Usually held over a weekend and popularly referred to as 'Sunset'. There's a fish cooking competition, a street fete, a thanksgiving service at the Catholic Church and a party on the beach with a bonfire.

Carriacou
Late Apr Carriacou Maroon Music Festival. Usually held after Easter, this festival is when villagers come together and cook traditional food and partake in Big Drum Dances. There's also a big party on Paradise Beach with steelpan, reggae, string-band and other music. See also page 13.

Petite Martinique
May Petite Martinique Whitsuntide Regatta May. This regatta is designed to foster competition between the fishing and sailing communities of Grenada, Carriacou and Petite Martinique as well as the Grenadines of St Vincent. There are many classes of boat races and lots of onshore competitions and activities too, including the greasy pole and tug of war.

Shopping

St George's
Arts and crafts
Art Fabrik, *Young St, T473-440 0568, www. artfabrikgrenada.com. Mon-Fri 0900-1700, Sat 0900-1600.* In an old St George's house on the other side of Young Street from the **House of Chocolate**, this lovely shop with colourful interiors is owned by artists and designers Chris Mast and Lilo Nido. They operate a cooperative of batik artists who either work in their homes or upstairs in the studio (which you can visit). For sale are some wonderful batiks made into dresses, bags, wraps, and home decor items, plus jewellery, good quality crafts, and at the back is a small art gallery featuring local painters.

Grenada Craft Centre, *Lagoon Rd, next to Tropicana Inn, T473-439 2603. Mon-Sat 0900-1700.* Houses vendors in booths selling jewellery, pottery, batik wraps, wood, basketry and T-shirts. Some of the vendors can be a bit persistent when a cruise ship is in, but it's otherwise quiet and hassle-free.

Susan Mains Gallery, *Spiceland Mall, Grand Anse, T437-439 3450, www.artandsoul grenada.com. Mon-Sat 1000-1800.* Fine and contemporary art and sculpture gallery, showcasing the work of local artists including owner Susan Mains, Oliver Benoit, Asher Mains, Marie Messenger and others.

Shopping malls
Esplanade Mall, *on the Esplanade, Melville St, at the Cruise Ship Terminal, T473-440 5356. Mon-Sat 0900-1700, Sun when a cruise ship is in.* Cruise passengers exit the ships through this mall, and it has duty-free shops (passengers only, and many only open when ships are docked), plus clothing and shoe boutiques, gift shops, juice bars, pizza and US fast food, and a tourist information kiosk which opens when a ship is in. A short walk

ON THE ROAD
Spice products

Grenada prides itself on its spices, and look out for spice gift baskets filled with cinnamon, nutmeg, mace, bay leaves, cloves, turmeric and ginger, which are ideal souvenirs. You can buy them for about US$5.50 in various places including the market in St George's, the Grand Anse Craft and Spice Market and the gift shops in the Esplanade Mall. Spices are of course cheaper in the supermarkets, but perhaps not so prettily packaged. Also head to:

All Things Nutmeg, Lagoon Road, St George's, T473-440 2117, www.grenadanutmeg. com. Monday-Friday 0800-1600. This is the shop for the Grenada Co-operative Nutmeg Association, and sells nutmeg oil for use in cooking, as well as massage oil and soaps, jams, jellies and sweets. The nutmeg itself goes through the Gouyave Nutmeg Processing Station (page 52), and some of these items are for sale in the shop there too.

Arawak Islands, Frequente Industrial Park, off Maurice Bishop Highway on the opposite side as the turn-off to True Blue Bay Road, T473-444 3577, see Facebook. Monday-Friday 0830-1630. This factory and retail outlet makes and sells a range of spices, sauces, herbal teas, candied nutmeg pods, natural perfumes, soap, bath goodies and massage oils, scented candles, insect repellents, lip balm and incense sticks.

De la Grenade Industries, T473-440 3241, www.delagrenade.com. Monday-Friday 0830-1700, Saturday 0900-1230. Makes nutmeg jams, jellies, syrups, sauces and drinks, available in supermarkets and groceries. Their nutmeg syrup is an essential ingredient for a Grenadian rum punch, also delicious on pancakes. Their shop and garden are open to the public, see page 37.

away is the market in Market Square for a more authentic experience.

Spiceland Mall, *Morne Rouge Rd, T473-439 9070. Supermarket Mon-Thu 0800-2100, Fri-Sat 0800-2200, Sun 0900-1900, other shops various hours.* This pleasant mall is the focal point of Grand Anse for shopping with 30 shops including a pharmacy, decent clothes and gift stores, a small food court, a taxi stand outside (T473-439 2233, you can come here from Grand Anse Beach if you want a taxi), and by far the best supermarket on the whole of Grenada, **Real Value IGA Supermarket** (T473-439 2121, www. realvalueiga.com), which has a bakery, deli counter, ready-made meals, liquor and wines.

Carriacou

If you are self-catering or need snacks, there are a couple of decent supermarkets in Hillsborough; the best is under **Ade's Dream** on Main St. Check the fish market on Main St for the daily catch, usually snapper, barracuda or tuna; you can get it cleaned and filleted and ice is available. Next door is the stall for **MNIB (Marketing and National Importing Board)**, a local cooperative that buys and sells fresh produce from local farmers and also import fruit and vegetables.

Patty's Deli, *Main St, Hillsborough, T473-443 6258, www.pattysdeli.com. Mon-Fri 0800-1630, Sat 0830-1230.* This fantastic shop stocks a wide selection of international products such as coffees, teas, preserves, condiments and wines, there's a well-stocked deli counter for hams, smoked turkey, herbed chicken etc. and cheeses like French brie and Italian mozzarella. The freezer might have steak, boned leg of lamb or salmon and some ready-made meals. Also excellent croissants and pastries and sandwiches made from baguettes are made to order. It is named after the owner's grandmother, Granny Patty, the original owner of the house.

What to do

Grenada
Cricket

Grenada National Stadium, *off River Rd, north of St George's, T473-437 2007, www. grenadastadium.com*. The island's main land sport is played from Jan-Jun. Informal cricket is played on any piece of flat ground or on the beaches, but international test matches are played at the **Grenada National Stadium**. Built in 1998, and formerly known as Queen's Park, it became the 84th Test venue when the West Indies played New Zealand there in 2002, but it was destroyed by Hurricane Ivan in 2004. It was refurbished for US$5 million for the 2007 Cricket World Cup (6 Super-8 matches were played there) with the help of the Chinese, to give it a capacity of 16,000 and it's also used for football and athletics. The West Indies' Cricket Academy is at the nearby St George's University. It is one of the grounds for the West Indies team (aka The Windies); see www.windiescricket.com.

Cycling

Mocha Spoke, *True Blue, just off the road going to the university, T473-533 2470, www. mochaspoke.com*. Not only a great little café (see page 71), but this bike rental place has a good range of mountain bikes and tourers, can offer lots of advice on the best routes or take you on a guided tour. Bike rental is US$5.55 per hr, US$22 per day, US$113 per week. Tours start from US$55 for a 2½-hr gentle coastal tour to US$68 for a 3½-hr uphill tour to Annandale Falls for the more advanced. They can pick up from local hotels.

Diving and snorkelling

There are around 35 dive sites off Grenada, and an exceptionally large amount of wreck dives (see box, page 80). Expect to pay in the region of 1 dive/US$55-65, 2 dives/US$100-120, up to 6-dive packages at around US$320. Also night dives, US$80, 4-day PADI Open Water course US$540-590. The best snorkelling is around Molinière Point and up to Dragon Bay and Flamingo Bay. Snorkelling trips by boat will usually bring you to this area, often in the afternoons so that divers on board can do a shallow dive as well. You can see a wide variety of fish and invertebrates on the rocks and coral, even moray eels if you look carefully. Snorkelling excursions by boat, including the trip to the Grenada Underwater Sculpture Park (see box, page 81) are around US$40-50.

Aquanauts Grenada, *bases at True Blue Bay Boutique Resort and Spice Island Beach Resort, see Where to stay, above, T473-444 1126, www.aquanautsgrenada.com*.

Dive Grenada, *at Flamboyant Hotel & Villas, see Where to stay, Grand Anse, above, T473-444 1092, www.divegrenada.com*.

Devotion 2 Ocean, *at the Grenadian by Rex Resorts, Magazine Beach, T473-444 3483, www.devotion2ocean.com*.

Eco-Dive, *Grenada, at Coyaba Beach Resort, see Where to stay, Grand Anse, above, and Port Louis Marina on The Lagoon, T473-444 7777, www.ecodiveandtrek.com*.

Native Spirit Scuba, *at the Radisson Grenada Beach Resort, Grand Anse, T473-439 7013, www. nativespiritscuba.com*.

Scuba Tech, *at the Calabash Hotel, Beach Lane, Lance aux Épines, see Where to stay, above, T473-439 4346, www.scubatech-grenada.com*.

Fishing

Deep-sea fishing takes place in the Atlantic off the west coast of Grenada where game fish included blue and white marlin, sailfish, wahoo and dorado. Fully equipped excursions can be arranged through both these for about US$500 for half day/4 hrs, and US$700 for full day/8 hrs for up to 4 people.

True Blue Sportfishing, *Port Louis Marina, Lagoon Rd, T473-407 4688, www.yesaye.com*.

Grenada's five best wreck dives

Bianca C

Also known as the '*Titanic of the Caribbean*' because of its sheer size (600-ft long), this Italian cruise liner sank in 1961. She caught fire whilst anchored off St George's, and approximately 700 passengers and crew scrambled to abandon the ship while Grenadian fishermen and boat owners rushed to help (only one crewman died). She sank perfectly upright on her keel at 165 ft. Often listed as one of the top 10 wreck dives in the world, the *Bianca C* is a must-do for advanced divers, and is home to eagle rays, nurse sharks, schools of Atlantic spadefish, large moray eels and barracuda. The opportunity to dive into one of her upper deck swimming pools is a particular thrill.

Hema I

In 2005 this coastal freighter had offloaded its cargo in St George's and was on its way back to Trinidad empty, but seas were rough and it started to take on water and the bilge pump didn't work. The captain tried to make it back to Grenada but failed (all crew members were rescued), and the ship sank three miles off the south coast. It now sits on its side at 100 ft, still swaying in the current, which makes this an advanced dive only. There are frequent sightings of nurse and reef sharks, and squadrons of eagle rays hover over the wreck.

King Mitch

This minesweeper sank on her side in 1981 four miles off the southern Atlantic coast after the ship leaked and its bilge pump failed (all of the crew survived). A challenging and another advanced dive due to strong currents, the wreck lies in the sand on its port side at 110 ft. The holds, ladders and walkways can be explored and are home to large marine species such as turtles, southern stingrays, nurse and reef sharks and other pelagics. The iridescent blue water makes a fantastic ascent and descent.

Shakem

This 180-ft-long cement-carrying cargo ship took on water and sank in 2001 within sight of the harbour at St George's. It now sits intact on the seabed at 105 ft, and solidified cement bags line the hold, overshadowed by a huge intact crane. Competent divers can explore the interior of the bridge, captain's quarters and engine room and her propeller and foremast make for great underwater photography. It's decorated with large gorgonian sea fans and soft corals, where seahorses, green moray and lobster can be found.

Veronica L

In contrast to the dramatic deep wrecks, the *Veronica L*, a small freighter, sits upright at 50 ft off Grand Anse Beach. It used to be outside the mouth of St George's Harbour but was moved to make way for the new Cruise Ship Terminal, when it was loaded onto a barge and dropped back upright. A highly photogenic wreck, it is festooned with colourful soft corals and sponges and the open hold and crane are home to seahorses, moray eels, sometimes turtles, barracuda, and shoals of purple wrasse. It's a great night dive, with the opportunity to see critters such as black brotula, shrimps and crabs. A shallow dive, it can be enjoyed by all levels.

Grenada Underwater Sculpture Park

One of the most popular and unusual diving and snorkelling sites is an underwater gallery of sculptures in the Grenada Marine Park (also known as the Molinière-Beauséjour Marine Protected Area) between Molinière Point and Flamingo Bay on the west coast. It lies about two miles north of St George's; roughly a 10-minute boat ride or 20 minutes from Grand Anse.

The Grenada Underwater Sculpture Park has a collection of sculptures which are fast becoming an artificial reef. The first statues were carved out of concrete in 2006 by Jason de Caires Taylor, who has been a prolific contributor to the park, followed by Troy Lewis, a Grenadian potter. There are Amerindian cultural influences to some of the works, together with a humorous cyclist and a man sitting at a desk, and the iconic Christ of the Deep statue, which commemorated 50 years since the *Bianca C* caught fire and sank. But it is perhaps the sculpture called *Vicissitudes* that has the most extraordinary visual impact: a circle of 26 life-size children holding hands and facing outwards.

The marine park is home to a shallow reef and the statues have been sympathetically making natural use of its varied topography of craggy gullies and sun-dappled sandy patches. The reef and its artificial components attract hard and soft corals, hawksbill turtles, moray eels and large amounts of schooling fish. There is a daily fee to enter the marine park; divers US$2, snorkellers US$1, which is paid with your trip. See also www.grenadaunderwatersculpture.com.

Half day charters with Captain Gary Clifford aboard the 31-ft *Yes Aye*.

Wayward Wind Fishing Charters, *Grenada Yacht Club, Lagoon Rd, T473-538 9821, www.grenadafishing.com.* With Captain Stewart on the 31-ft *Wayward Wind*.

Golf

Grenada Golf Course, *Golf Course Hill, off Grand Anse Main Rd, T473-444 4128. Daily 0800 to sunset, but only till 1200 on Sun.* A 9-hole golf course with 18 tee boxes. A round of 9 holes with club hire, balls and caddy is US$60. This is the only golf course on Grenada, and although it is not the most challenging (and can get quite brown in dry season), it's fine for visitors hoping to get in a round during their stay and has views of both the Caribbean and the Atlantic.

Kayaking

Conservation Kayak, *Whisper Cove Marina, Lower Woburn, T473-449 5248,* *www.conservationkayak.com.* Guided kayak trips on a variety of routes around Woburn Bay and out to Hog Island or Calivgny Island, checking out mangroves, coral reefs and the good birdlife. A fun and educational trip out on the water (lather up with sunscreen), they cater for novice and experienced kayakers, though you must be able to swim and be comfortable on the sea, and all trips include tuition and free use of waterproof cameras; some include lunch and time to enjoy the secluded beaches on Hog Island. Prices from US$70 for 2 hrs. You can have a meal or drink at the good **Steakhouse Restaurant** at Whisper Cove (see page 72).

Running

Hash House Harriers, *www.grenadahash.com.* Every other Sat afternoon at 1600, Grenada's Hash assembles at a chosen rum shop somewhere on the island, and then sets off to run or walk through the bush following a trail of flour or shredded paper. They end back at the rum shop a couple of hours later. Visitors are very welcome to join in.

Sailing

As well as yacht charter and sailing holidays from Grenada, see page 16 for more details, lots of companies offer day sails on catamarans, each with trampoline nets, sun shades and showers, and there's no shortage of choice, many of them catering for the cruise ship and resort markets. They usually last 6-7 hrs and either go up the Caribbean west coast or around the bays and islands on the south coast, and include a barbecue seafood lunch, rum punch and other drinks, snorkelling gear and sometimes fishing equipment. Prices start from US$100 for the day trip, discounts for children and groups, and other shorter options include 2-3 hr sunset, moonlight or party cruises from US$45.

Carib Cats, *the Carenage, St George's, T473-444 3222, see Facebook.*

Fast Fun Sailing, *the Carenage, St George's, T473-534 7290, www.fastfunsailinggrenada.com.*

First Impressions Catamaran Tours, *Coyaba Beach Resort, Grand Anse, T473-440 3678, www.catamaranchartering.com.*

Footloose Yacht Charters, *Lagoon Rd, St George's, T473-405 9531, www.sailing grenada.com.*

Shadowfax Banana Boat Tours, *Grand Anse, T473-437 3737, www. bananaboattoursgrenada.com.*

Tour operators

The standard day tour of the island includes stops to visit waterfalls, the Gouyave Nutmeg Processing Station, Belmont Estate, the River Antoine Rum Distillery and Grand Etang and includes lunch somewhere in the north. These are usually in minibuses or small buses and are primarily designed to give cruise ship passengers a taste of the island, so they can seem rushed, but are also enjoyable, especially if you're in a small group. Expect to pay around US$90 per person for the full

7-8 hr tour depending on numbers. There are lots of other options; explore the websites for ideas. Rates are around US$60 for a 3- to 4-hr tour for hiking in the rainforests and to waterfalls such as Concord Falls, Mt Qua Qua and, Seven Sisters Falls, and if you want to hire the services of a guide and vehicle and make up your itinerary, allow US$30 per person per hr.

A final option is to find a taxi driver you like, or get a hotel to recommended one (some of them make very good tour guides) and set off on your own; it's around US$170 for a full day, but again depends on duration. The cost would be split by passenger; some taxis are in fact minibuses.

For something a bit different, try **Adventure Jeep Tour** (T437-444 5337, www. adventuregrenada.com), with an all-terrain 4WD, high-clearance, open-top jeep/truck that seats up to 8, on an itinerary through the rainforests and to waterfalls along dirt tracks; US$93 including lunch. This can also be combined with seasonal river tubing on the Balthazar River, which runs from the mountains out to the ocean on the east coast near Grenville.

Caribbean Horizons, *T473-444 1555, www.caribbeanhorizons.com.*

Helvellyn Tours, *T473-444 3222, www.travelgrenadagrenadines.com.*

Henry's Safari Tours, *T473-444 5313, www.henrysafari.com.*

Mandoo Tours, *T473-440 1428, www.grenadatours.com.*

Sunsation Tours, *T473-444 1594/439 4447, www.grenadasunsation.com.*

Watersports

Plenty of watersports like windsurfing, waterskiing, sea kayaking and hobie cat sailing is offered at the beach resorts at Grand Anse and Lance aux Épines.

Native Spirit Scuba, *at the Radisson Grenada Beach Resort, Grand Anse, T473-439 7013, www.nativespiritscuba.com.* In the event you're not staying at Grand Anse, this dive shop also rents out hobie cats, US$26 per hr,

US$30 for a lesson; kayaks, US$17 per hr; and windsurfers, US$ 35 per hr, US$41 for a lesson. Also rents out snorkelling gear for use off the beach for US$7.40 per hr.
SUP Grenada, *at Morne Rouge Beach, T473-406 8624, www.supgnd.com.* Usually daily 1000-1800 but a good idea to phone first. Stand-up paddle boarding is best in Morne Rouge Bay where it's flat, shallow and calm. Located next to **La Plywood** beach bar, hourly rentals US$20, daily US$60. Novice paddlers will get a free safety briefing and dry land lesson.

Carriacou
Diving and snorkelling
Dive sites around Carriacou include **Kick Em Jenny** (a submarine volcano), **Isle de Rhonde**, **Sister Rocks**, **Twin Sisters** and **Sandy**, **Mabouya** and **Saline islands.** The reefs are unspoilt, with forests of soft corals growing up to 10 ft tall with a wide range of creatures living among them. Most are within a 10-min boat ride from Carriacou and visibility is very good. Costs are around US$55 for a single dive, US$100 for a 2-tank dive, US$70 for a night dive and US$550 for a PADI Open Water course. There is no shore diving, but plenty to see on the shallow reefs off the beaches by snorkelling. Both these companies rent out snorkelling gear too, which you can also rent from the beach bars on Paradise Beach.
Arawak Divers, *Tyrell Bay, T473-443 6906, www.arawakdivers.com.*
Deefer Diving, *Main St, Hillsborough, T473-443 7882, www.deeferdiving.com.*
Lumbadive, *Tyrell Bay, T473-443 8566, www.lumbadive.com.*

Tour operators
Minibus/taxi drivers will offer to take you on a tour of the island, and the hotels or the tourist office will give you a recommendation, but they are in fact so friendly, you'll easily find one you like. The official rate for a vehicle for a day is US$75, but you don't have to take it for this long;

negotiate how many hours you want one for, 2½-3 hrs should be plenty for a full trip around the island.
Water taxis will also take you on trips to the different bays and little islands offshore; be sure to check safety equipment, and request life jackets.

Transport

Grenada
Air
The airport in Grenada is small so there are few facilities but it does have an ATM, bureau de change and Wi-Fi, and a snack bar in the outside pickup/drop-off area (rather delightfully called 'curb-side'), while air-side are duty free shops and a café.
SVG Air operates between Grenada and Carriacou (see Getting around, page 148). For details of Transport between the airport and the centre, see box, page 29. For information on how to get to Grenada by air, including details of airlines, see Getting there, page 145.

Boat
The **Osprey Lines** ferry between St George's and Hillsborough on Carriacou (see page 84) docks and departs at Queen's Jetty on Wharf Rd on the Carenage (opposite the fire station and near the tourist office). However, the booking office is on the opposite side of the Carenage (T473-440 8126, www.ospreylines.com, Mon-Fri 0930-1600). On Sat and Sun when the office is closed you can buy tickets directly at Queen's Jetty, but it's a good idea to be there in plenty of time; the ferry departs Mon-Sat 0900, Sun 0800.

Bus
All public service vehicles – buses, minivans, taxis and vehicles for hire – are denoted by registration numbers beginning with 'H'. Buses (all are privately owned minibuses) run along the main roads around the island and are cheap: US$0.90 for any journey starting and finishing within the same parish and for

any journey of 3 miles or less (for example, St George's to Grand Anse), rising to US$2.20 for a journey to the top of the island, say to Sauteurs. You can pay for an extra seat if you have luggage. They start and finish at St George's Bus Terminus on Melville Street north of the Esplanade. A lively spot, there are kiosks for drinks and snacks here, lanes for the minibuses coming in and out which have the destinations well marked, and there are uniformed staff to help and show you which bus to get on. All vehicles carry numbered coloured stickers with their destinations – 1/Gold goes to Grand Anse, 2/Orange goes to Woburn, 3/Purple goes to Calivigny, and so on. They depart regularly Mon-Sat 0630-1900. Those to Grand Anse run until 2100, although start to thin out after 1300 on Sat. Note buses on all routes run very infrequently on Sun.

Car hire

Although none of the main international franchises are represented, there are dozens of local car hire companies in the southwest of Grenada around St George's and Grand Anse. Prices and standards are very similar; ask a hotel to recommended one, or Pure Grenada (the Grenada Tourism Authority) has a full list of companies on the website: www.puregrenada.com. All will be able to arrange a pick-up/drop-off at the airport and arrange the local drivers' permit (valid for 3 months, US$24). Expect to pay in the region of US$50-55 per day for a Suzuki jeep or normal/sedan car, US$60-65 for a more substantial 4-door 4WD, and US$70 for a minibus. There are significant discounts for weekly rates. See Getting around, page 148 for further details about hiring a car and driving.

Sanvic's, Grand Anse Shopping Centre, opposite the Radisson, T473-444 4753, www.sanvics.com. Recommended because of its central location and excellent service from English Karen and her team; they can drop off a car to you anywhere (hotels and restaurants) and vehicles are of a high standard. They also have desks at **True Blue**

Bay Boutique Resort and the **Grenadian by Rex Resorts**.

Taxi

Taxis are plentiful but are expensive and non-negotiable rates are set by the government and taxi associations; rates are US$10 for a short drop even within 1 mile, and US$16 for a 5- to 7-mile journey, say from St George's to Grand Anse or the airport. If you want to hire one for an hour or 2, standard fixed rates are US$25 per hr, and for the day, say for an around-the-island tour, around US$170. Taxis gather at the airport, the Cruise Ship Terminal and **Osprey** ferry in St George's, and at the **Spiceland Mall** in Grand Anse. Otherwise any hotel/restaurant can phone one, or if you find one you like get the driver's card/phone number.

Carriacou
Air

For details of flights to Carriacou from Grenada, see Getting around, page 148. For information on transport from the airport, see Finding your feet, page 57.

Boat

The jetty in Hillsborough is in the centre of town on Main St. The daily **Osprey Lines** catamaran takes 90 mins between St George's on Grenada and Hillsborough on Carriacou. It is a lovely route, following the length of Grenada's western coastline before crossing the channel to Carriacou and seeing the Grenadines coming into view. In heavy seas though you may get seasick, and the sea is said to be rougher going to Carriacou than coming back. On arrival/departure in Carriacou it is then linked by another much smaller boat that actually pulls alongside the main ferry (you just step on to the next boat and don't even have to put a foot on the jetty), which then takes 20 mins to/from Petite Martinique (Mon-Fri only). The **Osprey Lines** booking office is on the corner of Main St and Patterson St (T473-440 8126, www.ospreylines.com, Mon-Fri

0930-1600). On Sat and Sun, when the office is closed, you can buy tickets directly on the jetty before boarding, but it's a good idea to be there in plenty of time; the ferry departs daily at 1530.

There is also a twice-weekly ferry – Mon and Thu – on the *Lady JJ* to Union Island, which lies in St Vincent territory so you will be crossing between countries, as well as the option of organizing a private water taxi between the two; see page 150 for details about ferries between the Grenadines. You can also get to Carriacou by yacht.

Bus

Buses go from the small bus terminal between Patterson and Middle Streets in Hillsborough; but if it's quiet the drivers will do a cruise along Main St too in order to pick up wayward shoppers; the drivers will even help people loading their shopping bags. There are only 2 official bus routes, but inexplicably they are numbered 10 and 11; No 10 goes south via Paradise Beach, L'Esterre and Tyrell Bay to Hermitage; No 11 goes via Bogles to Windward on the northeast coast. To get between Tyrell Bay and Windward you have to change in Hillsborough. They generally run daily 0700-1700, although they also run at night if there's a party going on, but very few if any run on Sun. Fares are US$0.90-1.30 depending on how far you're going, and to go 'off route', say for a short distance to be dropped off on a minor road, you should pay US$0.75 extra.

Car hire

The tourist office can give you names/phone numbers of individuals that rent out a vehicle, and **Ade's Dream** (see page 68) rents out cars. Also try **Wayne's Auto Rentals & Services**, Main St, Hillsborough, T473-443 6120. Rates from US$50-60 per day for a small jeep. Like Grenada, you'll need a local driver's permit (see page 149, about hiring a car).

Taxi

Taxis are not regular cars but minibuses that become taxis if you are paying for single use, and thus pay the appropriate fare. From Hillsborough, expect to pay in the region of: to/from the airport US$7.40, Bogles US$9.25, Windward US$13, L'Esterre US$11 and Tyrell Bay US$13. The official rate for a vehicle at your disposal for a day is US$74, but you don't have to take it for this long. The tourist office has a rate sheet for taxi fares.

St Vincent

St Vincent

The largest island in the country of St Vincent and the Grenadines, 'mainland' St Vincent is 21 miles long and 11 miles wide. It is relatively uncommercial and is green and fertile with a lush rainforest and mountainous interior, beautiful black sand volcanic beaches and fishing villages, coconut groves and banana plantations. Hiking and birdwatching are rewarding activities, and underwater, diving and snorkelling on the unspoiled reefs offer a colourful adventure with a huge array of sea creatures to identify.

St Vincent is widely known for the superb sailing conditions provided by its 32 sister islands and cays in the Grenadines and many visitors start a leisurely yacht journey from here.

Accommodation on St Vincent is low key in small hotels and guesthouses, most of which cluster along the south coast east of Kingstown where there is a fine view across to Bequia.

Essential St Vincent

Finding your feet

ET Joshua Airport at Arnos Vale just less than 2 miles east of Kingstown. Buses (minibuses or 'vans') running along Windward Highway pull into the airport and stop right outside the terminal building. This makes it easy to get to both Kingstown and Indian Bay and Villa (the main hotel area); you can get off at the entrance gates to many of the hotels along Windward Highway (you pay for an extra seat for luggage). There is also a kiosk for taxis; a taxi to both Kingstown and Villa will cost around US$11.

The ferries that link St Vincent with the Grenadine islands arrive at the ferry dock off Bay Street in Kingstown, which is also where the Kingstown Cruise Terminal and jetty is. The usual and easiest point of arrival and departure for yachts is the **Blue Lagoon Hotel & Marina** in Calliaqua on the south coast (see page 101) where there is a customs and immigration office. See also Transport, page 108.

Best places to stay

Beachcombers Hotel, page 101
Blue Lagoon Hotel & Marina, page 101
Mariners Hotel, page 101
Young Island, page 101
Buccament Bay Resort, page 102

Getting around

Flamboyantly painted buses (vans) travel the principal roads of St Vincent and the central departure point is the bus terminal near the New Kingstown Fish Market off Bay Street; they stop on demand rather than at bus stops. While they are fun and easy, they tend to be overcrowded and cramped and noisy if the stereo is cranked up. Other options are taxis and car hire. Driving in St Vincent is fairly straightforward and it's difficult to get lost given that the main road is always on or near the coast. However, there are narrow sharp curves and turns in places and Kingstown has a very confusing one-way system.

Kingstown

small capital and chief port with narrow streets and a bustling wharf

The capital and commercial centre of the nation, Kingstown stands on a sheltered bay and is surrounded on all sides by steep, green hills, with houses perched all the way up. It was originally founded by French settlers, and had 196 years of British rule before the country's independence in 1979. However, it is a generally unattractive port city with the waterfront dominated by the container port, cruise ship terminal, fish market and bus station. There is no promenade along the seafront and buildings along the reclaimed land look inland rather than out to sea.

When coming in by ferry or cruise ship it looks disappointing to say the least and has nothing of the charm of the pretty arrival by sea into St George's in Grenada. Nevertheless, it has certain vitality and colour from the produce vendors along Bedford Street and the crowds at the fish market and rum shops, and it features a series of surviving 19th-century buildings, some built from the tile and red brick that was used as ballast on trading ships from Britain. The most attractive and historical buildings are inland along the three main parallel streets: **Bay Street**, **Long Lane** and **Grenville/Halifax Street**, also known as Front Street, Middle Street and Back Street.

Kingstown is a hub for trips by ferry to other islands. You can hop on a ferry or the mail boat southwards into the islands and travel as Vincentians do, starting with the busy port in Kingstown and chugging in and out of each delightful island harbour as you go. See also box, page 150.

St Vincent

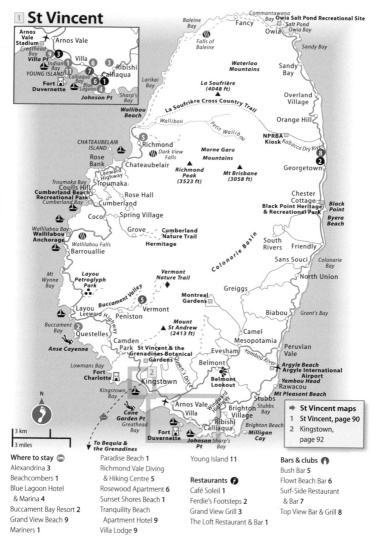

➡ St Vincent maps
1 St Vincent, page 90
2 Kingstown, page 92

Where to stay 🛏
Alexandrina 3
Beachcombers 1
Blue Lagoon Hotel
  & Marina 4
Buccament Bay Resort 2
Grand View Beach 9
Mariners 1

Paradise Beach 1
Richmond Vale Diving
  & Hiking Centre 5
Rosewood Apartment 6
Sunset Shores Beach 1
Tranquility Beach
  Apartment Hotel 9
Villa Lodge 9

Young Island 11

Restaurants 🍴
Café Soleil 1
Ferdie's Footsteps 2
Grand View Grill 3
The Loft Restaurant & Bar 1

Bars & clubs 🎵
Bush Bar 5
Flowt Beach Bar 6
Surf-Side Restaurant
  & Bar 7
Top View Bar & Grill 8

Sights

Kingstown is known as the 'city of arcades' and it is possible to walk around most of the centre under cover. There are even building regulations to encourage the practice in new construction. The shopping and business area is no more than two blocks wide, running between Bay Street and Halifax Street/Grenville Street. The **New Kingstown Fish Market**, built with Japanese aid, was opened in 1990 near the Police Headquarters. This complex, also known as **Little Tokyo**, has car parking and is next to the point of departure for vans to all parts of the island. **Market Square** in front of the Court House is the hub of activity, where the New Central Market is a covered market with cream and brown horizontal stripes; fruit and vegetables are downstairs and clothing and household items are upstairs.

On Halifax Street at the junction with South River Road is the **Old Public Library**, an old stone building with a pillared portico. Also known as the **Carnegie Building**, its construction was paid for by the US philanthropist, Andrew Carnegie, and the library opened in 1909. In the late 20th century the library moved into a newer, larger building and was replaced by the Alliance Française, who made it their headquarters. They still occupy the first floor, but the ground floor is the home of the **National Trust of St Vincent and the Grenadines** and houses the mildly distracting **National Archaeological Collection** ① *T784-451 2921, www.svgnationaltrust.org, Mon-Thu 0900-1700, Fri 0900-1600, US$2.* Archaeological evidence shows that Saladoid Amerindians from the Orinoco region of South America arrived in St Vincent around AD160 and there was a large settlement in the Argyle area. They knew how to weave, work stone and carve canoes. Artefacts and decorative pottery illustrate how they lived and ran their society, what tools they used, what they ate and how they cooked their food, as well as what jewellery they wore. There are several petroglyphs around the island, such as at Layou, Buccament, Barrouallie, Petit Bordel and Chateaubelaire, and some on Canouan and Petit St Vincent.

Kingstown has two cathedrals, both on Grenville Street; St George's (Anglican) and St Mary's (Roman Catholic). **St George's Anglican Cathedral**, consecrated in 1820, has an airy nave and a pale blue gallery running around the north, west and south sides. It became a cathedral in 1877 when the Diocese of the Windward Islands was constituted and the chancel and transepts date from 1880 to 1887. The cupula was blown down by a hurricane in 1898 and after that battlements were added to the tower. There is an interesting floor plaque in the nave, now covered by carpet, commemorating a general who died fighting the Caribs. Other interesting features include a memorial to Sir Charles Brisbane (1772-1829) who captured Curaçao. A lovely stained-glass window in the south transept was reputedly commissioned by Queen Victoria on the death of her grandson. She took exception to angels in red rather than the traditional white and it was put into storage in St Paul's Cathedral. It was brought to St Vincent in the 1930s.

St Mary's Catholic Cathedral of the Assumption is of far less sober construction, with different styles, Flemish, Moorish, Byzantine and Romanesque, all in dark grey stone, crowded together on the church, presbytery and school. Building went on throughout the 19th century, a steeple was added in 1877, with renovation in the 1940s. The exterior of the church is highly decorated but dark and grim, while the interior is dull in comparison but quite light and pretty. The **Methodist church**, also on Grenville Street, dates from 1841 and has a fine interior with a circular balcony. Its construction was financed largely through the efforts of freed slaves. There is a little bell tower at the south end, erected in 1907.

St Vincent and the Grenadines Botanical Gardens

Off Leeward Hwy, northeast of town, T784-453 1623, www.nationalparks.gov.vc, daily 0600-1800, US$1.85, under 12s US$0.90, guides available for US$3.70 per person. To get here, it's about a 20-min walk from Market Sq: go along Grenville St, past the cathedrals, turn right into Bentinck Sq, right again and continue uphill to the gate. Alternatively, take a van going along Leeward Hwy or a taxi.

Just below Government House and the Prime Minister's residence, these gardens are well worth a visit and are the oldest in the Western Hemisphere. Occupying 20 acres, they are peaceful, lush, green and colourful, and home to a wealth of tropical plants, flowers,

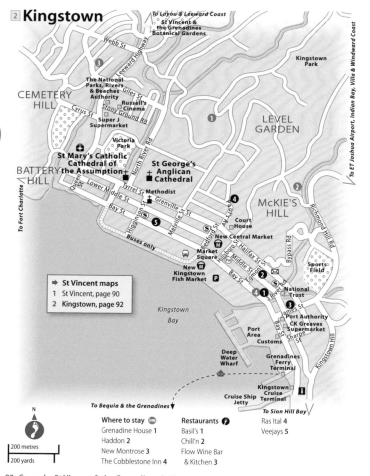

Where to stay
Grenadine House 1
Haddon 2
New Montrose 3
The Cobblestone Inn 4

Restaurants
Basil's 1
Chill'n 2
Flow Wine Bar
& Kitchen 3

Ras Ital 4
Veejays 5

trees and birds. They were created in 1765 by General Robert Melville, then Governor of the Windward Islands, as a plant breeding centre and 'to provide medicinal plants for the military and improve the life and economy of the colony'. At that time they were administered by the British War Office. Three acres were set aside for the established of a Government House. They are famous for being the destination of Captain Bligh's second visit to the Caribbean in 1798 (his first ended in the infamous mutiny on the Bounty) when he introduced breadfruit to the island from Tahiti; a descendant of one of his original breadfruit trees thrives today. He also wrote an early account of a visit to the volcanic crater of Morne Garou (now called Soufrière).

The gardens are compact but unfortunately the plants are not labelled, which forces you to take a guide to learn about them. There is a certain amount of hassling for business by the guides, particularly if a cruise ship is in port, but it's worth it as they are knowledgeable and the tours are interactive with the opportunity to taste and smell medicinal plants. A small aviary is home to a couple of dozen rare St Vincent parrots (*Amazona guildingii*), which is the national bird, originally confiscated from illegal captors.

Fort Charlotte

On Battery Hill at the top of Edinboro Rd, T784-456 1060, Mon-Fri 0800-1500, open weekends if a cruise ship is in, US$1.85, US$7.40 with a guide. The 2-mile walk up from town to the fort is a tough, steep and hot 45 mins. Or take a taxi (15 mins) or a van going to the village of Edinboro, and if you ask the driver they might take you 'off route' up to the fort.

On the promontory on the north side of Kingstown Bay, Fort Charlotte is 636 ft above sea level, and was completed in 1805 and named after the wife of King George III. It appears to be a conventional Napoleonic-era fort, guarding the harbour of Kingstown, but there is something unusual about it as all the 34 cannons (some of which are still in place) point inland. Although it was designed to fend off attacks from the sea, the commanders of the garrison were more worried about the Black Caribs – the descendants of the indigenous population and shipwrecked or escaped slaves. These fearsome people controlled the interior of St Vincent and had caused mayhem in 1779 when they had allied with a French invasion force. They had torn through settlements, burning sugar plantations and attacking the white English colonists. The British did not want a repeat of the violence.

The gatehouse, 1806, was where Major Champion of the Royal Scots Fusiliers was killed on 13 October 1824 (see plaque in St George's Anglican Cathedral) by Private Ballasty. The murderer was executed at the scene of the crime. In the old bakery, a series of paintings shows the early history of St Vincent. Painted by William Linzest Prescott in 1972, they suffer from poor lighting and their condition is deteriorating. There is also a coastguard lookout which controls the comings and goings of ships entering the port. The views are wonderful on a clear day, looking along the chain of Grenadine islands. Below, the ruins of a military hospital can be seen, as well as a bathing pool at sea level on the end of the point, used when the fort housed people suffering from yaws.

The ET Joshua Airport is just southeast of Kingstown at Arnos Vale, a residential area strung along Windward Highway which is also home to the football and cricket Arnos Vale Stadium. The road then runs round the runway and down towards the coast at Indian Bay. There are several hotels in this area, stretching along the seafront through Villa to Calliaqua Bay. It is very pleasant, with light sand beaches, Young Island just offshore, Bequia in the distance and dozens of moored yachts. Many people stay here rather than in the capital, as it is an easy commute into Kingstown if you need to go in, while there are marinas, dive shops, the best restaurants and watersports facilities here.

South coast

Indian Bay and Villa beaches along the south coast offer good snorkelling and swimming and are separated by a small hilly projection and are easily accessible from one to the other. They are popular as they have the lightest coloured sand to be found on the island (most beaches have volcanic black sand) and this area is very much the centre of tourism activities with a string of hotels between Windward Highway and the sea. There are constant views of Young Island, which covers 12.6 acres of tropical hillside surrounded by a white sandy beach, and is the most northerly island in the Grenadine chain, even though it lies only 200 yards off Villa Beach.

Named after British governor Sir William Young, the island today is privately owned and home to the resort of the same name (see page 101). It was in fact one of the first Caribbean private island resorts that opened in 1974. Its jetty is along the Villa Beach Boardwalk, a narrow wooden (concrete in places) walkway that links the hotels from Beachcombers to Mariners, making it easy to visit the restaurants at each without going back up to the main road.

On a tiny island just 50 yards south of Young Island is **Fort Duvernette** ① *US$1.85 officially, but not always collected, accessible any time by water taxi from the jetty on Villa Beach Boardwalk; about US$7.40 return, note: water taxis do not operate on Sun or public holidays.* Built in the 1790s, it is also known as 'rock fort' and previously as

Tip...

Avoid swimming in the water surrounding Fort Duvernette as it has strong currents; it's better to swim at Villa Beach after getting the boat back from the fort.

Young's Sugar Loaf, and has gun emplacements on top of a 190-ft-tall volcanic plug in the sea overlooking both Calliaqua and Indian bays. The battery was built to protect the colonial hub of Calliaqua where sugar was loaded onto ships bound for English ports. A staircase with 255 steps and a handrail winds up the rockface to two gun decks where you can find cannons from the reigns of both George II and George III, as well as the remains of the supply buildings. The views from the top battery to Bequia and Mustique are superb.

The next bay beyond Young Island is **Calliaqua** where there is a lovely long, crescent-shaped beach, **Canash**, which is perfect for young children. Within this large bay is a smaller inlet known as **Blue Lagoon** which is calm and sheltered by Johnson Point. Blue Lagoon is St Vincent's premier yachting destination, simply because it faces directly on to Bequia and there is easy passage from here straight southwards to the Grenadines.

Blue Lagoon Hotel & Marina ⓘ *off Windward Hwy, T784-458 4308, www.bluelagoonsvg. com, also see page 101,* is a port of entry with customs and immigration facilities and is the base for yacht charter companies. The property had a comprehensive makeover in 2015 (it was formerly **Sunsail Marina**) and now offers a range for facilities to sailors, overnight guests and day visitors. It has anchorages and berths, yacht services, a lovely beach, good restaurants and bars, very stylish rooms in the hotel, shops, a dive shop and all are connected by a pleasant wooden deck overlooking the marina.

Windward Coast

a wild Atlantic coast backed by fertile valleys and a looming volcano

There are two approaches to the Windward Coast of the island. From Calliaqua on the south coast, the Windward Highway cuts inland through Diamond and Stubbs and rejoins the coast again at the new Argyle International Airport, where the runway is parallel to the sea. This route, already served well by vans, will be the main route between Kingstown and the airport and is 8½ miles. The other route cuts across from ET Joshua Airport and meets the coast just north of the Argyle airport at Peruvian Vale, a distance of 9 miles, and is more winding and slower but has lovely views in parts. Whichever way you go, beyond Argyle is a rugged and windswept coastline of villages, rocky bluffs and black sand beaches.

Kingstown to the coast

From the roundabout at ET Joshua Airport, Mespo Highway (also known as Fountain Stretch) takes you into the hills northeast of Kingstown and gives splendid views all around. The Mesopotamia Valley is particularly beautiful and you can get a glorious view on the way up about midway to Peruvian Vale from the **Belmont Lookout** ⓘ *daily 0730-1700, free, toilets US$0.75.* From here you can look over lush farmland dotted with simple homesteads, where every strip of land irrespective of the gradient is cultivated in terraces: bananas, nutmeg, cocoa, breadfruit, coconut and a variety of root crops. Vendors selling fruit and vegetables may be seen on the roadside, but not on Fridays and Saturdays when they go to the market in Kingstown. The highest point is the **Bonhomme Mountain** (3192 ft) which overlooks the valley and streams tumble down and merge to flow over the rocks of the Yambou Gorge before heading out to sea. If you look south from the lookout you can see as far as Bequia.

Beyond the village of Mesopotamia (commonly known as Mespo), the lush, tropical gardens of **Montreal Estate** ⓘ *T784-458 1198, Mon-Fri, Dec-Aug 0900-1700, open at weekends if cruise ships are in, US$5.55,* are worth a visit where anthuriums are grown commercially for the domestic market. The owner, Timothy Vaughn, is a well-known landscape gardener in Europe and this is his tropical garden, full of organic flowers and colourful foliage. They sit on 7½ acres at 1500 ft, with glorious views of Argyle and the Mesopotamia Valley, and are surrounded by forest and banana plantations. There are three different sections: the Rain Forest Garden, the Colour Garden and the Formal Garden, and each offers something different and appealing so take your time to explore the winding paths.

> **Warning...**
> The Windward Coast is rocky with rolling surf and strong Atlantic currents; do not swim off the beaches as it can be very dangerous.

Windward Highway to Black Point

The interior road meets the **Windward Highway** at Peruvian Vale. It gets progressively drier as the road goes north hugging yellow sandstone cliffs which contrast with the white waves surging in towards the black volcanic beaches. A number of banana packaging stations are passed especially around **Colonarie**.

Black Point Tunnel is 350 ft long and was constructed by Colonel Thomas Browne using Carib and African slaves in 1815. A marvel of engineering for its time, it was blasted through volcanic rock from one bay to the other and the drill holes are still visible, as are storage rooms and recesses for candles. It is very atmospheric and there are a few bats as well as people washing in the water which pours out of the rock. It provided an important link with the sugar estates in the north and sugar was hauled through the tunnel to be loaded on to boats in Byera Bay. Black sand Byera Beach is the longest in St Vincent and the sea is rough, but in the days of the sugar plantations the coast curved round more giving protection to shipping and there was a jetty.

You cannot see the tunnel from the road, which goes over the top. Turn towards the sea between the fuel station and the river down a dirt road which leads to **Black Point Heritage and Recreational Park** ① *off Windward Hwy, about 20 miles from Kingstown, www.nationalparks.gov.vc, 0800-1800, US$2*, it comprises the tunnel, beach (not safe for swimming), Grand Sable River and recreational field where cricket is played and people gather for celebrations. It was also another film location for *Pirates of the Caribbean: Curse of the Black Pearl*.

Georgetown to the far north

Georgetown was the first capital of the island and is now the second largest town after Kingstown. For many years it was economically depressed after the loss of sea cotton and arrowroot and then problems with bananas. However, the area is now picking up and you can see many new or refurbished homes. It is not a tourist destination but there are places to eat and drink if you are passing through.

The road to **Sandy Bay** (beyond Georgetown), where St Vincent's remaining Black Caribs live, is now good. However, you have to cross the Rabacca Dry River, a jumble of rocks, grit, rubbish and dead wood swept down from the mountains above, which sometimes is not dry and therefore not passable. Rocks and sand are extracted for the building industry. Sandy Bay is poor but beyond it is an even poorer village along a rough dirt road, **Owia**. Here is **Owia Salt Pond Recreational Site** ① *about 32 miles from Kingstown, www.nationalparks.gov.vc, 0900-1800, US$1.85, changing rooms/toilets*, a natural area of tidal pools. The rough Atlantic crashes around the huge boulders and lava formations, then trickles into the protected pools; it's very picturesque. They are filled with small marine life and reef fish and it feels as if you are bathing in an aquarium but watch where you're stepping as there are black sea urchins. There is a small park at the top with gazebos for picnicking and 217 steps down to the Salt Pond area. Past Owia is **Fancy**, the poorest village on the island, also Black Carib and very isolated, reached by a rough jeep track of roughly 3 miles. The Falls of Baleine are another 2-mile hike from here around the tip of the island, rugged and not for the unadventurous they are more usually accessed by boat. Surrounded by steep cliffs this 60-ft-high waterfall tumbles into a rock-lined pool, perfect for swimming, but the rocks are very slippery. However, a bamboo pole bridge to get to them, a pathway to the coast, about a 10-minute walk, and a landing platform in Baleine Bay for boats has recently been added to the site.

Carving along cliff tops and scenic coastal stretches, the Leeward Highway is a 25-mile dramatic road running along the west coast from Kingstown. It goes through a crumpled landscape of local villages, black sand beaches and coconut plantations and the road is steep and twisty as it slips down into valleys and then sharply up to headlands. The views are wonderful, both inland to forest covered mountain ridges, and also seaward to where the Caribbean laps gently into numerous sheltered coves.

The route ends near Richmond Beach, a popular swimming area, and in the distance, is the view of **La Soufrière**, St Vincent's still-active volcano and the island's highest peak; see boxes, pages 98 and 107.

Vermont Nature Trail

Off Leeward Hwy, about 9 miles from Kingstown, www.nationalparks.gov.vc, daily 0700-1700, visitor centre and other facilities open from 0900, US$1.85. Vans from Kingstown go to Peniston from where it is a long walk.

The road leaves Kingstown and initially heads inland. There are views down into Campden Park Bay and the deep water Campden Park Container Port complex, and then the road passes through the small village of **Questelles.** About a mile after Questelles, turn right up the Buccament Valley to Peniston and Vermont to the Vermont Nature Trail. This is an area of great biodiversity with both primary and secondary rainforest providing a habitat for the St Vincent parrot and lots of other birds, lizards, opossum, agouti and the regionally endemic Congo snake (which is harmless). There is a marvellous 2-mile trail and, unless you want scientific information, a guide is not necessary; get a trail map from the visitor centre. There is a rest stop at 1350 ft, and a Parrot Lookout Platform at 1450 ft, which is probably the best place to see the St Vincent parrot. Designated by **BirdLife International** as an Important Bird Area (IBA), the Buccament Valley is also a good place to spot the whistling warbler, black hawk and purple-throated Carib. Be prepared for rain, mosquitoes and chiggars, and use insect repellent. At the car park, which is at 975 ft, the visitor centre has a kiosk for snacks and drinks, toilets and there are benches along the trail.

Layou Petroglyph Park

Off Leeward Hwy, about 9½ miles from Kingstown, www.nationalparks.gov.vc, Mon-Sat 0900-1600, US$0.75 and US$0.40 for the toilets. The visitor centre is basically a room with some photos on the walls.

After Questelles, the Leeward Highway rejoins the coast at Buccament Bay with its luxury beach resort (see page 102), and then goes down into Layou, a pretty village with a few excellent examples of gingerbread houses, a small beach and crescent-shaped bay. To reach Layou Petroglyph Park, look out for a signpost along a road to the north of the village. From the visitor centre there is a short trail down to the Rutland River and the petroglyphs (rock carvings) are at the foot of this trail.

Several Amerindian sites have been uncovered in St Vincent, and these are considered to be the best. They are carved on a huge boulder, about 20 ft wide, next to the stream, and are believed to date from AD 300-600 during the Saladoid, or Arawak, occupation of the island. It has been speculated that the largest drawing is of Yocahú, their principal

ON THE ROAD
Natural disasters on St Vincent

The first eruption of the volcano La Soufrière on written records was in 1718, and in 1812 it was noted that an eruption produced major explosions. As details of hurricanes began to be recorded, it was the Windward Islands Hurricane of 1898 that was reported as a strong, destructive hurricane that raged through the eastern Caribbean. Damage on Barbados and St Vincent was catastrophic and 300-400 people died in the storm. In 1902, La Soufrière erupted, killing 2000 people, just two days before Mont Pelée erupted on Martinique, killing 30,000. In 1979, the year St Vincent gained independence from Great Britain, there was another eruption of La Soufrière on Good Friday, 13 April. Fortunately, and thanks to advance warning, no one was killed as thousands were evacuated, but there was considerable agricultural damage. In 1980 Hurricane Allen caused further devastation to the plantations and it took years for production of crops such as coconuts and bananas to recover. Then Hurricane Emily destroyed an estimated 70% of the banana crop in 1987.

In 2004, Hurricane Ivan lashed St Vincent but the damage there was minimal compared to that of some of the Grenadine islands further south and the devastation it caused on Grenada. Christmas 2013 brought a freak storm outside the normal parallels of the hurricane season but caused destruction on a par with some of the worst hurricanes St Vincent has known. A low-level trough system brought severe rains and high winds which caused floods and landslides in St Vincent and the Grenadines, Saint Lucia and Dominica over a 24-hour period from Christmas Eve to Christmas Day. St Vincent reported nine deaths and over 500 people affected as dozens of homes were destroyed and hundreds damaged. The Leeward side of the island bore the brunt of the storm with rivers bursting their banks and sweeping all before them and many areas were without clean water and power for some time.

Things have been quiet on St Vincent since 2013. During the past 4000 years La Soufrière has had an average of one explosive eruption every 100 years. It has had two since 1902, so perhaps the mountain will be kind to the island for a while.

male god, yoca being the word for cassava and hú meaning 'giver of'. It is believed that the tribes of the Lesser Antilles, including St Vincent, associated this deity's power to provide cassava with the mystery of the volcanoes, since their carvings are conical. The Yocahú cult was wiped out by the invading Caribs before the arrival of the Europeans, but could have existed from about AD 200. There are picnic spots and a bathing pool in the river.

Mount Wynne and Barrouallie
Mount Wynne has two lovely black sand beaches with crystal clear water where Queen Elizabeth II once bathed in the late 1960s and the southern stretch of sand is named after her. There are changing rooms/toilets (US$0.75), plenty of shady trees and a grassy area with seats; it's a popular local picnic spot as well as a destination for cruise ship excursions from Kingstown. **Barrouallie** is the next village of any size, which was established by French settlers in 1719, the first European colony on the island and once was the capital of St Vincent and the Grenadines. With the rest of the island, it passed back and forth between the French and the British, finally remaining in the hands of the latter. In 1898,

a hurricane devastated St Vincent in general and Barrouallie in particular, and the church and almost all houses were destroyed. Today it is a fishing village and on the beach are fishing boats, nets, pigs and chickens scratching about. The local speciality catch is 'black fish', in reality a short-finned pilot whale, which grows to about 18 ft. The whale meat is usually dried or steamed before being eaten.

Wallilabou Bay

The road also passes through the remains of a sugar mill (the furnace chimney is still standing) and then heads inland from the popular anchorage and restaurant at Wallilabou Bay. A stone gateway marks the entrance to the **Wallilabou Falls** (Wally-la-boo), or **Wallilabou Heritage Park** ① *Leeward Hwy, 14 miles from Kingstown, www.nationalparks. gov.vc, daily 0800-1700, US$1.85, restaurant, changing rooms/toilets*. Large samaan trees give shade to the area and keep it cool. The waterfall is small but it can give you quite a pressure shower and you can bathe in the pool. The park was once a plantation and the remains of a stone wall cross the river. On the opposite side of the road is a nutmeg plantation.

Wallilabou Bay was one of the settings for Disney's *Pirates of the Caribbean* movies, *Curse of the Black Pearl* and *Dead Man's Chest*, with copies of 18th-century piers and storage houses being built here to replicate the pirate's town of Port Royal in Jamaica. The whole bay was bustling with hundreds of cast and crew for the duration of the filming and pirate ships ruled the sea. Today the site is occupied by the **Wallilabou Anchorage** ① *T784-458 7270, ww.wallilabou.com, restaurant daily 0800-2100,* which has sheltered moorings and a small marina for yachts, a simple restaurant (see page 104) and memorabilia of the *Pirates of the Caribbean* including photos and props displayed in what was Disney's 'green rooms'. Unfortunately, the film set has not been well maintained and each storm destroys a bit more so it is becoming increasingly dilapidated and most visitors are disappointed. Many of the Grenadine islands were also used for location shooting, including Union Island and the Tobago Cays.

Cumberland to Wallibou

The road goes inland along the **Wallilabou Valley** before quickly rising over the ridge into the North Leeward district, and then descending down to Cumberland Bay. **Cumberland Beach Recreational Park** ① *Leeward Hwy, 21 miles from Kingstown, www.nationalparks. gov.vc, daily 0800-1800, changing rooms/showers/toilets US$1.85,* has a pretty beach with small restaurant/bar, and there is a view of the palm-lined slopes up towards the Morne Garu Mountains. Cumberland Bay provides a protected anchorage for yachts because it is deep and boats can anchor close to shore. Another attraction inland from here at the village of Grove is the **Cumberland Nature Trail** ① *daily 0700-1700, US$1.85,* which meanders through the rainforest of the Cumberland Forest Reserve in the Upper Cumberland Valley for 1.6 miles. It is very good for birdwatching and there are hides along the trail where you can watch for the St Vincent parrot, whistling warbler, brown trembler, tanagers, fly-catchers and many other birds. From Grove, where it starts, the trail follows a wooden water pipe taking water to three hydroelectricity plants on the Cumberland River. However, it's difficult to get to, vans don't go up the road to Grove, so if you're not in a car it's an hour walk uphill from Leeward Highway to begin with. You then need about two hours to complete the trail and get back to the ticket booth and some parts are steep and overgrown, becoming slippery and dangerous if it rains.

From Cumberland, the Leeward Highway climbs quickly to the small village of **Coulls Hill** with perhaps the best view on the coast, through **Chateaubelair,** a sprawling fishing village with small islands offshore, and then goes through **Richmond** and before ending at the beautiful black sand beaches at **Wallibou**. To the right of the road between Chateaubelair and Richmond are the **Dark View Falls** ① *off Leeward Hwy, 24 miles from Kingstown, daily 0900-1700, US$1.85, changing rooms/toilets,* which lie on a tributary of Richmond River. They consist of two cascades, one above the other, plunging down cliff faces into pools. The hike through the rainforest to the first one is easy and short, about 10-15 minutes from the parking area, and crosses the Richmond River on a bridge made from long bamboo poles. Once on the other side it passes through a bamboo grove, where there is a picnic area and viewing platform. The trail up steps and across the river on slippery rocks to the second waterfall is more difficult, but doesn't take long. A quiet and peaceful spot most of the time and exquisitely beautiful, the water is cold and refreshing and the falls' water pressure will leave your skin tingling. Swimming is better in the upper pool.

Listings St Vincent *maps pages 90 and 92.*

Tourist information

Kingstown

St Vincent & The Grenadines Tourism Authority (SVGTA)
2nd floor, NIS Building, Bay St, Kingstown, T784-457 1502, www.discoversvg.com. Mon-Fri 0800-1600.
There is also a kiosk at the nearby Kingstown Cruise Terminal, which is open when ships are in. If you're coming from Barbados, SVGTA also runs a desk at Grantley Adams International Airport, T01-246 428 0961, which is manned daily from around 1300 until the last flight to St Vincent departs. There is also tourist literature and maps to pick up at the hotels.

Where to stay

Unless otherwise stated, all hotel rooms have a/c, TV and Wi-Fi. Hotel tax (10%) and VAT (10%) is charged by all accommodation options, usually as a single charge of 20%. Check if this has been included in quoted rates.

Kingstown

$$$ Grenadine House
Kingstown Park, T784-458 1800, www.grenadinehouse.com.

Originally the British governor's residence (parts of the building date to 1765), this delightful boutique hotel featuring old-world decor and a nice ambience has 18 comfortable rooms, with patios or terraces and views of the garden or mountains, 2 elegant restaurants, 1 with exposed stone walls and the other on a terrace, bar, pool, spa and gym. On the downside, it's quite a walk into town.

$$ Haddon Hotel
McKies Hill, T784-456 1897, www.haddonhotel.com.
Recently renovated to a good modern standard, this business-style hotel is nestled on a hillside on the outskirts of Kingstown and is within walking distance of the centre but away from the bustle. The 11 rooms and 8 1- or 2-bedroom suites have kitchenettes. **El Patio** is an excellent restaurant and bar run by a Cuban chef, and has friendly and efficient service.

$$ New Montrose Hotel
New Montrose, T784-457 0172, www.newmontrosehotel.com.
Straightforward, family-run hotel in a quiet semi-residential area close to the centre and a short walk to a good supermarket, slightly old-fashioned with wicker furniture and floral colours, but the 25 rooms, studios

and 1-2 bedroom apartments are more than adequate and there's a decent restaurant, and rooftop bar with a view of Kingstown.

$$ The Cobblestone Inn
Bay St, T784-456 1937, www. thecobblestoneinn.com.
A 10-min walk from the ferry in a charming former sugar and arrowroot warehouse dating from 1814, the 26 rooms have been renovated to highlight the Georgian architecture with hardwood floors and exposed stone. An informal rooftop restaurant and bar has harbour views but is only open for breakfast and lunch until 1500, though there is a smaller, darker wood-panelled bar in the lobby that's open in the evening (but no food).

The south
The hotels along Windward Highway can be reached by van from Kingstown and the airport; just asked to be dropped off at the top gate.

$$$$ Young Island
T784-458 4826, www.youngisland.com.
A tiny, privately owned islet, 200 yds off the coast at Villa and reached by a 5-min boat transfer. The 29 delightful stone cottages have sea views, patio, open-air shower and some have plunge pools and interconnect to accommodate families. Spa treatments, meal packages available, tennis, sailing, diving, wedding and honeymoon packages offered. There is a lovely lagoon swimming pool, surrounded by tropical flowers and a golden-sand beach overlooking Indian Bay.

$$$ Blue Lagoon Hotel & Marina
Windward Highway south of Villa, T784-458 4308, www.bluelagoonsvg.com.
This recently thoroughly overhauled complex offers a range of facilities including the hotel, The **Loft Restaurant & Bar** and **Café Soleil** (see page 104), **Flowt Beach Bar** (see page 105), shops selling groceries and souvenirs, a pleasant pool, and **Indigo Dive** is based here (see page 106). Each of

the 19 rooms is well-equipped, stylish and bright with luxuriously large beds and good linen, and most have a balcony overlooking the boats. Great service, cool Caribbean colours and decor, and friendly atmosphere throughout. Also owns the equally good newly opened **Bequia Plantation Hotel** (see page 128).

$$$-$$ Beachcombers Hotel
Windward Highway, Villa, T784-458 4283, www.beachcombershotel.com.
Friendly beach resort with 48 rooms in 6 different categories from family suites with kitchenettes to small good-value garden rooms – all comfortable and essentially you pay more for space and view. Excellent high-ceilinged and breezy **The Dock** restaurant/ bar (open to non-guests 0700-2200), with sail cloth walls and wooden floors overlooking the pool, Sat steelpan band, Sun afternoon tea.

$$$-$$ Grand View Beach Hotel
Off Windward Highway, Villa Point, T784-458 4811, www.grandviewhotel.com.
A former cotton plantation house in 8 acres of grounds in a commanding position on 300-ft-high Villa Point overlooking Indian and Greathead bays, this 50-year-old hotel has aged gracefully and features black and white tiled floors, a grassy courtyard with pond, great artwork, 19 neat rooms (it's worth paying extra for a balcony) and impeccable service from staff that have been here many years. Facilities include pool on the headland, tennis courts, gym, and excellent breakfasts are taken in the atmospheric dining room with a view.

$$$-$$ Mariners Hotel
Windward Highway, Villa, T784-457 4000, www.marinershotel.com.
Jaunty blue and white hotel with 20 comfortable rooms in tropical gardens arranged in a U-shape around the pool overlooking Young Island. On the Villa Beach Boardwalk to the other hotels and the **French Verandah** restaurant here is very

good (see page 104) and the bar does great healthy smoothies. Can organize sunset cruises and dive/accommodation packages with **Dive St Vincent** (see page 106).

$$$-$$ Villa Lodge Hotel
Off Windward Highway, Villa Point, T784-458 4641, www.villalodge.com.
Next to **Grand View** (above) on the headland with views of Indian Bay, 11 bright newly decorated rooms and 8, 1- or 2-bedroom fully equipped apartments, pool, and relaxed restaurant/bar with nautical decor and patio dining (meal plans are available).

$$ Hotel Alexandrina
Hercules Dr, off Windward Highway, Ribishi, T784-456 9788, www.hotelalexandrina.com.
A little off the beaten track, but within a 15-min drive to Blue Lagoon and Villa Beach, this family-run hotel is on a hillside overlooking a lusciously green valley with amazing views down the Grenadines to Mustique. An unusual building with many curves, wraparound balconies and red-tiled roofs, it offers 27 comfortable rooms, some in garden cottages, and has a rather grand, but warm feel to it. Good meals, lovely swimming pool in beautifully maintained gardens, and friendly staff.

$$ Paradise Beach Hotel
Windward Highway, Villa, T784-570 0000, www.paradisesvg.com.
Small hotel with 17 modern rooms with balconies and good beds and quality furniture, some with kitchenettes, arranged in neat double-storey bright yellow units along the Villa Beach Boardwalk; the beachfront ones have the best view of sunset and Young Island. Good restaurant serving traditional local dishes and a popular Fri night barbecue. **Fantasea Tours** is based here (see page 106).

$$ Sunset Shores Beach Hotel
Windward Highway, Villa, T784-458 4411, www.sunsetshores.com.
Next door to **Paradise Beach** (above), simple resort but the 32 spacious rooms in blocks are cheerful and well-priced, some sleep families/groups of up to 5, with balconies/patios, pay more for sea views. Casual restaurant with reasonable food, a pool with bar, and the beach and Villa Beach Boardwalk is just over a white picket fence.

$ Adams Apartments
Off Top Rd, Arnos Vale, T784-458 4656, www.adamsapts.com.
Right next to the runway at ET Joshua Airport in a bright purple building with 6 rooms and 3 studios. Very simple and no breakfast but cheap and convenient for flights and supermarkets nearby. The Arnos Vale Stadium (cricket) is on the opposite side of the airport.

$ Rosewood Apartment Hotel
Rose Cottage, Villa, T784-457 5051, www.rosewoodsvg.com.
Minutes from the beach in a quiet street in Villa, this is a little dated but spotless with 7 studios with kitchenette, and 3 smaller standard rooms without, each additional person US$20, all opening up to a shared spacious patio or balcony with a glorious view towards Young Island. Supermarket close by or opt for a continental breakfast.

$ Tranquillity Beach Apartment Hotel
Off Windward Highway, Villa Point, T784-458 4021, www.tranquillityhotel.com.
Great value for the location on the Indian Bay side of Villa Point with excellent views and a short walk to Villa Beach, this no-frills spot is run by helpful Lucelle Providence, 7 self-catering apartments with balconies overlooking the bay (studios, 1-, 2-, 3-bedrooms), some up flights of steps, the exterior could do with some updating but clean and well equipped.

Leeward Coast

$$$$ Buccament Bay Resort
Reservations UK T44-(0)1268 242463, www.buccamentbay.com.
The only all-inclusive resort on the island at the mouth of the Buccament River, with

100 polished suites and villas with all mod-cons, some with furnished balconies, plunge pools and ocean views. Good for families, with 2 outdoor pools and a kids' pool, lots of activities and sports including football, yoga, tennis, and dining options include a steakhouse, a beachside bar and an upscale Indian restaurant.

$ Richmond Vale Diving & Hiking Centre
Richmond, T784-458 2255,
www.richmondvalehiking.com.
Almost at the top of the road on the Leeward Coast, this centre focuses on teaching sustainable living and is primarily a destination for school groups from across the Caribbean and the UK and US to partake in various projects like tree planting and working in the organic garden, as well as a base for preparing international volunteers for development work. But it welcomes budget travellers and families in the 8 simple rooms (from US$50), there's a shared kitchen and food is available at US$7.50 per meal. Also good for a day or overnight visit for the activities including the La Soufrière volcano climb, horse-riding and diving (see What to do, below).

Restaurants

VAT on restaurant bills is 15%, but this is nearly always included in menu prices; 10% service charge is, however, usually added to the bill.

Kingstown

$$$-$$ Basil's Bar and Restaurant
Bay St, T784-457 2713 www.basilsbar.com.
Mon-Sat 0800-2400.
Owned by Basil Charles, the same proprietor of the legendary **Basil's Bar** on Mustique (see page 134), like the **Cobblestone Inn** next door, this has an interior of high-reaching arches and rough-hewn stone. Buffet lunch Mon-Fri 1200-1400 for hungry people, acceptable but not startling, also à la carte lunch and dinner like burgers,

barbecue chicken or seafood platters. Pleasant for an evening drink.

$$ Flow Wine Bar & Kitchen
Allen Building, James St, T784-457 0809,
www.flowwinebar.com. Mon-Thu 1100-2200,
Fri 1100-2400, Sat 1800-2400.
Contemporary upstairs spot with pleasant setting indoors with fat leather couches or at tables on the rooftop terrace bar, specializing in good wines and craft beers, plus there's a tasty menu of local and international dishes; try the flatbread pizzas, tapas and yummy desserts.

$ Chill'n
1st Floor Trotman's Building, Egmont St,
T784-456 1776. Mon-Thu 0730-2000,
Fri-Sat 0730-2300.
Nothing fancy but tasty and reasonable lunches in this upstairs spot that has open windows to catch the breeze and free Wi-Fi, breakfast, patties, rotis, burgers, passable pizzas, barbecue and jerk chicken wings, sugary cakes and pastries; with luck they'll have rum n' raisin cheesecake.

$ Ras Ital
Paul's Av. Mon-Fri lunch only 1100-1430.
Rastafarian café serving mostly vegetarian dishes but also some meat and fish. Each day, there 8-10 dishes to choose from the counter plus bread and a beverage (fresh juice, tea or mauby). From Halifax St walk past the Court House on your right, then take your next right. At the end of the road, turn left and Ras Ital is on the right.

$ Veejays
Lower Bay St, T784-457 2845. Mon-Sat 0900-2000, Fri until late with live band.
Friendly and popular with locals for lunch (especially taxi drivers who all know it), offers good, wholesome local food, either cafeteria-style with buffet food in big catering pans, or an off-the-wall menu (though you'll have to wait for a meal to be cooked from scratch), fried steak, fish, prawns or lambi, and best rotis in town.

The south

All the hotels on the Villa Beach Boardwalk have restaurants.

$$$ The French Verandah

At Mariners Hotel, Windward Highway, Villa, T784-453 1111, www.marinershotel.com. Daily for dinner, reservations required.
Great atmosphere at this candlelit romantic restaurant on a beach-facing terrace, small but really interesting menu that might include lambi gratin, stuffed crab backs or lobster tail in sherry and there's a good choice of wine. The bar next to the pool is open all day and does delicious smoothies among the usual cocktails.

$$$ The Loft Restaurant & Bar

At Blue Lagoon Hotel & Marina, off Windward Highway south of Villa, T784-458 4308, www.bluelagoonsvg.com, also see Facebook. Daily 1800-2200.
With a gorgeous blue, white and silver interior this first-floor venue with balcony looks directly on to the marina. Offers a fine dining menu with the likes of fish, lobster and lamb, vegetarian choices and some Thai dishes, and regular events including Caribbean Fest on Tue with a steelpan band.

$$-$ Café Soleil

At Blue Lagoon Hotel & Marina, off Windward Highway south of Villa, T784-458 4308, see Facebook. Daily 0700-2330.
On the wooden deck overlooking the yachts, this always buzzing coffee shop/bar offers anything from full hot meals of fish and meat to filled paninis, salads, cakes and ice cream. Great proper coffees, fresh juices, cocktails and cold beers, and free Wi-Fi. Good spot to eat before walking along to **Flowt Beach Bar** (see below).

$$-$ Grand View Grill

On the beach below Grand View Beach Hotel, off Windward Highway, Villa Point, T784-457 5487, see Facebook. Tue-Sun 1500-2200.
Under separate management from the hotel, a colourful double-storey building with lively bar, on a grassy bank with outside tables and next to the beach with great views; the location is perfect, the food however can be hit and miss (overcooked chicken/fish and boring burgers). The pizzas are the best bet (also does takeaway) as are the delicious rum cocktails.

Windward Coast

$$-$ Ferdie's Footsteps

On the main street in Georgetown, on the corner with Cambridge St, T784-458 6433. Daily 0900-1700.
Ferdie's is a favourite with organized tour groups hiking La Soufrière for a big meal at lunchtime after the climb, when you can expect a delicious buffet of callaloo soup, chicken, fish, rice, salad, fried plantains and stewed greens. At other times he doesn't have a menu but can be persuaded to rustle up something like a fish sandwich or roasted breadfruit, and you can stop for drinks.

$ Top View Bar & Grill

On the main street in Georgetown, T784-492 2641. Mon-Wed 0900-1700, Thu-Sat 0800-0100, Sun 1000-2200.
Colourful pink and green haphazardly built local bar and takeaway with wooden seats on a deck and ocean views, serving what's available but it could well be grilled or steamed fish, chicken kebabs, barbecue wings or burgers and fries.

Leeward Coast

$ Beach Front Restaurant & Bar

Chateaubelair, T784-458 2853, see Facebook. Mon-Sat 0800-2400, 1600-2400.
Rustic beach bar where you can swim and eat and drink outdoors or on the roof terrace with shade, good view of the bay, specializes in rotis (chicken, beef, fish, lambi or vegetable) more substantial fish, fries and salad or fried plantains for lunch, cold drinks and coffee.

$ Wallilabou Anchorage

Wallilabou Bay, T784-458 7270, www.wallilabou.com. Daily 0800-2100.

Caters mainly for yachties as it has mooring facilities in the picturesque bay, serves snacks, sandwiches, local dishes and fish, none of it great and sometimes there's not much available, but worth a stop to see the remains of the *Pirates of the Caribbean* movie sets (also see page 99).

Bars and clubs

St Vincent

The island is not famed for a particularly raucous nightlife, although there's usually good crowds at the bars in the hotels along the Villa Beach Boardwalk where most of the hotels take turns hosting a barbecue once a week. In Kingstown and the rural villages, there is no shortage of rum shops.

Bush Bar
Vermont, T784-491 8127, see Facebook for Zen's Organic. Daily 1400-2200.
Up in the hills near the Vermont Nature Trail and popular with locals and tourists venturing off the beaten track, the Bush Bar was built by the ethereal Zen Punnett in the forest high above the Buccament Valley surrounded by birds, butterflies and pets. Materials used are rustic bamboo and thatch and quite a few empty rum bottles cemented together and used as windows. There is electricity, a clean toilet and you can play dominoes or lie in a hammock in the garden. Cold beers and rum, and her brother Kyle is an excellent cook who can rustle up something from a tiny wooden shack at the back, or call and book in advance if a meal is required. It isn't easy to find, there is no public transport so get a taxi or phone for directions, but worth it for the authentic Caribbean feel.

Flowt Beach Bar
Blue Lagoon Hotel & Marina (see Where to stay, above), T784-456 8435, see Facebook. Wed-Sat 1400-2200, Sun 1200-2200.
With a fun and friendly atmosphere and always popular with yachties, offering snacks and main mails like burgers, grilled fish or jerk pork, tables in the sand and on wooden decks under thatched roofs, plenty of drinking and there's often a DJ on Sat night. Under the same ownership as **Flow Wine Bar & Kitchen in Kingstown** (see Restaurants, above).

Surf-Side Restaurant and Bar
Windward Highway, Villa, T784-457 5362, see Facebook. Mon-Sat (except Wed) 1200-2200, Sun 1500-2220.
With a deck overlooking Calliaqua Bay, more of a bar than a restaurant although the pizzas are excellent, huge choice of rum and other drinks, popular happy hour 1900-2100 Fri and Sat and often plays calypso and soca music.

Entertainment

St Vincent
Cinema
Russell's Cinema, *Stoney Ground Rd, Kingstown, T784-4579308, www.russells-cinema.com.* Show times Wed, Fri-Sun 1700 and 2000; US$5.55, under 14s US$3.70 and there's popcorn and soft drinks.

Shopping

St Vincent
Food
You can buy excellent fresh fruit and vegetables at the New Central Market in Kingstown; the best days to go are Fri and Sat mornings when vendors from around the island bring their produce to sell.
CK Greaves Supermarket, *T784-457 1074, www.ckgreaves.com.* A well-stocked chain of supermarkets with the most useful branches near the ferry terminal on Bay St, Kingstown (Mon-Thu 0800-1700, Fri 0800-1900, Sat 0700-1300, and across the road from ET Joshua Airport in Arnos Vale (Mon-Thu 0745-2000, Fri 0745-2100, Sat 0700-2000, Sun 0800-1200).
Super J, *www.superjsupermarkets.com/stvincent.* Supermarket at **Russell Shopping Centre**, Stoney Ground Rd, Kingstown, T784-457 2984 (Mon-Thu 0700-2100, Fri-Sat

1900-2200, Sun 0700-1300), and at Arnos Vale, T784-457 2981 (Mon-Sat 0700-2200, Sun 0700-1500). Both have delis and ATMs.

What to do

St Vincent
Cricket
Arnos Vale Stadium, *next to the airport.* This is a multi-use sports complex and is also better known locally as the Playing Fields, and is where Test Match cricket is played. It is one of the most picturesque cricket grounds in the world with a view of the Grenadines, has a capacity of 18,000, and the 2 ends are Airport End and Bequia End. It's also used for football and alongside there are netball and tennis courts. Arnos Vale is one of the grounds for the West Indies team (aka The Windies), check the website for fixtures; www.windiescricket.com.

Diving
The St Vincent reefs are fairly deep, at 55-90 ft, so scuba diving is more rewarding than snorkelling. Dive sites include Bottle Reef, the Forest, the Garden, New Guinea Reef and the Wall. In Kingstown Harbour there are 3 wrecks at one site, the Semistrand, another cargo freighter and an ancient wreck stirred up by Hurricane Hugo, as well as 2 cannons, a large anchor and several bathtubs.
Dive St Vincent, *at the Young Island jetty near Mariners Hotel on the Villa Beach Boardwalk,* T784-457 4714, www.divestvincent.com. The oldest dive operation on the island, owner Bill Tewes has been here since the 1970s and benefits from a wealth of local knowledge and experience. PADI certification courses, daily dives (prices similar to below), equipment and camera rental, specializes in small groups and lots of package options are available, including a week's accommodation at one of the hotels and 10 dives from US$1000 per person.
Indigo Dive, *at Blue Lagoon Hotel & Marina,* T784-493 9494, www.indigodive.com. Offers a full range of diving from single dives for

US$75 and double dives for US$135 to a PADI Open Water course for US$600. Also PADI discover scuba and kid's programmes using the pool at the hotel, plus a range of snorkelling or glass-bottom boat trips from US$45.

Sailing
Blue Lagoon Marina, *www.bluelagoonsvg. com.* The centre of yachting activities on St Vincent given its position on the south coast and its proximity to the Grenadines – Bequia is only 9 miles away. It's the most popular anchorage and mooring for private yachts and a number of yacht charter companies are based there. For full details of these, see page 16.

Tour operators
Bamboo Adventures, *Georgetown, T784-570 8000, www.booksvgnow.com.* Based in Georgetown near the start of the trail on the windward side of the volcano, one of the best options for the La Soufrière hike but can also customize island tours.
Fantasea Tours, *at Paradise Beach Hotel, Windward Highway, Villa, T784-457 4477, www.fantaseatours.com.* Jeep safaris, birdwatching, La Soufrière hikes and waterfall visits, and also has a fleet of 4 boats of different sizes for cruises, snorkelling, dolphin and whale watching and day excursions to Bequia and Mustique, and Mayreau and the Tobago Cays.
Richmond Vale Diving & Hiking Centre, *Richmond, T784-458 2255, www.richmond valehiking.com.* This centre offers a number of activities in the north of the island including the guided hike of La Soufrière from the leeward side from US$75 (it's an early night and you can stay overnight), see box, opposite, and other hikes to Dark View Falls or other nearby trails. There's a PADI dive school on Richmond Beach, prices are from US$45 for a single dive to US$450 for a PADI Open Water course. The centre has horses, and 2-hr rides in the countryside or along the beaches cost from US$85.

Hiking La Soufrière

Dominating the north of St Vincent and the highest peak on the island, La Soufrière volcano rises to 4048 ft. Hiking the volcano is very popular, but you must leave very early in the morning and allow a full day for the trip. It is accessible from either the leeward or windward coasts. The leeward trail starts at the village of Richmond, and takes about two and half to three hours up, while the windward trail starts inland from Rabacca and takes about two hours. The windward trail is the more popular route, covering 4 miles on a well-marked track from the trailhead where there is a manned kiosk, toilets and car park (0730-1530) run by **The National Parks, Rivers and Beaches Authority** (NPRBA; corner Leeward Highway and Stoney Ground Road, Kingstown T784-453 1623, www.nationalparks.gov.vc).

It is not mandatory to take a guide, though it's advised for inexperienced hikers as the route is moderately difficult (but older children will manage it). Always hike in a group. To get here, about 2 miles north of Georgetown you cross the Rabacca Dry River, then take a left fork and walk/drive along the paved farm track that heads inland through banana plantations until it reaches the trailhead and kiosk. Get a taxi all the way there, or a van from Kingstown to Georgetown (US$2), and you can ask the driver to make a detour for an extra charge. From there it is a two-hour steady uphill climb to the crater's edge.

The first 3 miles are through the Rabacca plantation, then up through rainforest, montane thicket and cloud forest along Bamboo Ridge and all the way to the crater's magnificent volcanic rock and ash-strewn rim; the top can be cloudy, windy, chilly and rainy, so take adequate clothing (although most people hike in shorts) and footwear, as well as water, snacks and insect repellent. If you have some extra energy once you reach the top, you can go down into the crater on a path which has rope to assist in places; in 1970 an island reared up out of the lake in the crater which smokes and the water round it is very warm. It will take about an hour to walk around the entire interior, and requires some light climbing and possibly wading. Where the wind is forceful at the rim, the inside of the volcano is always calm and the temperature comfortable.

For the alternative, unmarked, overgrown and even more challenging route from the leeward side starting from the end of the road after Richmond, you will need a guide and there are no facilities at the trailhead. The views are even better on this route, especially across to the Caribbean and on an exceptionally clear day you can see as far as St Lucia. You also need a guide for the La Soufrière Cross Country Trail – a combination of both routes – which snakes across the width of St Vincent. It covers 9 miles and takes about six to seven hours. It is better to start on the windward side and end on the leeward side as you can take a welcome swim in the Caribbean at the end.

Tour operators (see opposite) can organize day tours for the volcano climb. Costs vary depending on arrangements and transport but expect to pay from US$85 per person, depending on how many passengers are in the vehicle to get to the trailhead. For the windward trail, try **Bamboo Adventures** in Georgetown (T784-570 8000, www.booksvgnow.com) or **Sailor's Wilderness Tours** in Kingstown (T784-457 171, www.sailorswildernesstours.com). For the leeward trail, try **Richmond Vale Hiking** in Chateaubelair (T784-458 2255, www.richmondvalehiking.com).

Sailor's Wilderness Tours, *Middle St, Kingstown, T784-457171, www.sailors wildernesstours.com.* Day trips to Bequia on a catamaran, La Soufrière hikes, and half-day tours combining sites such as Fort Charlotte, the Botanical Gardens, Mesopotamia Valley and Montreal Gardens.

Sam's Taxi & Tours, *Kingstown, T784-456 4338, www.samtaxiandtours.com.* City tours (1-3 hrs) including the cathedrals and Fort Charlotte, half-day tours up the Leeward Coast to the Layou Petroglyph Park, Barrouallie and Wallilabou, or full-day island tours up the windward side as far as Owia Salt Pond.

Sea Breeze Nature Tours, *Arnos Vale, T784-458 4969, www.seabreezenaturetours.com.* Hal Daize runs coastal boat tours of St Vincent as well as whale and dolphin watching, snorkelling and fishing charters.

Transport

St Vincent
Air
See page 146, for information on getting to the island. ET Joshua Airport is named for Ebenezer Theodore Joshua, the first chief minister of Saint Vincent and the Grenadines. It is quite tiny, with a couple of basic shops selling snacks and drinks (**CK Greaves Supermarket** across Windward Highway has a better choice), a Bank of Saint Vincent & the Grenadines bureau de change (Mon-Fri 0830-1230, 1530-1730) with an ATM, and airside a duty-free kiosk with a limited choice of booze and a coffee machine. For details of Transport from the airport, see Finding your feet, page 89.

The new Argyle International Airport is presently under construction on the east coast between Windward Highway and Argyle Beach 8½ miles from Kingstown.

Boat
See page 150 for details of the ferry services between St Vincent and the other Grenadine islands. St Vincent is often the departure point for ferry-hopping between them, or otherwise beginning in Grenada and working your way north to St Vincent is an option too.

Bus
Vans (minibuses) leave from the terminal near the New Kingstown Fish Market off Bay Street; they stop on demand rather than at bus stops and go to all parts of the island, including a frequent service to **Indian Bay** and **Villa** along Windward Highway; the main hotel area. At the terminal they crowd round the entrance competing for customers rather than park in the bays provided. They generally run Mon-Sat 0530-2000 in the busier south, but perhaps only until about 1700 or 1800 further north. There is generally no service on Sun or public holidays, although a few do run along the south coast on Windward Highway as far as Calliaqua. Fares range from US$0.40 for any distance less than one mile, US$0.90 to Villa and the hotel area, to US$2.60 as far north as Fancy. Pay for an extra seat if you have luggage, and if the van is not full of passengers in a hurry to get somewhere, the driver may agree to make a short deviation 'off-route' for about US$0.75. The number of vans starting in Kingstown and running as far as **Sandy Bay**, **Owia** or **Fancy** in the northeast is limited; the best times are actually school runs – secondary children in this region actually come in daily to go to school in Kingstown. Otherwise go to Georgetown and try to catch one of the few vans running between Georgetown and Fancy. Again to the far northwest, direct vans from Kingstown are limited so take one to Barrouallie or Chateaubelair and seek transport from there on to Richmond.

Car hire
Avis is the only international franchise represented at ET Joshua Airport (in a shipping container in the car park) but there are several local car hire companies that will arrange to meet you off a flight. Prices and standards are very similar; ask a hotel

to recommended one, or St Vincent & The Grenadines Tourism Authority (SVGTA) has a list of companies on the website: www.discoversvg.com. All will be able to arrange the local drivers' permit (valid for 6 months, US$26). Expect to pay in the region of US$55 per day for a normal/sedan car, and US$70 for a small jeep/4WD, with significant discounts for weekly rates. See page 149, for further details about hiring a car and driving.

Avis, at the airport, T784-456 6861, www.avis.com. **Sam's Taxi & Tours**, Kingstown, T784-456 4338, www.samtaxiandtours.com. As well as a good tour and taxi operator, this company is also a reliable option for car hire.

Cycling

Cycling is rewarding, but expect long, steep hills and lots of them.

Sailor's Wilderness Tours, Middle St, Kingstown, T784-457 171, www.sailors wildernesstours.com. Can arrange guided mountain bike tours such as, among other options, a 3-hr tour which involves a drive up to the Belmont Lookout and a cycle downhill to the Mesopotamia Valley and the coast at Peruvian Vale. Contact them about hiring a bike.

Taxi

Taxis are plentiful but are expensive and non-negotiable rates are set by the government and taxi associations; rates are Kingstown to the airport US$11, and the airport to Villa and Calliaqua US$11. Beyond that, standard fixed rates are US$22 per hr. Taxis gather at the airport, the Kingstown Cruise Terminal and the Grenadines ferry terminal. Otherwise any hotel/restaurant can phone one, or if you find one you like get the driver's card/phone number; taxi drivers usually make knowledgeable guides for an island tour.

The Grenadines

The Grenadines

The Grenadines, divided politically between St Vincent and Grenada, are a compact archipelago less than 70 miles in length of 100 or so tiny rocky islands and cays stretching across the sea between the two. They are still very much off the beaten track as far as mass tourism is concerned, but are popular with private yachts and for yachting holidays, exploring while spending all their time afloat, and indeed it was yachtsmen who first popularized the Grenadines as a destination.

The seven picturesque, hilly and inhabited islands are particularly appealing, each with a distinct character and easy-going way of life, and with glorious white-sand beaches and rocky coves, excellent harbours and lots of opportunities for snorkelling, diving and other watersports.

The Grenadines have a certain exclusivity, and some of the smaller islands are even privately owned such as Mustique, which is famous for its villas owned by the rich, royal and famous. There are some fabulously expensive and luxurious places to stay, served by small planes zipping around the airstrips, but the island chain is also ideal for the independent traveller on a more modest budget. There are affordable hotels, guesthouses and rental homes and Grenadine ferry-hopping is a journey that is one of the most delightful tourist routes in the Caribbean.

Bequia

lots of yachts, a delightful waterfront walkway, and gorgeous sandy beaches

Nine miles south of St Vincent and 7 square miles, Bequia (pronounced Bek-way) is derived from a Carib word meaning 'island of the clouds', and is the largest of the St Vincent dependencies. It is home to roughly 5000 people, some of which are descendants of 19th-century Scottish sailors, and is steeped in seafaring traditions such as boat-building, fishing and whaling. Bequia attracts quite a number of tourists; chiefly those on yachts and smaller cruise ships, but increasingly land-based tourists who get here from St Vincent on the fast ferry services (less than an hour).

Essential Bequia

Finding your feet

JF Mitchell Airport is at the island's southwest tip. Hotels normally arrange for their guests to be collected by taxi, otherwise taxis meet arriving flights. The ferry terminal/dock is right in the middle of things in Port Elizabeth and is served by the *Jaden Sun*; *Bequia Express* and *Admiral II*. Sometimes the mailboat *Barracuda* stops in Bequia but it's not on the scheduled route. From the dock you can get a 'dollar van' or walk along Belmont Walkway to hotels (even with luggage); this concrete path is directly on the water's edge and runs from Port Elizabeth right along the southern side of Admiralty Bay. For those arriving on yachts, customs and immigration is opposite the jetty in Port Elizabeth (Monday-Friday 0830-1800, Saturday-Sunday 0900-1200 and 1500-1800). There are anchorages all round Admiralty Bay, Princess Margaret Beach, Lower Bay, Friendship Bay and off Petit Nevis. See also Transport, page 140.

Best for yacht and sunset views

Bequia Plantation Hotel, page 128
Frangipani, page 133
De Reef, page 133
Jack's Bar, page 133
Tante Pearl's, page 134

Tip...

For an island tour take a taxi; most drivers are very knowledgeable and three hours should be enough, and you may enjoy a ride in an open-back pick-up truck. Ask the tourist office to make a recommendation or talk to the drivers at the almond tree on the Belmont Walkway.

Getting around

Buses (minibuses and open pick-up trucks with bench seats in the back called 'dollar vans') wait under the almond tree just to the right (or south) of the tourist office and ferry jetty. As public transport they only go to the south of the island but are available for private hire as taxis. Water taxis scoot about in Admiralty Bay, Princess Margaret Beach and Lower Bay for the benefit of the many yachts and people on the beach. Whistle or wave to attract their attention, or they gather at the little jetties outside the **Frangipani Hotel** and **Gingerbread Café** on the Belmont Walkway. Fares are around US$7.40 per trip to the beaches, less for a journey across the harbour at Port Elizabeth. Car hire can usually be arranged through your hotel, or ask at the tourist office.

The main developed tourist and yachting area is in Admiralty Bay on the west side, where lush hillsides dotted with bougainvillea tumble to beaches and boat-filled bays, and where a charming walkway runs along the waterfront passing hotels and restaurants. But the island is also quite hilly and well forested and you can hike just about anywhere, including across to the rugged and windswept east coast, which is thinly populated and has stunning views of the Atlantic.

Port Elizabeth

Bequia's village-style capital is Port Elizabeth and here Admiralty Bay offers one of the most popular yachting hangouts in the Grenadines. Boat building and repair work are the main local industries, and you can see fishing boats and their nets strung out on the narrow beach along Belmont Walkway. When you get off the ferry you will find to your left the fruit and veg market, with some clothes and souvenir stalls, and across the road is the immigration and customs building, and next to it the **Bayshore Mall**; a blue and white building with a few shops and a café. Behind this on the next block is the **Bank of St Vincent & the Grenadines**, which has an ATM.

On the right, the **Belmont Walkway** runs along the shoreline and narrow strip of sand in front of the hotels and restaurants, and has recently been extended all the way around the rocky headland as the Princess Point Trail to Princess Margaret Beach. It is a delightful

Bequia

Where to stay	Bequia Plantation **2**	Sugar Reef Bequia **7**	De Reef **2**
Bequia Beach **5**	Firefly Plantation **11**	Sweet Retreat **8**	Fig Tree **3**
	Frangipani **4**	The Old Fort Boutique	Ginger Bread **4**
	Keegan's **12**	Hotel & Estate **9**	Jack's Bar **5**
	Ramblers Rest	Village Apartments **10**	L'Auberge de
	Guesthouse **1**		Grenadines **6**
	Spring House Bequia **3**	**Restaurants**	Sugar Reef Café **7**
	Sugarapple Inn **6**	Chameleon Café **1**	Tante Pearl's **8**

walk taking in the crystal clear water with lots of tiny fish and views of the whole bay dotted with colourful fishing boats and smart shiny white yachts.

The street a little back from the waterfront is Belmont Road, also known as 'Front Street' and Belmont itself is the residential area running up the hillside. Look out for the **Anglican St Mary's Church** on Belmont Road, which was built of local limestone and ballast bricks in 1829, replacing an earlier church which was destroyed by a hurricane in 1798. It is open and airy and has some interesting memorial stones.

Above and to the north of Port Elizabeth a paved road runs to **Hamilton Village** and the **Hamilton Battery**, which used to guard the bay. The original structure is no more, but French and British cannon retrieved from local waters have been placed there, looking out to sea. The view is indeed very fine over the harbour.

West coast beaches
Just beyond the end of the Belmont Walkway at the Bequia Plantation Hotel, Princess Point Trail climbs up wooden steps and around the headland (there are benches to enjoy the views) and then descends on to a flat concrete causeway over the sea, past a small cave and on to Princess Margaret Beach (the causeway may be covered at high tide, in which case you might have to splash along it). Alternatively, access is via a steep track off Belmont Road or water taxi. Princess Margaret Beach is the quintessential Caribbean beach, fringed by cedar and almond trees with perfect white sands. It was so named after the princess in 1958 when she swam there while visiting the island by yacht.

It is, remarkably, undeveloped except for a single beach bar; **Jack's Bar** in a glorious position above the beach with a broad deck under sailcloth and which rents out sun loungers for the day (US$9.25 or US$5.55 for customers). As does Faye's place a little further along, not a beach bar but a friendly vendor who sits under a tree and also sells cold drinks and rum punch out of her cooler box. At its south end there is a small headland, around which is Lower Bay and its beach which is equally beautiful, but livelier, with three beach bars, and a sleepy fishing village at the bay's southern end. Local cricket matches are held regularly on the flat sand, usually on Sundays. It is a bit more exposed to the breeze, although the snorkelling is better and you can rent beach loungers from **De Reef** beach bar (US$3.70 per day).

The west coast is the location for several yacht races, including the **Bequia Easter Regatta** in April; see Festivals, page 137.

> **Warning...**
> Beware of the clearly marked manchineel trees at Lower Bay; their shade may look tempting but their fruit is poisonous and the sap can cause a very severe skin reaction. See also box, page 154.

To Mount Pleasant and Hope Bay
The highland area of Bequia is a patchwork of woods and open moorland on the steep sheltered leeward approach from Port Elizabeth. The walk up to **Mount Pleasant** is worthwhile and takes about 45 minutes but go by taxi if it is too hot. The shady road is overhung with fruit trees and the view of Admiralty Bay is ever more spectacular. There is a settlement of airy homes (local and holiday villas) at the top, all with sweeping views of most of the Grenadines. There is a general store with a restaurant and bar, which sometimes has entertainment by local string bands in season, and the **Old Fort Country Inn Boutique Hotel & Estate** set on an historic plantation dating to the 18th century when the first French settlers arrived.

By following the road downhill and south of the viewpoint at Mount Pleasant you can get to **Hope Bay**, an isolated and usually deserted sweep of white sand. At the last house (where you can arrange for a taxi to meet you afterwards), the road becomes a rough track, after half a mile turn off right down an ill-defined path through cedar trees to an open field, cross the fence on the left, go through a coconut grove and you reach the beach. Bring your own food and drinks, as there are no facilities. This is on the windward side so while the sea is usually gentle, sometimes there is powerful surf and a strong undertow, so take care.

The northeast coast

Take a taxi or drive over the hills through coconut groves to **Spring Bay**, where there is a hotel and many desirable villas offering a tranquil outlook and breezy living. Spring Plantation once dominated this part of the island and the ruins of the old sugar mill can still be seen. **Firefly Plantation Hotel** ① *T784-458 3414, www.fireflyhotels.com, tours by appointment so call ahead, US$3.70*, is built on the foundations of the old plantation house. Sugar is no longer grown but you can tour the 30-acre grounds with the head groundsman, who will show you the orchards of oranges, grapefruit, bananas, breadfruit, guava, Bequia plums, sour cherries, mangoes and other tropical produce and animals, let you sample the fruits and vegetables and tell you something about the estate's history. The tour takes around 45 minutes after which you can have a drink or meal at the hotel.

Industry Bay has another attractive beach surrounded by palms known as Crescent Beach, which is narrow and has a fair amount of weed, but is still good for a cooling dip with good snorkelling on the reef when the water is calm. It also has a brilliant view across to Bullet Island, Battowia and Balliceaux where the Black Caribs were held before being deported to Roatán. Set above the road looking down on the bay, **Sugar Reef Bequia** is a new hotel and luxuriously intimate with just eight suites in a 65-acre coconut plantation dating to the 18th century. You can visit its separate **Sugar Reef Café** for lunch which sits on the sand at Crescent Beach.

The next bay on from Industry over a rocky headland is **Park Bay**, with its beach of the same name and the **Old Hegg Turtle Sanctuary** ① *T784-458 3245, www.turtles.bequia.net, tours by appointment only so call ahead, US$5 entrance fee, but donations warmly welcomed*. This is an extremely worthwhile project for the conservation of the hawksbill turtle (*Eretmochelys imbricata*), founded and maintained by a former fisherman, Orton 'Brother' King. The project involves monitoring beaches and checking nests, and collecting the hatchlings to care for them in a nursery during their most vulnerable years (from predators, poachers and being accidently caught up in fishing nets) before releasing them back into the ocean when they have grown and reached maturity at about 2½ years old. There is only about a 50% success rate and a lot of injuries from the turtles biting each other, but it is still better than the natural survival rate and Orton has released well over 1000 turtles since he began in 1995.

The south coast

Friendship Bay is a sheltered south-facing bay also on the island's windward side, with a broad golden sweep of golden sand, although again weed can be a problem here. From the road down to it are good views across to Mustique, and this area is where traditional staple crops of cassava, corn and pigeon peas are cultivated. The hillsides around the bay are also dotted with small houses, rental apartments and villas, and the excellent **Bequia Beach Hotel** with its restaurant and bars sits right on the beach; see page 127. On the eastern side of the bay near the now defunct Friendship Bay Hotel, is the new small **Bequia Boat Museum** ① *T784-457 3649, tours by appointment only so call ahead, entry by donation but US$5.55 would be appropriate*, which officially opened in 2013 and is still a work in progress, but 40 minutes here is well worthwhile to hear the stories about Bequia's seafaring heritage from the curator. The museum currently houses a 36-ft Amerindian canoe, two Bequia-built whaleboats and a 12-ft whaleboat tender, as well as photographs, model boats and traditional woodworking tools. A second building is planned for further exhibits documenting Bequia's history.

Tip...
It takes about 30 minutes to walk from Port Elizabeth to Friendship Bay, or dollar vans follow Belmont Road past the Bequia Beach Hotel and on to La Pompe and Paget Farm.

The western end of Friendship Beach reaches the village of **La Pompe** where fishing boats are drawn up on the beach, and is famous for its 'Gumboat' (model sailing boat) racing on Sundays. Beyond La Pompe the road continues to **Paget Farm** and then the airport.

Offshore from here, whale harpooning is still practised from February to May (the breeding season) by a few fishermen who used to traditionally use three 26-ft long cedar boats, powered by oars and sails (power boats are used today). A Scot, William Thomas Wallace, introduced whaling to Bequia having worked on one of the New England whaling ships that came to the Caribbean chasing humpback whales. He started his own whale station in the mid-1870s in Friendship Bay, and the Ollivierres family from France followed suit in 1876 with a fishery at Petit Nevis (a small offshore island just south of Bequia). Whale meat was a staple food for the population in those days. Today one small whale fishery still exists on Petit Nevis, and despite pleas from conservationists, Bequia does have an annual quota of up to four whales to be killed for meat, although in reality these days it's usually one and many whalers have given up the practice.

Mustique *See map, page 118, and box, page 120.*
exclusive private island famous for rock stars and royals

Lying 18 miles south of St Vincent, Mustique is 3 miles long and less than 2 miles wide, about the same size as Hyde Park in London. Mustique has a glamorous background and the reason the wealthy still flock here is partly to do with the island itself; it is a beautiful place with rocky headlands, dramatic hilltops and seven pristine palm-fringed beaches.

A private island, it is owned by the Mustique Company, comprising the island's home owners, and there are about 100 villas, many of which are rented out through the Mustique Company when their owners are not using them. There is also a hotel, **The Cotton House**, also owned by the Mustique Company, and a seven-bedroom hotel, **Firefly**. But given that the villas are all divided into neat plots across the island, it is described by some as 'manicured', like a large luxury housing estate. Nevertheless, the whole of the island, its beaches and surrounding waters are a conservation area and in recent years environmental conservation is an increasingly important aspect of life on Mustique and many of the villa developments are incorporating new green, sustainable methods of technology and design.

Although there is no intention to commercialize the island, it is accessible to tourists, but privacy and quiet is prized by those who can afford to live there. Most visitors are day-trippers from Bequia or other neighbouring islands on private or chartered yachts, who enjoy the beaches and eat at **Basil's Bar** (see page 134).

Along the leeward coast is **Britannia Bay**, the main anchorage where there are very expensive moorings for medium-sized yachts. At the northern end of the bay is **Basil's Bar**, the focal point for social life on Mustique, and **Lovell** village, where the island's 500 or so local inhabitants live. North of Britannia is **Endeavour Bay**, where the Mustique Company's **Watersports Centre** is located, and from here there is a well beaten path to **The Cotton House**, which is the island's other congregating point. You can also take a picnic lunch to the island's best-known beach, **Macaroni Beach,** on the Atlantic side. This white-sand beach is lined with small palm-thatched pavilions and a well-kept parking/ picnic area. Swimming and snorkelling is good too at **Lagoon Bay** south of Britannia Bay, a narrow strand fringed with coconut palms. Or walk a little further south along the rocky path at the base of the headland and to **Gelliceaux Bay**, a secluded, sheltered bay where the sand shelves steeply and there is great swimming (this was Princess Margaret's favourite beach).

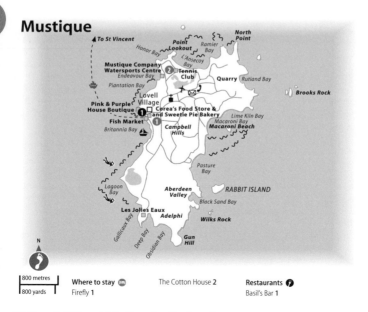

Mustique

To St Vincent
Honor Bay
Point Lookout
L'Ansecoy Bay
Ramier Bay
North Point
Mustique Company Watersports Centre
Endeavour Bay
Tennis Club
Quarry
Rutland Bay
Plantation Bay
Brooks Rock
Lovell Village
Pink & Purple House Boutique
Corea's Food Store & and Sweetie Pie Bakery
Fish Market
Britannia Bay
Campbell Hills
Lime Kiln Bay
Macaroni Bay
Macaroni Beach
Pasture Bay
RABBIT ISLAND
Lagoon Bay
Aberdeen Valley
Black Sand Bay
Les Jolies Eaux
Adelphi
Wilks Rock
Gelliceaux Bay
Deep Bay
Obsidian Bay
Gun Hill

N

| 800 metres | **Where to stay** | The Cotton House 2 | **Restaurants** |
| 800 yards | Firefly 1 | | Basil's Bar 1 |

A quiet, peaceful crescent-shaped island, Canouan (pronounced Can-ah-wan), lies 25 miles south of St Vincent, and is a small island, measuring only 3½ miles by 1¼ miles. It has excellent reef-protected beaches and hidden coves, and a barrier reef runs along the Atlantic side.

The island was valuable for plantation crops during the colonial period, for sugar then cotton, which was grown until 1924. The Snagg family who owned the land were unable to keep the plantation going and the north reverted to acacia scrub and thicket. The estate was sold to the government in 1946. Other local families include the Comptons and the Mitchells, shipwrights who arrived in the 19th century. At that time there was plenty of cedar (for the hull), mahogany (for planking) and bamboo (for masts) for ship building. In 1939 Reginald Mitchell built the largest schooner ever in the Lesser Antilles. The three-masted *Gloria Colita* was 165 ft long, 39 ft wide and weighed 178 tons. Unfortunately only two years later it was found abandoned and awash in the Gulf of Mexico and no one knows what happened to Captain Mitchell and his crew.

Much of the north of the island, 1200 of the island's 1866 acres, has been owned by the Canouan Resort Development Company (CRD) since the early 1990s. At the time, the CRD built roads (previously there were only dirt tracks), installed electricity to the island and residents' houses and provided desalinated water for the first time. This area was

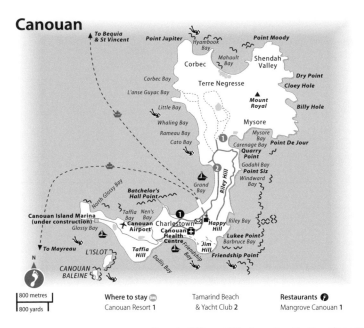

Canouan

Where to stay 🛏	Tamarind Beach	**Restaurants** 🍴
Canouan Resort 1	& Yacht Club 2	Mangrove Canouan 1

BACKGROUND

Mustique

Although Mustique, like the rest of the Grenadines, had small European sugar cane and cotton industries in the 18th and 19th centuries, most of the plantations were abandoned and the island was eventually swallowed up by scrub. In 1958, it was acquired by a single proprietor for just £45,000 – Colin Tennant, or Lord Glenconner, a Scottish aristocrat and the 3rd Baron Glenconner (1926-2010). There were no roads, jetties or running water, and Tennant's initial ambition was to establish a cotton plantation, and he developed the infrastructure, including one of the world's chicest little airports with a thatched terminal surrounded by a white picket fence. He also built a village for its few inhabitants (fishermen), and planted coconut palms, vegetables and fruit. But this venture was not financially successful and he looked for other ways to develop the island.

In 1960 the British royal yacht Britannia cruised around the Caribbean with Princess Margaret and her new husband, now Lord Snowdon, on their honeymoon. They visited Mustique and Tennant gave the princess a plot of land as a wedding present (his wife was an avid socialite and a lady-in-waiting to the princess). This caused considerable media interest in Mustique as a destination and Tennant formed The Mustique Company to develop a private island hideaway, his own exclusive resort where he could entertain the rich and famous. Two architects helped shape the island during its formative years: Arne Hasselqvist, a construction engineer from Sweden, and Oliver Messel, a leading British theatre set designer who had developed a reputation for the flamboyant houses he had designed on Barbados. Their first project was to convert the old cotton warehouse into a small hotel, The Cotton House, and to split the islands into plots, which were sold to shareholders to build villas. Its appeal was its privacy and exclusivity, and plots were bought by an eclectic group of socialites, rock stars, artists and other wealthy private individuals.

then taken up by **Raffles Resort**, then **Canouan Resort** at Carenage Bay (rebranded from Raffles), a villa development and the **Tamarind Beach Hotel**.

Canouan has now gone under another metamorphous, and in early 2016, much of a new US$200 million development opened. Some of it incorporates the old facilities – the Tamarind Beach Hotel is still there, for example – while there's a new ultra-luxurious 26-suite and 6-villa **Canouan Resort**, and 27 residences under the banner of **Grenadine Estate**. Additionally, the airstrip has been extended so it can accept private jets, and a new marina is currently under construction in Glossy Bay with 80 berths; six of which will be able to accommodate superyachts. Access to most of this is gated and only employees and guests are allowed entry. Although the **Tamarind Beach Hotel & Yacht Club** welcomes yachts and day visitors, and the 18-hole **Grenadines Estate Golf Club** running up and over the hill in the centre is open to all; some well-heeled tourists fly over from Mustique or the other super-luxurious resorts in the Grenadines for a day of golf.

The international press has said that Canouan is the place "where the billionaires go to get away from the millionaires", but if you're not quite in this league there are other

Princess Margaret herself built Les Jolies Eaux as a private royal residence on her 10-acre plot in 1972 – the only property she ever owned – and the main five-bedroomed villa was designed by Messel in the neo-Georgian-style. At the time Tennant was quoted for saying, "She filled it with things she had seen at the Ideal Home Show: there was an awful lot of Formica". Margaret adored Mustique, and spent lengthy holidays there for more than 20 years to escape freezing British winters, royal stuffiness and the paparazzi. It was somewhere very private where she could let her hair down, and by the mid-1970s the parties at Les Jolies Eaux had become legendary. Nude sunbathing was de rigueur, there were evening cocktails, dinner parties, parlour games, the weekly 'jump up' at the beach bar, and lavish picnics were set out on the beach on fine china; allegedly MI5 kept a discreet watch from a nearby hilltop.

Mustique's jet set fame reached its zenith with Tennant's week-long 50th birthday party in 1976, when guests included Mick and Bianca Jagger among other royals and celebrities. A deeply tanned Margaret, dripping in jewellery, was photographed as she 'crowned' Tennant as the 'King of Mustique'.

It was here too, that she conducted her affair with Roddy Llewellyn, a landscape gardener 17 years her junior. After a photo of Margaret and Llewellyn together in swimsuits on a Mustique beach was published in 1976, the Snowdons publicly acknowledged their marriage had broken down and they were divorced two years later. Lord Snowdon himself only ever visited the island once, on their honeymoon in 1960, and in later years he called it 'Mustake'.

Meanwhile the cost of running Mustique depleted Tennant's family fortune and, beset by financial problems, he had severed his connections with the island by the late 1970s and moved to St Lucia (where he died in 2010). Margaret eventually gave Les Jolies Eaux to her son, Lord Linley, when he married in 1998, but, much to her distress, he quickly sold it. Like many of the 100 or so villas on Mustique, it is now available for weekly lets through The Mustique Company. There is a small museum at The Cotton House, where there are some interesting photos and artefacts that document the story of Mustique.

options. You can get there by ferry and visit on a day trip, and the Tamarind Beach Hotel & Yacht Club is in the mid-range category.

The village, on the leeward side in Grand Bay, is **Charlestown**, founded after a devastating hurricane destroyed the settlement at Carenage Bay in 1921. It is architecturally uninteresting, untidy and scruffy, having grown too quickly and unplanned, but has a few shops and the **Bank of St Vincent & the Grenadines**, which has an ATM. The white-sand beach is superb, running the length of the bay and broken only by the jetty. The beaches in the south around Dallis and Friendship bays are also splendid with views of numerous islands to the south, while there are sheltered yacht anchorages in Friendship Bay, Glossy Bay and off the **Tamarind Beach Hotel & Yacht Club**.

Mayreau

About 5 miles south of Canouan, and 3 miles east of the Tobago Cays, Mayreau (pronounced my-row) is the smallest inhabited island in the Grenadines and is only 1½ square miles in size. Roughly 300 people live there permanently; many descendants of slaves imported by the Saint-Hilaire family who acquired the island after fleeing France in the Napoleonic Wars.

The Eustace family inherited it through marriage on the death of Miss Jane-Rose de Saint-Hilaire in 1919 and their descendants still own most of the land, with 21 acres belonging to the government of St Vincent, on which the village is built.

Officially unnamed but called Old Wall by the locals, the village is tightly packed on Station Hill and is crested with a small school, the telecommunication masts, and the beautiful brick and stone **Catholic Church of the Immaculate Conception**, built in 1930. From the church there are lovely views east to the Tobago Cays and Union Island to the south. The ferries call in at Mayreau on their way between St Vincent and Union Island, and there is a single-lane tarred road leading from the jetty on Saline Bay through the village to Saltwhistle Bay. You can hike this route which takes about an hour, though be prepared for a little climb up to the village.

The beaches are glorious and are easily accessed on foot. The southern leeward beach in Saline Bay is long and sandy and closer to the village, and where cruise ships anchor offshore, but it is **Saltwhistle Bay** that is the highlight of the island, a perfect horseshoe-shaped bay in the northwest with calm turquoise water and powdery white sand. This is a popular stop-off point for yachts, and many day charters include the bay as a lunch stop when visiting the Tobago Cays. The **Saltwhistle Bay Club** restaurant and bar serves great food and cocktails and there are other more modest shacks along the beach. On the windward coast, Upper Bay, Windward Bay and Windward Careenage have pretty beaches and the presence of large offshore reefs means that the sea does not get particularly choppy (unlike other Atlantic coasts) so are suitable for swimming.

Tip...
Mayreau has no airstrip and access is only by sea; the nearest airport is on Union Island, 4 miles to the south, from where you can take a water taxi or scheduled ferry.

Tobago Cays

The Tobago Cays are a collection of five tiny islands and numerous cays and sandbars lying about 3 miles to the east of Mayreau, collectively protected from the open sea by a horseshoe reef and surrounded by aquamarine water in shallow sand-bottom lagoons. The beaches are some of the most beautiful in the Caribbean, there is diving and snorkelling on Horseshoe Reef where the coral gardens are rich in marine life including stingrays, barracuda, and shoals of reef fish, and a turtle-watching area has been marked by buoys around the beach on Baradel.

The Tobago Cays were used for the filming of *Pirates of the Caribbean*; Petit Tabac is where Captain Sparrow and Elizabeth were marooned by Barbossa at the end of *Pirates of the Caribbean: Curse of the Black Pearl*. Many yachties anchor here, it's a popular day trip from the other islands, cruise ships anchor in the open sea and transport their passengers across by dingy, and everyone frolics in the crystal clear waters and basks on the beaches.

It is protected in the **Tobago Cays Marine Park (TCMP)**, which was established in 1997 to simply try and halt the damage and pressure on the ecology caused by the massive volume of visitors. Some of the damage is unfortunately irreversible. Numerous anchors, together with hurricanes, over-fishing and removal of black coral has killed some of the reef, while hard coral lies broken on the bottom. The national park now covers nine islands; the five uninhabited islands of Petit Tabac, Petit Bateau, Jamesby, Petit Rameau, Baradal that lie within the Tobago Cays, the populated island of Mayreau as well as its uninhabited offshore islets to the north of Catholic Island, Jondall and Mayreau Baleine, as well as the uninhabited cays, the 4-km Horseshoe Reef and a 1400-acre area of sand-bottom lagoons.

Although it has not always well policed, rangers on boats will come to collect the daily fee, a five-knot speed limit is in force for all craft, which must use dedicated moorings and anchorages (a zone map can be downloaded from the website). Other restrictions include scuba diving must only be with a registered local dive shop, no fishing is permitted, you must remove all rubbish, and not touch anything underwater, notably the coral.

Despite all these restrictions, which have helped tremendously, the Tobago Cays can still be very crowded with unlimited yachts (an estimated 3000 visit each year), and day charter catamarans out of St Vincent, Bequia, Canouan and Union Island; it's feasible that there are up to 150 boats here per day in high season. Many visitors are surprised too by the vendors, who are permitted to come in by boat (they also pay a park fee).

Mayreau & the Tobago Cays

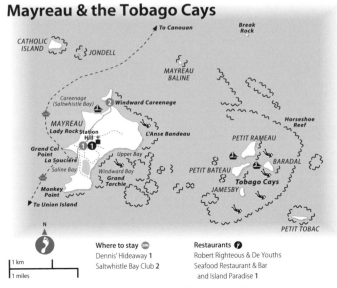

To Canouan
Break Rock
CATHOLIC ISLAND
JONDELL
MAYREAU BALINE
Careenage (Saltwhistle Bay)
Windward Careenage **2**
Horseshoe Reef
MAYREAU
Lady Rock
Station Hill
L'Anse Bandeau
PETIT RAMEAU
Grand Col Point
La Soucière
Upper Bay
PETIT BATEAU
BARADAL
Saline Bay
Windward Bay
Grand Tarchie
JAMESBY
Tobago Cays
Monkey Point
To Union Island
PETIT TOBAC

N

1 km
1 miles

Where to stay
Dennis' Hideaway **1**
Saltwhistle Bay Club **2**

Restaurants
Robert Righteous & De Youths
Seafood Restaurant & Bar
and Island Paradise **1**

Nevertheless, the Tobago Cays Marine Park is one of the loveliest places in the Grenadines; the environment is quite stunning. A trip out here is not to be missed.

Tobago Cays Marine Park Office ① *Main St, Clifton, Union Island, T784-485 8191, www. tobagocays.org. Mon-Fri 0800-1600*, is the visitor centre, with displays on the ecology for the park and helpful staff who can recommend boat trips (as can the Union Island tourist office across the road). Note this is not where you pay park fees. These are either included in the tour price of organized excursions such as sailing trips or diving, or collected by rangers on boats within the Tobago Cays from visitors on yachts, water taxis or cruise ship dinghies. The fees are US$3.70, under 12s US$1.85, per day.

Union Island
a buzzing centre for the southern Grenadines and springboard for trips to the Tobago Cays

The most southerly of the islands belonging to St Vincent and the Grenadines, Union Island is 40 miles from St Vincent and 4 miles south of Mayreau. It is only 3 miles long by 1 mile wide, and has two settlements; Ashton is the working village while Clifton is home to most of the tourist facilities, the ferry dock and the airport. Popular with yachts, Union is one of the busier Grenadine islands with a population of around 3000 and has excellent facilities for a shore-based visit including dive shops, a kite-surfing school, hikes into the hills, good restaurants, shops and a

Essential Union Island

Finding your feet

The airport lies on a rather impressive spit of reclaimed land on the northeast corner of the island near Clifton and has a neat terminal building with a snack bar and taxis pull up outside to meet the flights.

All the ferries arrive at the dock in the middle of Clifton and it is the end of the line for the *Jaden Sun*; *Barracuda*, and *Gemstar*, which have come from St Vincent. You'll notice there is nearly at least one of these at the dock waiting to commence the return trip in the next day or two. The exception is the twice-weekly *Lady JJ* ferry

(Monday and Thursday) to/from Carriacou in Grenada territory, which goes from the jetty in Ashton. Union Island serves as the south point of entry to St Vincent and the Grenadines for yachts and there are anchorages at Clifton, Frigate Island and Chatham Bay, while the Anchorage Yacht Club has some moorings. If you are coming to/from Grenada by yacht or the ferry, the immigration and customs offices are at the airport (daily 0800 until the last flight, but after 1500 you must pay overtime of US$7.40). See also Transport, page 142.

Getting around

All the tourist facilities and most of the hotels are within walking distance of each other along the main street in Clifton, and to get further afield minibuses run between Ashton and Clifton and will go 'off route' for a small fee and will convert to taxis on request. You can also hire bikes and water taxis zip around.

Best bars
Sparrow's Beach Club, page 135
The AYC Bar & Restaurant, page 136
Happy Island, see box, page 136
The Loft, page 136
The Snack Shack, page 137

choice of accommodation for all budgets. There are a lot of French businesses on the island, so is a good place to get fresh baguettes and good coffee, and it is also one of the best places to arrange a trip to the Tobago Cays, only a 15-minute boat ride away, if you are travelling independently.

Sights

About 75% of the population live in Ashton, but most of the action takes place in **Clifton**, where the harbour is always animated with yachts, fishing boats, the ferries and water taxis. The main street is a very pleasant place to idle away some time where you will find a good selection of bars, coffee shops, eateries, supermarkets, stalls selling souvenirs (do not buy shells), places selling specialist yacht provisions and a little market opposite Hugh Mulzac Square and the wharf sells fresh fruit and vegetables.

Union is distinguished by some dramatic peaks, which are visible from St Vincent on a clear day. **Mount Olympus** (637 ft) is in the northwest, while **Mount Parnassus** (920 ft) and **Mount Taboi** (1002 ft) stand side by side in the centre-west and in the centre-east are the jagged **Pinnacles** (925 ft). A walk around the interior of the island (about two hours on a circuit of Clifton–Ashton–Richmond Bay–Clifton) is worth the effort, with fine views of the sea, half a dozen neighbouring islands, brown pelicans and frigatebirds and Union itself. Parnassus, or 'Big Hill', is a good hike. Take the upper level road in Ashton. In front of a clearing are some steps leading to a path; after two or three minutes, fork to the left. The path winds round the hill to the top, from where the views are as fine as you would imagine. North of the airport is **Fort Hill** (450 ft), where the site of a 17th-century French fort gives another panoramic view of dozens of islands.

The closest beach to Clifton, and a short walk through coconut palms around the point from the Anchorage Yacht Club, is **Kite Beach**, which has a great view over the airport's

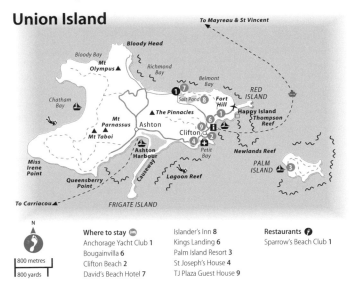

Union Island

Where to stay 🛏
Anchorage Yacht Club **1**
Bougainvilla **6**
Clifton Beach **2**
David's Beach Hotel **7**

Islander's Inn **8**
Kings Landing **6**
Palm Island Resort **3**
St Joseph's House **4**
TJ Plaza Guest House **9**

Restaurants 🍴
Sparrow's Beach Club **1**

runway that sticks out into the ocean, Happy Island and Palm Island (there's a small rock above the beach that you can climb for photographs). It is home to, as the name suggests, the **JT Pro Center Kitesurfing School** (see page 139), which also has a little beach bar, day beds under shade and is a good spot to spend an afternoon snorkelling and watching the kite-surfers. Every full moon during high season (December-May) they hold a full

Tip...
There is only one bank on Union Island, the **Bank of St Vincent & the Grenadines** in Clifton which has an ATM, but it's often empty of cash by the weekends. Most places accept cards though, but you will need cash for ferry tickets, buses, taxis and water taxis.

moon party on the beach with a barbecue and kite-surfing demonstration by moonlight. Further round the point, although reached by a steep road over the hill from near the airport terminal, Belmont Bay, or Big Sands, is a crescent-shaped sandy beach where **Sparrow's Beach Club** is a fine place to go for the day and it offers free pickups from Clifton. It has good swimming and is calm, thanks to an offshore reef.

To the west of it **Richmond Bay** is also pleasant, good for swimming and easily reached as the road runs alongside it. However, it is not well looked after and there is broken glass and rubbish on the sand, so take care. On the west coast, **Chatham Bay** is beautiful and deserted with clear water and sunset views, and has far fewer yachts moored than in front of Clifton. But it's not particularly good for swimming as there is a coral ledge along most of it just off the beach, although snorkelling and diving are worthwhile. There's a rough track to get there from Ashton so water taxi is the best option.

Palm Island and Petit St Vincent

idyllic private island resorts offering a peaceful escape

The privately owned 135-acre Palm Island and its luxury all-inclusive resort, about a mile from Union Island, has abundant coconut palms, five lovely white-sand beaches and coral reefs on three sides. On the west coast, Casuarina is the most beautiful beach and has the casual Sunset Grill restaurant and bar facing Union Island that is open to yachties and passengers of small cruise ships, but the rest of the island is reserved for guests of the 43 rooms and villas. Even access to the beach from the jetty is prevented by ropes and notices. From the airport on Union Island, guests are met and brought over by the resort's launch, a 10-minute boat ride.

To the southeast of Palm Island, and locally referred to as PSV, Petit St Vincent is another beautiful, privately owned, 113-acre island and has one of the Caribbean's most secluded resorts, which is a part of the Small Luxury Hotels of the World hotel chain. Laid-back and stylish, with an excellent standard of service, guests are ensconced in 22 secluded ocean-view villas sprinkled around the hillsides and bays. It is uniquely known for not having phones, Wi-Fi or TV for those that really want to escape modern life. It has a 2-mile perimeter of beaches and the highest point is Marni Hill (275 ft). There are lots of trees and flowers providing a peaceful atmosphere and you can see most of the southern Grenadines from one view or another, and even Mustique on a really clear day. The resort's launch picks guests up from Union Island, and again yachties can come ashore to the bar.

Tourist information

Bequia *map page 114.*

Bequia Tourism Association
T784-458 3286, www.bequiatourism.com. Mon-Fri 0830-1800, Sat-Sun 0900-1400, slightly reduced hours out of season (May-Oct) but still open daily in the mornings.
Straight in front of the ferry terminal is a small hexagon building that is home to this exceptionally helpful information office. They have plenty of leaflets and maps to pick up, maintain an excellent folder of information for all the local tour companies and activities (including yacht charter), and publish *Bequia This Week*, which has listings of what's on.

Union Island *map page 125.*

Union Island Information Centre
T784-458 8350, www.union-island.com. Mon-Fri 0900-1600.
On your left as you come off the ferry. They can recommend water taxis and boat excursions to the Tobago Cays, there are leaflets/maps to pick up and staff can phone the ferry companies to check schedules are running (or not). The Tobago Cays Marine Park visitor centre and head office is a few yards along the road, T784-485 8191, www. tobagocays.org. Mon-Fri 0800-1600.

Where to stay

Unless otherwise stated, all hotel rooms have a/c, TV and Wi-Fi. Hotel tax (10%) and VAT (10%) is charged by all accommodation options, usually as a single charge of 20%. Check if this has been included in quoted rates.

Bequia *map page 114.*
Many villas on Bequia are available for rent; the website of the **Bequia Tourism Association** (www.bequiatourism.com), lists private properties, and **Grenadine Escape**

(www.grenadine-escape.com), and **Bequia Net** (www.bequia.net), act as agents. As does **Grenadine Island Villas** (T784-457 3739, www.grenadinevillas.com), which has a drop-in office on Belmont Walkway.

$$$$ Spring House Bequia
Port Elizabeth, T784-457 3707, www.springhousebequia.com.
Luxury 10-suite hotel set in 2 acres of private grounds in the hills above Port Elizabeth, popular for its privacy and quality. Features include high wooden ceilings and louvered doors, 4-poster beds, gazebos in the gardens, pool, hot tub, gym, guest kitchen, pool table, rooftop deck, a drawing room for afternoon tea, plenty of helpful but discreet staff, and meals are cooked to order by the resident chef.

$$$$ Sugar Reef Bequia
Crescent Beach, Industry, T784-458 3400, www.sugarreefbequia.com.
A 10-min walk from the Old Hegg Turtle Sanctuary, this refined adults-only resort is set in a 65-acre coconut plantation dating to the 18th century. Totally idyllic, it has 8 super-stylish rooms with stone walls, colourful textiles, 4-poster beds and French doors leading out to verandas; each is named after a Grenadine island. Delicious gourmet food at the **Beach House** restaurant (non-guests can call to make a reservation for dinner), plus the **Sugar Reef Café** (see page 133) on the beach, pool, massages and watersports.

$$$$-$$$ Bequia Beach Hotel
Friendship Bay, T784-458 1600, www.bequiabeach.com.
Lovely location right on the beach, 59 rooms, suites and 1- to 2-bedroom villas with kitchens and plunge pools, all with tropical or nautical-inspired decor and balconies or terraces, some with sea views. Excellent service, very relaxing with 2 pools, spa, gym, watersports centre, beachside or hillside restaurants, and entertainment some nights.

Moonhole

On the westernmost tip of Bequia lies the unique series of houses and structures built into the rocks above the ocean called Moonhole. It derives its name from a massive arch formed in volcanic substrate through which the setting moon is sometimes visible. If you are coming to Bequia by ferry or yacht, look out for it on Lower Bight Bay as you approach Port Elizabeth.

It was founded in the late 1960s by Thomas and Gladys Johnston, who retired from the advertising business in New York and built a house beneath the arch with the aid of local stonemasons. With no formal training as an architect, Tom relied on plans he sketched in the sand and a trial-and-error approach to construction. He picked up whalebones, driftwood and shells and incorporated them into the structure, and the rooms are partially open with stone verandas and magnificent views of the sea. Rather than cut down trees, Tom built around them, and trees still grow up through the middle of living rooms, bedrooms and decks. Over time, Tom formed the Moonhole Company and his crew designed and built 17 more houses on the 30-acre property.

Today 11 of the homes are privately owned, but five houses still owned by the Moonhole Company are available to rent by the week, month or season; www.moonholecompany.com.

$$$$-$$$ Bequia Plantation Hotel
Belmont Walkway, T784-534 9444, www.bequiaplantationhotel.com.
Now under the same ownership as the **Blue Lagoon Hotel & Marina** in St Vincent (see page 101), this underwent a complete overhaul/rebuild in 2016 and now competes as one of the best places to stay on Bequia. In a marvellous position in spacious palm-filled gardens at the southern end of Belmont Walkway, it has rooms in The Main House (a former colonial residence) and currently under construction are individual elevated cabins, each with fretwork detail, French doors and terraces. Lovely bright white decor with splashes of aquamarine colours, 4-poster beds, gorgeous bathrooms, a pool, and the beachfront restaurant and bar are open (see Restaurants, page 133).

$$$ Firefly Plantation Hotel
Spring Bay, T784-488 8414, www.fireflybequia.com.
On a hillside to catch the breeze, and part of a working plantation dating to the18th-century, which can be explored on a guided tour (see page 116). The 6 suites with high wooden ceilings and 4-poster beds have lovely views, the open-air restaurant serves modern, locally sourced Caribbean cuisine, there's a pool, and good walks to Port Elizabeth over the hills, or down to the Old Hegg Turtle Sanctuary.

$$$ The Old Fort Boutique Hotel & Estate
Mount Pleasant, T784-485 8888, www.theoldfort.com.
A quiet and peaceful boutique hotel in a 17th-century French-built fortified farmhouse, probably the oldest building on Bequia, on top of Mount Pleasant surrounded by breadfruit, tamarind and mango trees, and with magnificent island views. 6 rooms in the main house and 2 built within the foundations of the old sugar mill, stunning pool with a view, restaurant/bar with terrace and grand inside dining room.

$$$-$$ Sugarapple Inn
Friendship Bay, T784-457 3148, www.sugarappleinn.com.

Overlooking the bay, this classic Caribbean inn has 8 rooms with lovely interiors and lots of natural light from the large shuttered windows, a pool in landscaped gardens, a spacious veranda where continental breakfast is served, and it's a 5-min walk to the beach (cool boxes, towels and beach chairs are provided). Also rents out 2 self-catering 2-bedroom cottages on the beach itself.

$$$-$$ Sweet Retreat Hotel
Lower Bay, T784-498 3921, www. bequiasweetretreathotel.com.
Surrounded by greenery just above the southern end of Lower Bay Beach, just 4 rooms in a timber building with rustic charm and lovely wooden balconies, Robert and Shelby are attentive hosts and provide delicious meals, as well as a good selection of wine and coffee and home-made cakes.

$$$-$ Frangipani Hotel
Belmont Walkway, Admiralty Bay, T784-458 3255, www.frangipanibequia.com.
Based around a double-storey shingle-sided house that was originally built by a Bequia sea captain in 1898, this was Bequia's first hotel that opened in 1967, and continues to be one of the best places to stay with super-friendly service. It now sits in a commanding position on Belmont Walkway and spreads prettily up the hillside. 15 rooms from large, comfortable suites on the hillside featuring Caribbean hardwood and stone detailing and views of Admiralty Bay, to economy rooms in the original house with shared bathrooms and a balcony (from US$65). Open-sided restaurant/bar (see below) that is a focal point for the island.

$$ The Village Apartments
Belmont Rd, Belmont, T784-458 3883, www.villageapartments.bequia.net.
George and Val Whitney are the charming hosts of these 7 1- and 2-bed apartments on a hillside in residential Belmont overlooking Admiralty Bay, each furnished and equipped to an excellent standard, with kitchen and terraces and either garden or ocean

views. The walk to restaurants on Belmont Walkway is down a number of steps and takes about 5 mins.

$$-$ Keegan's
Lower Bay, T784-458 3530, www.keegansbequia.org.
Lovely position on the beach, with 10 rooms from a small twin with fan on the ground floor to a 2-bedroom a/c apartment on the top floor, plus a cottage in the grounds with another 2 apartments and 3 more further down Lower Bay Beach (Apartment 007 is the best with lovely huge windows, balcony and views). All are bright, spotless and well-kept, and there's a beachside restaurant for breakfast and evening meals.

$$-$ Rambler's Rest Guesthouse
Port Elizabeth, T784-430 0555, www.accommodation-bequia.com.
Irishman Donnaka is a fantastic character, he's informative and takes you around Port Elizabeth to show you where everything is (and offers hiking tours, see below). He has converted his house into a small guesthouse with 2 rooms upstairs sharing a bathroom and a 2-bedroom apartment downstairs sleeping 4 with extra mattresses available (great value for a group). Lovely view of Admiralty Bay from the balcony, especially at sunset with a drink in hand. A 10-min walk uphill from the centre and ferry. Minimum stay 2 nights.

Mustique *map page 118.*

$$$$ Firefly
Overlooking Britannia Bay, T784-456 8414, www.fireflymustique.com.
On a hillside with lots of steps, this was once a private villa that has been transformed into a charming hotel with eclectic decor. It's small and intimate with a house-party feel. It has only 7 gorgeous individually decorated and named rooms, special features include outdoor showers, plunge pools or 4-poster beds. There's a 2-tiered pool with a view of the bay in the landscaped gardens, and

the **Firefly Restaurant** and **Patrick's Bar** get busy with Mustique's residents in the evening (see page 134).

$$$$ The Cotton House
Overlooking Endeavour Bay, T784-456 4777, www.cottonhouse.net.
This iconic and very expensive luxury hotel was converted in the 1960s by Oliver Messel from an 18th-century cotton warehouse into an elegant plantation house hotel. Today it has the Great Room (the main public area) which is open to the rafters and furnished with white sofas, 20 very pretty cottages with colourful interiors and latticework verandas, some with plunge pools, dotted throughout acres of tropical gardens leading down to Endeavour Bay, and there's a spa and gym, pool, the fine **Veranda Restaurant** (see page 134) and, on the beach, the informal **Beach Café** serves pizzas, grills, seafood and cocktails.

$$$$ The Mustique Company
See box, page 142, T784-488 8500, www.mustique-island.com.
Manage the letting (and the sales) of 75 of the private residences on the island, which usually come with a full complement of staff of at least a chef, housekeeper and gardener – the larger villas may have up to several additional staff including butlers and house managers and babysitting and childcare services can be arranged. Eye-watering rates are from US$5000 per week in summer for a 1-bedroomed villa to US$50,000 per week in winter for a large villa.

Canouan *map page 119.*

$$$$ Canouan Resort
T784-458 8000, www.canouan.com.
The most luxurious resort in the Grenadines, which reopened in early 2016 after a major rebuild with 26 suites and 6 villas overlooking a beautiful white-sand beach and one of the largest swimming pools in the Caribbean at 12,900 sq ft. There are 4 restaurants, 4 tennis courts, a ballroom, fitness centre, luxury spa,

casino, kids' club and activities including windsurfing, sailing and other watersports, as well as boat trips to the other islands and the 18-hole **Grenadines Estate Golf Club**. A private 9-seater jet provides transfers from Barbados, and a 19th-century church, dismantled in England and rebuilt stone by stone on the island, is available for weddings.

$$$$ Tamarind Beach Hotel & Yacht Club
T784-458 8044, www.tamarindbeach hotel.com. Closed 1 Sep-15 Oct.
Part of the **Canouan Resort** but less exclusive and set in lovely mature gardens, with 40 comfortable rooms and suites with wood and wicker decor, all with sea views and right on the beach. There are **Palapa** and **Pirate Cove** restaurants and a beach bar (all humming with yachties at night), an Italian café/deli, complimentary kayaks, pedal-boats and snorkelling gear, a PADI dive shop, and moorings and facilities for dinghies and yachts. Out of season doubles start at US$265.

Mayreau *map page 123.*

$$$$ Saltwhistle Bay Club
T784-458 8444, www.saltwhistlebay.com. Closed Sep and Oct.
This resort occupies 22 acres of the northern end of Mayreau with Saltwhistle Bay on one side and the unspoiled beach on the windward side of the spit. 10 rooms in stone and hardwood cottages, comfortable with ceiling fans, broad decks and hammocks in the tropical garden, some with roof terraces. Serene with breathtaking views, though some complain it's way overpriced. The restaurant and bar (open daily 0800-late) is a popular stopover for the yachting set, who come ashore for a meal and drinking. Boat transfers can be arranged from Union Island.

$$ Dennis' Hideaway
T784-458 8594, www.dennis-hideaway.com.
The only other place to stay on Mayreau, this guesthouse above Saline Bay near the village offers 5 twin or triple rooms, fairly

basic but with a/c, fans, fridge and balcony overlooking the ocean for sunset views. Bar/restaurant and Dennis is a good cook; tell him what you want to eat earlier in the day and be sure to try his creole fish and Vincentian curry, pool with spectacular view, and fishing with a local skipper and boat trips to the Tobago Cays can be organized.

Union Island *map page 125.*

$$$$ David's Beach Hotel
Belmont/Big Sands Bay, T784-485 8447, www.davidsbeachhotel.com.
Recently refurbished boutique hotel on the isolated western end of Big Sands, with 10 beachfront suites and 8 smaller garden rooms, in startlingly white buildings with balconies/patios, some are interconnected. Quiet and relaxing with great views of the bay, but it's pricey, although all-inclusive rates include good set meals, massages and tours of the island in their own speedboat and minibus.

$$$-$$ Anchorage Yacht Club Hotel
Clifton, T784-458 8221, www.aycunionisland.com.
On a large property with palm trees and little beach, this casual mid-range hotel has been going since 1975 and shows its age in the blocky architecture. But recent new owners are making improvements to the 15 rooms, which are comfortable enough with rattan furnishings, wood-beamed ceilings, tiled floors, balconies/patios with bay views. Open-air restaurant/bar (see page 136) from where you can watch the yachts come into the marina.

$$ Bougainvilla Hotel
Clifton, T784-458 8678, www.grenadines-bougainvilla.com.
The 12 spacious rooms here are well-decorated with a mix of French-style lime washed furniture and African masks, 4 have kitchenettes, some have balconies but no views, the larger ones have a separate lounge area and terrace; extra beds US$30. **Mare**

Blu Boutique is here, plus a there's a small supermarket, and the base for **Wind & Sea** for day tours. No Wi-Fi except in the attached restaurant, L'Aquarium (see page 135).

$$ Kings Landing Hotel
Clifton, T784-458 8823, www.kingslandingunionisland.com.
Old fashioned 2-storey blocks but affordable and clean, with 17 rooms and bungalows in gardens on the harbour, each has balcony/terrace and some have kitchenettes. There's a restaurant/bar, staff are always willing to help with organizing excursions, and it's the only hotel on the island with a pool.

$$ The Islander's Inn
Belmont/Big Sands Bay, T784-527 0944, www.theislandersinn.com.
Run by Clyde (Trinidadian) and Sandra (German), 15 neat rooms in a cheerful yellow block with terrace/balcony facing the beach, colourfully decorated with kettle and fridge but only 3 with a/c and the rest with floor fans, restaurant/bar but limited food if there are not many guests. Peaceful but not convenient for Clifton which is a 10-min flat walk along a path or steep drive over the hill.

$$-$ St Joseph's House
Clifton-Ashton Rd, book through Erika's Marine Services, T784-485 8335, www.erikamarine.com.
A 10-min walk west of Clifton towards Ashton, this guesthouse is in the grounds of the St Joseph's Catholic Church, and is built above with stupendous views of Palm Island, Petit St Vincent, Petite Martinique and Carriacou. Delightfully breezy and peaceful on the spacious balconies, it has 4 self-catering apartments, the 2 on the middle floor share a kitchen so can be booked by a family/group, plus there's another self-contained wooden garden cottage. You don't have to be religious to stay; all visitors are made to feel at home.

$ Clifton Beach Hotel
Clifton, T784-458 8235, www.cliftonbeachhotelsvg.com.

Opened in 1952, this is the oldest hotel on the island, and the Adams family is now in their 3rd generation of innkeepers. 12 rooms with fans, 2 have kitchenettes, very basic with leaky bathrooms so are a bit overpriced for what you get (doubles from US$70). But the central location is excellent, the staff are friendly, and they make a mean rum punch in the bar/restaurant. They also run the little souvenir shop close by.

$ TJ Plaza Guest House
Clifton, T784-4588 930,
www.tjplaza.weebly.com.
On one of the back streets behind the bike hire shop, this is one of the cheapest places to stay and is not bad, with 10 rooms; '1st class' have hot water, '2nd class' don't but are half the price at just US$38. Spotless and friendly, most have fridge, microwave and kettle and John's Bakery is on the ground floor which sells excellent bread, cakes and pastries.

Palm Island and Petit St Vincent

$$$$ Palm Island Resort
Reservations UK, T+44-(0)1245 459906,
www.palmislandresortgrenadines.com.
Luxurious but also with an informal feel, with 43 rooms – from modest-sized lofts to 2-bedroom villas with their own plunge pools – all airy with vaulted, wood-slat ceilings and terraces, some on the beach, others in the gardens. Lots of watersports and activities including cycling, a spa, gym, and there's 2 restaurants, 2 bars and entertainment like barbecues and cocktail parties. No children under 12.

$$$$ Petit St Vincent Resort
Reservations US, T+1 (954) 963-7401,
www.petitstvincent.com.
High-quality resort with 22 1- and 2-bedroom cottages and villas, discreetly tucked into the hillside or along the shore and is part of the **Small Luxury Hotels of the World** chain. Facilities include a Balinese spa, yoga pavilion, 2 restaurants/bars, wine cellar, boutique and art gallery, floodlit

tennis court, a fleet of kayaks, hobies, paddle- and windsurfing boards, and speed boat and sailing tours to Tobago Cays or elsewhere can be arranged at a whim.

Restaurants

VAT on restaurant bills is 15%, but this is nearly always included in menu prices; 10% service charge is however usually added to the bill.

Bequia *map page 114.*
There is a wide range of restaurants, from gourmet French to local West Indian, with pizzas, burgers and sandwiches also on offer. Reservations are recommended in high season, particularly during the Easter Regatta, when things get very busy. Jump-ups and live music can be heard on different nights in the hotels and restaurants in high season; pick up a copy of *Bequia This Week* (www.begos.com) at the tourist office which has daily listings.

$$$ Fernando's Hideaway
Lower Bay, T784-458 3758. Dinner only at 1900 Mon-Sat, reservations required.
A real Caribbean experience in a lovely setting in the trees above Lower Bay Beach with a candle-lit terrace, local-style dinner, usually fish such as snapper caught by Nando earlier in the day and perhaps a meat option like lamb chops, on Sat there is always goat water, all served with sides like baked garlic toast, plantains, squash and greens, followed by a tasty dessert. Dinner is not a rushed affair, but you need to be there promptly at 1900.

$$$-$$ L'Auberge de Grenadines
Hamilton, T784-457 3555, www.carib restaurant.com. Sun-Fri 1130-2130, closed Sep-Oct and on Sat May-Aug.
Pretty setting in a colourful double deck wooden building overlooking the water on the north side of Admiralty Bay, gourmet French cuisine with the emphasis on lobster in season (large tank of live specimens), light lunches including sandwiches made from

baguettes, salads and filling lobster burgers, and reservations required for à la carte or 3-course set dinners.

$$$-$$ Sugar Reef Café
Crescent Beach, Industry Bay, T784-458 3400, www.sugarreefbequia.com. Daily 1200-2100.
Magical setting with a stylish interior of sculptures made from shells and driftwood and large barn doors opening on to the palm-lined beach, where tables and sun loungers sit on the sand. The menu might include beetroot and chickpea salads, lobster tail soup, callaloo lasagne and local fish, plus yummy desserts and good coffees. Very busy in high season, when reservations are essential.

$$$-$ Bequia Plantation Hotel
Belmont Walkway, T784-534 9444, www.bequiaplantationhotel.com. Daily 0800-2200, bar later.
This lovely new hotel is just next to the start of the Princess Point Trail to Princess Margaret Beach. There's a formal menu for breakfast, lunch and dinner, **Stelton's Bakery** offers excellent coffees and freshly baked pastries, and the broad bar area has a patio overlooking the bay, a wood-fired pizza oven and friendly service. Happy Hour special cocktails 1700-1900.

$$$-$ Frangipani
Belmont Walkway, T784-458 3255, www.frangipanibequia.com. Daily 1100-2100, bar later.
Known locally as Frangi, the hotel's charming open-sided waterfront restaurant/bar serves seafood including fish and lambi, as well as snacks all day, great cocktails – try a Frangi Fever, Mango Potion or Passion Colada – and the Thu night 'Jump Up' with a steelpan band and barbecue buffet is so popular you must drop in earlier in the day to book.

$$$-$ Gingerbread
Belmont Walkway, T784-458 3800. Restaurant, daily 1800-2200, café 0800-1900.
So named because of its gingerbread fretwork and with an airy, comfortable dining room for dinners by candlelight (steaks, seafood and curries are specialities). Breakfast, lunch, fresh juice, cappuccinos and lattes, and baked goodies are available all day downstairs in the café by the water. Also here is **Maranne's Ice-Cream** (Mon-Sat 1000-1730), a kiosk selling delicious ice cream, fruit sorbets and frozen yogurt.

$$ Mac's Pizzeria
Belmont Walkway, T784-458 3474. Daily except Wed 1100-2200.
Between **Gingerbread** and **The Fig Tree** with another terrace overlooking the bay, Mac's has been serving excellent pizza since the 1980s, 17 toppings including lobster in season, daily specials, soup, salads, lambi fritters, lasagne and desserts such as lime pie and cheesecake. Very popular, get there early or reserve a table earlier in the day.

$$-$ Chameleon Café
Belmont Rd, Port Elizabeth, T784-593 9764, www.chameleonbequia.com. Daily 0800-2100.
This lovely café and boutique is set back from the Belmont Walkway but has a lovely terrace with comfortable sofas and potted palms (and free Wi-Fi) and serves great coffees, smoothies, cooked and cold breakfasts, paninis, wraps, couscous and quinoa salads and freshly baked quiches and cakes.

$$-$ De Reef
Lower Bay, T784-458 3958. Daily 0900-2000.
Informal beach bar and restaurant in a lovely position on Lower Bay Beach, popular with yachties and locals, food includes curried lambi, fish, salads and bar snacks like toasted sandwiches, often a live band in the afternoon on Sun, and in high season Sat dinner of a seafood barbecue including lobster. Service can be very slow, but there's no hurry, especially if you rent a sun lounger.

$$-$ Jack's Bar
Princess Margaret Beach, T784-457 3762. Daily 1100-2100, later in high season.
With a unique design of enormous sails providing a high shady ceiling over a vast wooden deck, this upscale new beach bar

is right at the end of Princess Point Trail. The menu offers main meals with Mediterranean influences like herb-crusted mahi mahi and tuna niçoise salad, plus burgers and sandwiches, plenty of rum punch and cocktails, and there's a Tue night beach barbecue with live entertainment.

$$-$ Tante Pearl's
Cemetery Hill, T784-457 3160.
Daily 1130-1400, 1730-2200.
Up on Cemetery Hill, 2 mins by taxi above Port Elizabeth up a very steep hill, West Indian cooking, callaloo soup, jerk chicken and mahi mahi, lobster and conch, all the usual trimmings, the wonderful rum punch or virgin cocktails make excellent sundowners with a great view of Admiralty Bay from the breezy terrace.

$ Green Boley
Belmont Walkway. Daily 1100-2100.
A traditional Caribbean beach bar in a green shack made out of split bamboo, shady and cool picnic benches outside, in the heart of things, and an ideal place for a lunchtime roti (US$4.40) or a plate of good fried fish and salad (US$7.40), cold beer, rum punch, mauby or ginger beer, while watching the world go by and the yachts in the bay.

$ The Fig Tree
Belmont Walkway, T784-457 3008,
www.figtreebequia.com. Wed-Mon
Nov-Mar 0800-2200, Apr-Oct 1100-2000.
With a pleasant wooden deck on the Belmont Walkway and views, serves well-priced and tasty local meals including a variety of rotis (chicken, fish, beef and vegetarian), callaloo soup, grilled fish, curried mutton and the like. Welcoming owner Cheryl also has 4 simple guest rooms ($).

Mustique *map page 118.*

$$$ Firefly Restaurant and Patrick's Bar
At Firefly, see Where to stay, above, T784-456 8414, www.fireflymustique.com.
Like the hotel in which it's housed, this restaurant is an oasis of casual chic, and many famous faces have dined here. The menu mixes French and Caribbean influences and dishes are beautifully presented. Arrive early for a sunset drink at Patrick's Bar, and try the Firefly Special; a cocktail made with rum, nutmeg, papaya and coconut cream. There's also a choice of premium French wines and over 25 champagnes. Reservations required.

$$$ Veranda Restaurant
At The Cotton House, see Where to stay, above, T784-456 4777, www.cottonhouse.net.
With small outside intimate tables wrapped around the Great Room, this serves leisurely breakfasts, light lunches and a sophisticated menu for dinner with local and Mediterranean influences, accompanied by an extensive wine list. Sample dishes might be callaloo risotto, West Indian curry, grilled barracuda, or tagliatelle with crab. Reservations required.

$$$-$ Basil's Bar
Britannia Bay, T784-488 8350, www.basilsbar.com. Daily 0800-2200, bar open later.
Built on stilts over the ocean, Basil's was established in 1976 and has a long reputation as the place where the beautiful people hang out. Though not quite the scene it was then, most people staying on the island flock here, particularly for the Wed night barbecue and 'Jump Up', and Sun sunset jazz. Food is anything from banana pancakes for breakfast to lobster for dinner, and there are plenty of lime daiquiris and rum punch. Owner Basil Charles hosts the **Mustique Blues Festival** (late Jan/early Feb) and invites international musicians to perform (check the website for details).

Canouan *map page 119.*
The restaurants at the **Canouan Resort** are for guests only; but the **Tamarind Beach Hotel & Yacht Club** allows non-guests and it's a popular spot for yachties. In the village are a few local kiosks selling saltfish and bake, rotis and fried fish/chicken, but sit down options are limited.

$$$-$ Tamarind Beach Hotel & Yacht Club

T784-458 8044, www.tamarindbeachhotel.com. Palapa Restaurant, daily 0700-2200; Pirate's Cove Bar, daily 1700-2300, later at the weekend.

Palapa Restaurant is the more formal place and has a delightful open terrace surrounded by tropical flowers, while **Pirate's Cove Bar** is the livelier and sometimes has a band or a DJ. Being Italian owned both serve pizza, pasta, fish and meat dishes, and on occasion there's a buffet night. An additional beach bar serves cocktails and sandwiches until about 1700 when Pirate's opens.

$$-$ Mangrove Canouan

Western end of the main street, Charlestown, T0784-482 0761. Daily 1100-2200.

Local spot popular with day visitors and resort guests about a 20-min walk along the beach from the **Tamarind**, although it is easier to walk along the road, tables indoors or on the sand under trees and you can swim, the kitchen is made from a recycled shipping container. Good rotis and club sandwiches at lunchtime, dinners of lobster in season, steak, lambi, grouper, snapper and burgers, and strong rum punch. Do not sit under the manchineel trees here.

Mayreau *map page 123.*

$$ Saltwhistle Bay Club

Saltwhistle Bay, T784-458 8444, www.saltwhistlebay.com. Daily 0800-2300.

Yachties come ashore here and there are stone-built small circular buildings with thatched roofs to sit in on the sand, food is grilled fish, conch fritters and the like but it takes a long time to materialize and some complain sometimes there is no food at all. However it's a beautiful spot for a chilled rose wine or rum cocktail. There are a couple of other shacks on the beach for local food.

$$-$ Island Paradise

In the village, T784-458 8941. Mon-Sat 1200-2200.

A steep walk up the hill from the dock, or get a taxi, with a great view out over Saline Bay towards Union Island and it's not far from the church, for even better views of the Tobago Cays. Run by James, this jaunty little blue and white shack has a deck and food may include lobster, snapper and curried conch.

$ Robert Righteous & De Youths Seafood Restaurant & Bar

In the village. Open 'any day, any time'.

This fantastically named ramshackle spot is run by Rasta Robert Righteous, who everyone on the island knows, and is just beyond **Dennis'** up the hill. The eclectic bar is a fine place to enjoy a pina colada or rum punch (or instant coffee) and take in all the photos, Bob Marley art and random graffiti and messages from yachties the world over. Robert will cook lobster, fish, ribs and chicken and talk while he does. Watch out for his heavy hand with the drinks measures and he is always willing to partner anyone on the dance floor.

Union Island *map page 125.*

There's a decent choice of restaurants and bars on Union, almost all concentrated along the main street in Clifton.

$$$-$$ L'Aquarium

Main St, Clifton, in front of and attached to the Bougainvilla Hotel (although under different ownership), T784-458 8311, see Facebook. Daily 1200-1400, 1800-2200, bar open all day.

Facing the harbour and with a delightful little dingy dock with bridges to negotiate, there is an aquarium in the dining room with sand sharks in it, and another with lobsters (to choose). This place has a lovely location and atmosphere with big leather couches and friendly staff. However, the pricey food – beef, chicken, fish and lobster – can be a bit hit and miss. The lunchtime pizzas, crepes and club sandwiches are the better bet.

$$$-$$ Sparrow's Beach Club

Belmont/Big Sands Bay, T784-458 8195, www.sparrowsbeach club.com.

Located just off Kite Beach, **Happy Island** (T784-433 7647, open 'any day, any time') is a tiny bar and the home of Janti Ramage, and sits on a foundation of scavenged conch shells. Like in many places in the Caribbean, conch, or lambi is popular to eat, and the conch shells are discarded by fishermen and piles of them litter the beaches. Janti devised a unique solution to this natural pollution while working as a volunteer environmental officer in 2002, and began gathering up conches and similar-sized rocks, and piling them up in the shallow waters to build his own private island. Constantly a work in progress, it now has a flat concrete surface on top of it, a little house and bar and a patio area planted with palms. Underwater it has also become a breeding ground for fish and other creatures such as crabs and conch. It's only accessible by boat (get a water taxi), and JT Pro Center Kitesurfing School organizes boat transfers every Friday evening for US$3.70 per person.

Come for the day and use the beach facilities (there's even a spa for massages), or for a romantic evening when the lights twinkle in the water. Bertrand runs this excellent French and Caribbean restaurant with flair, serving delicious food including his home-smoked marlin. The beer is cold and the wine list is good. There's a free shuttle service from anywhere on the island, although the main pick up is at the little roundabout on Main St in Clifton; just ask anyone in town what time the bus is there.

$$ Barracuda
Main St, Clifton, T784-458 8571, see Facebook. Daily 1100-2200.
Italian-owned restaurant and bar with authentic pasta and pizza as well as grilled chicken, ribs, pork chops and beef tenderloin and some more local dishes. Reliably good food, friendly service and atmosphere with a pleasant outside deck and a softly lit interior.

$$ The Loft
Main St, Clifton, T784-528 8550. Daily 1100-2300.
Superb harbour views from the upstairs balconies, this wine bar is run by Reynald who used to work at the **Cotton House Hotel** on Mustique. It's a great place for a drink with lots of excellent appetizer/tapas

choices – hamburger sliders, nachos, salmon cakes with chilli dip and chilli prawns – and one of the best selections of wine on the island also available by the glass, plus cocktails and free Wi-Fi.

$$-$ The AYC Bar & Restaurant
At the Anchorage Yacht Club Hotel, Clifton, T784-458 8221, www.aycunionisland.com. Daily 0800-2200, bar open until last person leaves.
Popular with yachties and overlooking the marina, this has a good varied menu from pasta and excellent burgers, to fresh fish and lobster. The bar offers tropical cocktails, an extensive list of rums plus smoothies and ice cream.

$$-$ The West Indies Restaurant
Main St, Clifton, T784-458 8911. Mon-Sat 1100-1500, 1830-2200.
Located on the waterfront next to the dive shop in Clifton, and run by Joelle and Jean-Jacques, this offers a combination of French and Creole cuisine including seafood, excellent beef tenderloin and local conch, plus home-made daily soups, paninis and ice cream.

$ Big Citi Grill
Main St, Clifton, above the tourist office, T784-458 8960, see Facebook. Mon-Sat 0800-2130.

Also known as **Teroy's Place** after the amicable owner/chef, veranda seating with view over the street where the fruit and veg sellers are. Dependable grill, with meat and seafood options or sandwiches and burgers at lunchtime, all well-priced and tasty. Beer available and BYO wine.

$ The Snack Shack
Main St, Clifton, T784-434 0764, see Facebook. Daily 0730-2230, closed Sun in low season. Built with the use of recycled material found on Union Island, this eclectic little café has outdoor furniture made from driftwood, chilled music, free Wi-Fi and is always buzzing. Good coffees and fresh juices, English breakfast, pancakes and syrup, paninis, salads and sweet and savoury crepes. It livens up as a bar in the evening and is attached to an excellent little craft shop and the office for **JT Pro Center Kitesurfing School**.

Festivals

Bequia *map page 114.*
1st week of Apr Bequia Easter Regatta.
The centre of activities for the regatta is the Belmont Walkway and races start from in front of the **Frangipani Hotel**. There are races for all sizes and types of craft, even coconut boats chased by their swimming child owners or model sailing yachts chased by rowing boats. Everyone is welcome and there are crewing opportunities. There are other contests on shore (sandcastle building) and the nights are filled with events such as dancing, beauty shows and fashion shows.

Shopping

Bequia *map page 114.*
Books
Bequia Bookshop, *on Belmont Rd near the church, Port Elizabeth, T458 3905. Mon-Fri 0830-1630, Sat 0900-1300.* An excellent stock of books, particularly of Caribbean literature, maps and charts, cooking and cocktails, and a selection of postcards and prints.

Crafts
There are 2 model boat-builder workshops; **Mauvin's** (T784-458 3344), just beyond the fruit and vegetable market in Port Elizabeth, and **Sargeant Brothers'** up the hill going out of town. The craftsmen turn out replicas of traditional craft and visiting yachts, and each is expertly rigged and authentically detailed.
Oasis Art Gallery, *Belmont Rd, Port Elizabeth, T784-497 7670, see Facebook. Mon-Sat 1000-1600, longer hours in high season.* Locally created art from oil paintings to banana-leaf pictures, plus crafts such as model boats, ceramics and greeting cards.

Food
Bequia is a centre for yacht provisioning. There is a market for fruit and veg by the jetty and small supermarkets in Port Elizabeth with a good selection of groceries. Fish is sometimes on sale along the Belmont Walkway.
Doris Fresh Food, *Back St, Port Elizabeth, T784-458 3625, www.dorisfreshfood.com. Mon-Sat 0800-1600.* Gourmet grocery store and yacht provisioning hub selling meats imported from the US (beef steaks, duck and veal), French cheeses, Italian cold cuts and pasta, and specializes in local smoked fish and pâtés. In high season also bakes baguettes and pastries. Doris can have everything delivered to yachts by water taxi, at no extra charge, and skippers can email orders in advance.
Vintages Bequia, *downstairs at the Gingerbread Café, Belmont Walkway, T784-533 0502, www.vintagesbequia.com. Mon-Sat 0800-1800, Sun 0900-1200.* Excellent choice of booze, wines and rums, local and imported beer, soft drinks and Nespresso coffee. Again, can deliver to yachts.

Mustique *map page 118.*
There are only a handful of shops on the island and many food items are not always available, but if you are renting a villa, all catering will be organized. For visiting yachts,

a fresh fruit and vegetable stall can be found near the moorings at Britannia Bay.

Corea's Food Store, *T784-488 8634, and Sweetie Pie Bakery T784-488 8529, are next door to each other at the bottom of the hill on Britannia Bay opposite the fish market. Both open Mon-Fri 0700-1200 and 1600-1800, Sat-Sun 0800-1200.* Corea's sells most things including basic groceries and toiletries and some wine, while the bakery is run by the highly accomplished Ali Medjahed, who came to the island from France, and produces exquisite pain au chocolat, baguettes, croissants and brochettes.

Pink and Purple House Boutique, *Britannia Bay, T784-488 8521, www.pinkhousemustique. com.* British designer, Lotty Bunbury, lives on the island and sells an extensive range of jewellery, beachwear, and luxurious women's silk sarongs and kaftans, and men's linen shirts (also available online). Her husband is the island doctor.

Canouan *map page 119.*
Food
Buon Appetito, *at the Tamarind Beach Hotel & Yacht Club, T0784-532 8044. Mon-Sat 0800-1700.* An Italian deli and takeaway offering cold cut meats, cheeses, caviar, pâté, wine, hot meals like pasta and sauce or fish, rice and salad, fresh bread and imported groceries. The hotel's **Le Petit Bazaar** is a boutique and gift shop selling crafts and beachwear.

Canouan Foods, *on the main street in Charlestown, T074-482 0679. Mon-Sat 0800-2000, Sun 0900-1200.* Good selection and will deliver to the dock if you are on a yacht. There are also market stalls along the road from the dock.

Union Island *map page 125.*
Food
There are a few small supermarkets/groceries in Clifton and a couple of stalls near the ferry dock selling fruit and veg.

Captain Gourmet, *Main St, Clifton, T784-458 8918, www.capgourmet.com. Daily 0800-1830.* Part deli, part café owned by a French couple

with tables on the street, this offers imported treats from chocolate to cornflakes, plus cold meats and cheeses, baguette sandwiches, croissants, coffees and juices. Also provisioning for yachts; contact in advance.

What to do

Bequia *map page 114.*
Diving
Diving is good around Pigeon Island, afternoon and night dives are usually on the Leeward side of the southwest peninsula, there are a few sites around Isle à Quatre and shallow dives for training can be done around Petit Nevis. Expect to pay in the region of US$70 for a single dive, US$85 for a night dive, 5-10 dive discounts are available, and US$575 for PADI Open Water course. Snorkelling trips out on the dive boats are from US$20.

Bequia Dive Adventures, *next to Mac's Pizzeria, Belmont Walkway, T784-458 3826, www.bequiadiveadventures.com.*

Dive Bequia, *near the Gingerbread Café, Belmont Walkway, T784-458 3504, www.divebequia.com.*

Hiking
Ramblers Hiking Tours, *T784-430 0555, www.hiking-bequia.com.* Irishman Donnaka who owns the **Rambler's Rest Guesthouse** (see page 129) takes guided hikes across the island for all abilities and tailors his tours to your interests. The normal drill is to set off from Port Elizabeth around 0800 and end somewhere where you can buy lunch or picnic on a beach. Prices are around US$35 per person.

Sailing
Friendship Rose, *office on Belmont Walkway, T784-458 3739, www.friendshiprose.com.* This magnificent 2-mast 100-ft auxiliary schooner with its billowing sails was many years ago the only lifeline for Bequians to 'mainland' St Vincent, carrying passengers, mail and supplies. Now fully restored it offers day trips

to the Tobago Cays, US$170, and Mustique US$140, under 12s half price, under 5s free. All-inclusive, there are hammocks on board, deck cushions, snorkelling gear, and a smaller launch for island exploring.

Octopus, *T784-432 5201, www.octopus-caribbean.com*. Also day sails to the Tobago Cays, US$150 and Mustique, US$140, under 12s half price, with meals and drinks on the 63-ft Isle-à-Quatre yacht that accommodates 8 people. Also available for overnight charters, and the owners rent out 2 luxury villas on the island.

Mustique *map page 118.*
The Mustique Company, *T784-488 8500, www.mustique-island.com*. Has the watersports centre on Endeavour Bay, where an extensive range of activities is arranged for island residents including snorkelling, fishing, a PADI dive school, windsurfing, hobie cat sailing, stand-up paddle boarding (SUP), and glass-bottomed boats. Much of the equipment can be dropped off at the closest beach to where you might be staying. They also run a tennis club, an equestrian centre, there are boat or plane transfers to the golf course on Canouan, and there's a spa and gym at The Cotton Club.

Canouan *map page 119.*
The hotels organize boat trips to the Tobago Cays and non-hotel guests are permitted to make up numbers if the boat is not fully booked.

Canouan Scuba Center, *at the Tamarind Beach Hotel & Yacht Club, T784-532 8073, www.canouandivecenter.com*. Single dives from US$95, night dives US$130. Also the dive operator serving the **Palm Island Resort** and dives can also be arranged at the Tobago Cays, Mayreau and Union Island.

The Grenadines Estate Golf Club, *at the Canouan Resort, T784-458 8000, www.canouan.com. Daily 0700-1830*. An 18-hole, par 72 course designed by Jim Fazio covering 60 acres along the bay and up the hillside with stunning ocean views. Non-residents

of the resort and villas can play for US$350 per day which includes golf cart and clubs. There's a bar at the 9th hole and a clubhouse.

Union Island *map page 125.*
Diving
The best dives at Union are Round About Reef, an easy dive with lots of corals, schooling fish and the occasional manta ray, which is also good for night dives, and Clipper's Point, a drift dive where you might see turtles, sting rays and moray eels. Trips also go to the Tobago Cays and to the reefs around Petit St Vincent.

Grenadines Dive, *next to King's Landing Hotel, Clifton, T784-458 8138, www.grenadinesdive.com*. Run by the very experienced Glenroy Adams, diving mostly around the Tobago Cays from US$90 and can organize accommodation packages on Union Island with 10 boat dives over a week.

Kitesurfing and stand-up paddling
JT Pro Center Kitesurfing School, *Kite Beach, and also office at the Snack Shack in Clifton, T784-527 8363, www.kitesurfgrenadines.com*. Union Island has become one of the top kitesurfing destinations in the Grenadines thanks to this set-up which offers beginner's lessons to pro-clinics. Off Kite Beach, a beautiful lagoon with shallow areas and very flat water, formed by an offshore reef, but on the north side is the airport runway – definitely a 'no-kite' zone. The best wind is from mid-Dec to late Jun. Not the cheapest place to try this sport with beginner's packages from US$195 for 3 hrs, but the location is certainly special. Gear is available to rent to experienced kiters. Guided SUP tours can also be arranged from US$50-65 per person depending on group size; 2-3 hrs along the coast and to mangroves.

Sailing Day trip boats to the Tobago Cays go from the jetty at Clifton and there are a number of options; from a fun day under full sail on the wonderful schooner, the *Scaramouche*, used in the filming of *Pirates of the Caribbean*; to a small water taxi with a local skipper who will take you wherever you want to go. Most go via Mayreau, and once at the Tobago Cays, visitors are usually taken ashore on Petit Bateau. Some of the boats only go with a minimum amount of people; your preferred boat may not be going out on your chosen day. On the plus side, if they are going out, you should have no problem jumping aboard at the last minute. The tourist office can assist with arrangements.

Sail Grenadines, *The Anchorage Yacht Club, Clifton, T784-533 2909, www.sailgrenadines. com.* The option here is to charter the whole boat with skipper, crew and catering for a day sail to the Tobago Cays and other islands; from US$650-1750 per day depending on the size of the yacht/remember to divide this price by the number of people, which makes it worth considering for 6-plus passengers.

Scaramouche, *T784-458 8418, www. scaramouchegrenadines.com.* This 82-ft traditional schooner was hand-built in Windward on Carriacou (see page 60) in the late 1960s and worked as a cargo boat up and down the islands. She was almost destroyed by Hurricane Ivan in 2004, but was restored, again in Windward, and now serves as a tourist boat to the Tobago Cays. On the day trip she usually drops anchor at Mayreau, the Tobago Cays and Palm Island with time for snorkelling and to enjoy the beaches; US$80, under 12s half price, under 4s free, including meals and drinks.

Southern Grenadines Water Taxi Association, *Clifton, T784-532 1373/533 4833.* Look for the board of rates on the main street, and enquire at the jetty or tourist office for a boat. Prices are set at US$100 per person for a return trip to Tobago Cays, and only if there are 4 people can prices be negotiated; this in fact makes it more expensive than the larger boats, especially if there are children and you need to add the cost of taking your own food and drink. However it may appeal if you want to make up your own itinerary, or spend the maximum time snorkelling once at the Tobago Cays.

Wind and Sea, *at the Bougainvilla Hotel, T784-458 8878, see Facebook.* On the Sunspirit catamaran with the 1st stop at Mayreau's Saltwhistle Bay for a morning swim, then Tobago Cays and a buffet lunch, and a sail to Palm Island before returning to Union; US$85, under 12s half price, under 5s free.

Transport

Bequia *map page 114.*

Air

Given that the *Bequia Express* ferry only takes 1 hr from St Vincent, fewer people get to Bequia by air than the other islands, but **SVG Air** (www.svgair.com) has 1 daily scheduled flight to/from Barbados. **Grenadine Air Alliance** (www.grenadine-air.com) and **Mustique Airways** (www.mustique.com) may drop down on Bequia on request on a flight between St Vincent and one of the other islands further south.

Boat

For ferry information, see box, page 150. Bequia is served by the *Jaden Sun*; *Bequia Express* and *Admiral II*. Sometimes the mail boat *Barracuda* stops but it's not on the scheduled route.

Bus and taxi

Dollar vans leave from under the almond tree near the jetty at Port Elizabeth. As public transport they only go to the south of the island (US$0.75-1.50 per ride) and stop anywhere to pick you up. All are available for private hire as taxis; rates are set at US$22 per hr or part thereof, and there's a list of fares in the tourist office (next to the almond tree).

Car hire

Car hire is available, which might be useful if you are staying in self-catering accommodation and need to shop, but is hardly necessary if you don't mind taking the cheap public transport or taxis over the short distances. All will be able to arrange the local drivers' permit (valid for 6 months,

US$26). Expect to pay in the region of US$50-60 per day for a small jeep. See also page 149. **Affordable Jeep Rentals**, T784-431 8760, www.affordablejeeprentals.com. **Bequia Jeep Rentals**, T784-458 3760, www.bequiajeeprentals.com. **Big J Rental**, T784-527 8173. **King Rental Service**, T784-532 4821/454 9138.

Mustique *map page 118.*
Air
Being in the centre of the island the airstrip is clearly visible, so check-in time is 5 mins before take-off (after you've seen your plane land). **Mustique Airways** (www.mustique.com), fly to/from St Vincent and Barbados, and **SVG Air** (www.svgair.com) to/from St Vincent. **The Mustique Company** (www.mustique-island.com) has an 18-seater plane that also operates scheduled flights to/from Barbados and St Lucia to connect with international flights. It also goes over to the much longer airstrip in Canouan to pick up from the private jets that are too big for the Mustique airstrip.

Boat
Endeavour is the dedicated ferry between St Vincent and Mustique, T784-457 1531 (Kingstown); the other ferries do not stop on the island. It runs Mon, Tue, Thu and Fri (and the 1st Wed of every month), takes 2 hrs and departs Kingstown at 1400, and returns from Mustique at 0730; one-way US$9.25. Sadly the timings don't allow for a day on the island and the boat mostly ferries workers and provisions across. It is possible to visit on private or chartered yachts.

Canouan *map page 119.*
Air
The runway has been extended on reclaimed land to take larger private jets. **Grenadine Air Alliance** (www.grenadine-air.com), **Mustique Airways** (www.mustique.com) and **SVG Air** (www.svgair.com) fly to/from Barbados and St Vincent. The **Canouan Resort** also has 2 private jets that shuttle guests to and from Barbados.

Boat
For ferry information, see box, page 150. Canouan is served by *Barracuda, Jaden Sun* and *Admiral II.*

Bus and taxi
Given that most of the island is taken up by the **Canouan Resort**, whose guests are ferried around by golf cart or mule (see box, page 142), everything is within walking distance from the ferry jetty. If you have difficulty climbing the hill, there are a few local minibuses that can be commandeered as taxis.

Union Island *map page 125.*

Air
Grenadine Air Alliance (www.grenadine-air.com), **Mustique Airways** (www.mustique.com) and **SVG Air** (www.svgair.com) fly to/from Barbados and St Vincent. **Mustique Airways** also operate a shared charter flight to/from St Lucia.

Bike hire
Bicycles can be hired from the **TJ Plaza Guest House** (T784-458 8930) in Clifton. More accurately, the little office is in a bright pink building above **Roots Boutique** on the main street and you will have to negotiate your bike from it down a spiral staircase on to the street; US$22 per day, US$11 half a day.

Boat
For ferry information, see box, page 150. Canouan is served by the *Barracuda*, *Jaden Sun* and *Admiral II*. There is an international ferry service between Ashton and Hillsborough on Carriacou on the *Lady JJ*,

and Troy the captain takes you through immigration procedures on arrival, but on departure you have to go to the airport at Clifton the day before at 1500; again Troy or his assistant is likely to be there to help you, see Finding your feet, page 124.

Bus
Minibuses run between Clifton and Ashton and will go 'off route' for a small extra fee. They will convert to a taxi on request and no journey will cost more than US$3.70-7.40.

Water taxi
Southern Grenadines Water Taxi Association (T784-532 1373/533 4833) is in principle in Clifton. Look for the board of rates on the main street, and enquire at the jetty or tourist office for a boat. Prices are set; anything from the equivalent of US$3 to a yacht in the harbour or US$5 for a short hop over to Happy Island to US$200 for a return journey to Canouan.

Practicalities

Getting there

Air

Grenada

Grenada's airport is **Maurice Bishop International Airport** ⓘ *Maurice Bishop Memorial Highway, T473-444 4555, www.mbiagrenada.com*, which is about 7 miles southwest of the capital, St George's, at the southwestern tip of the island. It's close to most of the hotels in the Grand Anse area. It's well served with flights from Europe and North America as well as having good connections with other Caribbean islands for a two-centre holiday or some island-hopping by air. See also Finding your feet, page 29, for details of transport from the airport, and Transport, page 83, for airport information.

Grenada's sister island of Carriacou has the tiny Lauriston Airport, located west of Hillsborough. It is served by a shuttle service between the two with **St Vincent Grenada Air** ⓘ *SVG Air; www.svgair.com*; see Getting around, below, for details of flights. See also Finding your feet, page 57, for details of transport from the airport.

Flights from the UK and Europe British Airways ⓘ *www.britishairways.com*, and **Virgin Atlantic** ⓘ *www.virgin-atlantic.com*, both fly weekly from London Gatwick via St Lucia, and **Condor** ⓘ *www.condor.com*, weekly from Frankfurt December-April. From the UK, the other option is to take the **British Airways** or **Virgin Atlantic** flights to Barbados (which both fly on different days of the week than the Grenada service) and connect from there. Europeans also have the option of flying with **KLM** or **Air France** to one of the Dutch or French islands in the Caribbean and again taking a flight with one of the regional airlines to Grenada.

Flights from North America Delta ⓘ *www.delta.com*, and **American Airlines** ⓘ *www.aa.com*, fly from New York JFK and Miami (some of which touch down in Puerto Rico), **JetBlue** ⓘ *www.jetblue.com*, twice weekly from New York, and **Air Canada** ⓘ *www.aircanada.com*, weekly from Toronto during December to April (and year-round from Toronto to Barbados and Montreal to Trinidad from where you can connect). **Caribbean Airlines** ⓘ *www.caribbean-airlines.com*, fly from New York, Orlando, Fort Lauderdale, Miami and Toronto to their hub in Port of Spain, Trinidad, from where you can connect on to another Caribbean Airlines flight to Grenada.

Flights from South America The only airline with direct flights to Grenada from South America is **Conviasa Airlines** ⓘ *www.conviasa.aero*, who fly twice weekly from Porlamar, Margarita, via Caracas in Venezuela. There is also the option of going to Trinidad and connecting there; **Caribbean Airlines** fly to Trinidad from Caracas in Venezuela, Georgetown in Guyana and Paramaribo in Suriname, and **LIAT** fly to Trinidad from Georgetown in Guyana.

Flights from the Caribbean Caribbean Airlines ⓘ *www.caribbean-airlines.com*, and **LIAT** ⓘ *Leeward Islands Air Transport; www.liat.com*, are the major carriers in the southern Caribbean. **Caribbean Airlines** has direct flights to/from Grenada and Port of Spain in Trinidad, where you can connect to Antigua, Barbados, Jamaica, St Lucia and Sint Maarten.

LIAT fly to/from Grenada and Barbados, St Vincent and Trinidad. At these than you can connect on direct or a combination of flights on the **LIAT** network which includes Anguilla, Antigua, Curaçao, Dominica, Dominican Republic, Guadeloupe, Martinique, Nevis, Puerto Rico, St Lucia, Sint Maarten and St Kitts.

St Vincent and the Grenadines

On St Vincent, ET Joshua Airport is at Arnos Vale just under 2 miles east of Kingstown. It does not receive direct international long-haul flights but for connections from North America and Europe, **LIAT** have direct flights to/from Grenada, Barbados, Puerto Rico (which stop in St Vincent to/from Barbados), St Lucia and Trinidad.

A new, larger airport, Argyle International Airport, is under construction, and has been since 2008; at the time of writing it was largely completed and due to open 'imminently', possibly by the end of 2016. However, as yet there has been no information about what airlines might serve it. For progress check the website of the International **Airport Development Company Limited (IADCL)** ⓘ *www.svgiadc.com*.

ET Joshua Airport is also a hub for **Grenadine Air Alliance** ⓘ *www.grenadine-air.com*, **Mustique Airways** ⓘ *www.mustique.com*, and **SVG Air** ⓘ *www.svgair.com*, for travel between the Grenadines; there are small airports/airstrips on Bequia, Mustique, Canouan and Union islands (see Getting around, below).

For details of transport from ET Joshua Airport see Finding your feet, page 89. For airport information, see Transport, page 108.

The other option to get to the Grenadines is directly from Barbados with the same airlines. Alternatively, each of them operates flights to/from St Lucia on a shared charter basis (which means they run on demand, but often connect to one of the international flights in St Lucia). To get from Grenada to the Grenadines, the usual option is to go on scheduled flights via Barbados. However, **SVG Air Grenada** ⓘ *www.grenada-flights.com*, can organize direct charters to any of the islands.

Sea

You can get to Grenada, St Vincent and the Grenadines from the north by private yachts and cruise ships. In Grenada cruise ships dock at St George's Cruise Ship Terminal, which is big enough to accommodate four ships at once and has extensive facilities including a shopping mall. In St Vincent, fewer ships make the stop but when they do it's at the two-berth Kingstown Cruise Terminal on Customs Wharf in the port at Kingstown, which also has shops and facilities. Some ships also stop offshore at Bequia, Mayreau and Tobago Cays. There are no international passenger ferry services between the other islands outside the territories of either Grenada or St Vincent and the Grenadines, but there is one ferry service between Union Island (St Vincent) and Carriacou (Grenada). This allows for some wonderful island hopping throughout the Grenadines; see box, page 150.

Yachts These islands are a yachties dream; the Caribbean Sea is easily navigable, distances between each island is short, and there are anchorages in beautiful bays. The ports of entry on Grenada (where there are customs and immigration facilities) are St George's, Prickly Bay, St David's Harbour and Grenville, and on Carriacou, Hillsborough and Tyrell Bay. The **Grenada Ports Authority** ⓘ *www.grenadaports.com*, has full details of port fees, anchorages and marinas. The ports of entry in St Vincent are Kingstown, Blue Lagoon and Campden Park, and on the Grenadines, Port Elizabeth on Bequia, Britannia Bay on

Mustique, Charlestown Bay on Canouan, and Clifton on Union Island. These are operated by the **SVG Port Authority** (www.svgpa.com). Most of the customs and immigration facilities at each of these are open 24 hours, but normal business hours are Monday-Friday 0800-1600, and an overtime fee is applicable for processing at weekends, public holidays and 1600-0800, so it pays to arrive during normal working hours. A clearance out certificate from your last port is required.

After clearing into the country, yachts are free to move between anchorages, but if a vessel wishes to enter Grenada (and Carriacou) and clear out of St Vincent and the Grenadines (or vice versa), the captain must notify the immigration/customs officers at the entry port so that necessary papers can be transferred to the planned exit port. The same goes if you are leaving a boat at the islands and are departing by air.

Getting around

Air

SVG Air ① *T473-444 3549 (Grenada), T473-443 8159 (Carriacou), www.svgair.com*, operates two to four daily (one on Sunday) 20-minute flights to/from Grenada's Maurice Bishop International Airport; US$57 one-way, US$110 return. If you get the first flight at 0745, and the last return at 1700 (depending on the day of the week), it's entirely possible to spend just the day in Carriacou, but that would be a shame. Note if you are connecting from an international flight into Grenada, the last flight to Carriacou is 1600 (1430 on Sun). Carriacou's Lauriston Airport is also served by charter flights from Barbados and some of the other islands.

Grenadine Air Alliance ① *www.grenadine-air.com*, **Mustique Airways** ① *www.mustique.com*, and **SVG Air** ① *www.svgair.com*, have daily flights between St Vincent (and Barbados) and the Grenadine islands of Bequia, Mustique, Canouan and Union Island.

Charter flights to these and other neighbouring islands, including Grenada and Carriacou, can be organized with any of these airlines. They operate small aircraft with a maximum of 18 passengers and the weight of luggage allowed is determined by the weight of the passengers. You should expect to be weighed. The flights are generally reliable, but schedules may change, they run on 'island time', which has got its advantages; they could wait for you if an international connection is delayed.

Road

On all the islands the main roads are in reasonable condition and connect most points, which make it relatively easy to get around. Some coastal roads can be narrow and winding, and on secondary and rural access roads look out for potholes, deep storm drains at the edges, as well as speed bumps or dips. Car hire, regular taxis, buses (always small vehicles like a minibus), or an island tour with a tour operator are the options of getting around by road. Hitchhiking is not advised; neither is giving lifts to strangers.

Bus

Most, but not all, of the islands have a cheap bus service, which can be a minibus or, on Bequia, a pick-up truck with seats in the back. They are all privately owned vehicles but usually belong to an association of drivers and are registered as public service vehicles with the necessary insurance and licences. They share the public terminals; on Grenada this is the large and well-organized St George's Bus Terminus, for example, while on a small island it's somewhere far less formal; in Bequia, they simply gather under the shade of an almond tree in Port Elizabeth. They follow a fixed route and stop on demand rather than at bus stops. There is usually the option of paying extra for a short deviation ('off route'), and will convert to a taxi for the appropriate rate. They are a popular and colourful means of transport and give an opportunity to see local life and hear the music. On the busier routes, there are conductors who can help you get off at the right place if you ask. Fares range from US$0.90-2.60, depending on distance, and you can pay for an extra seat if you have luggage. However, they are renowned for driving fast on the twisty roads, so if you are prone to car sickness this may not be for you.

Car

Driving on any of the islands is not especially challenging, there aren't that many roads, and even fewer signposts, but wandering from your intended route is seldom more than a minor inconvenience and you can never get really lost on an island. Driving is on the left, and cars are right-hand drive. All passengers must wear seatbelts in the front and back seats, and the use of mobile phones is illegal while driving, except in hands-free mode. In urban areas, petrol stations are located on main thoroughfares, but are scarce in rural areas.

Car hire is readily available; the minimum age for hiring is usually 21, you need to have a full driving licence and a credit card. You don't need an international licence; your home country one will do as long as it's got a photograph, with an English translation if necessary, If it's not busy, then you should be able to arrange a car almost immediately. Most companies require a rental period of three days or more in high season (November to April) and deals can be made for more than seven days' car hire. Basic hire generally only includes statutory third-party insurance; it is advised to take out the optional collision damage waiver premium at US$15-20 per day as even the smallest accident can be very expensive. On Grenada (and Carriacou) a local driver's permit valid for three months costs US$24; on St Vincent and the Grenadines, a local permit valid for six months costs US$26. The car hire companies organize these.

There are numerous car hire companies in Grenada, several in St Vincent, a couple of small outfits with a few cars on Carriacou and Bequia. There are none on the tiny islands; you can walk or cover the small distances on short bus or taxi rides.

Taxi

Taxis are plentiful but are expensive and rates are set by the government and taxi associations so there is no negotiation. You can pay about US$10 for a short ride of no more than a couple of blocks to US$50 for a 30-minute drive or 15-20 miles. Lists of fares are available at the Maurice Bishop International Airport in Grenada and ET Joshua Airport in St Vincent, as well as the tourist offices on some of the other islands. Any hotel can phone a taxi for you and if you find a driver you like, get their card and phone number, and he/she may also offer to be your driver on a tour of the islands, usually informative and fun. Always book ahead if you have a flight to catch.

ON THE WATER
Island hopping

Getting around the islands by ferry offers terrific views and gives you a taste of life on the water but at a fraction of the price of chartering your own yacht or water taxi. The small islands are highly dependent on sea transport and all the docksides are lively places where you will meet locals and see vessels being loaded and unloaded. Ferries are usually punctual. Always check that your chosen boat is operating by asking at the jetties, the tourist office or your hotel; they can phone the ferry companies (or even the captains).

Between Grenada, Carriacou and Petite Martinique

These are linked by the Osprey Lines catamaran (T473-440 8126 (Grenada), www.ospreylines.com) between St George's on Grenada and Hillsborough on Carriacou (90 minutes to two hours), and between Hillsborough and Petite Martinique. It departs St George's Monday-Saturday 0900, and Sunday 0800, returning from Hillsborough every day at 1530; one-way US$31, children (5-12 years) US$19, under fives US$4. There's another service between Hillsborough and Petite Martinique; in Hillsborough a much smaller boat pulls alongside the main ferry (you just step on to the next boat). This in theory takes 20 minutes but can take longer so they do not always run on time. If intending to go to Petite Martinique for a few hours, only buy your ticket when you are sure there will be no delays. It runs Monday-Friday and departs Hillsborough at 1130 and 1530, returning 0715 and 1415; one-way US$8, children (5-12 years) US$4, under fives US$2. There are Osprey ticket offices in St George's and Hillsborough and you can also pay on the ferry.

Between Carriacou (Grenada) and Union Island (St Vincent)

As they are in two different countries, crossing between Carriacou and Union Island involves clearing out of one country and clearing in to the other. The process can take time, but the views are better than any airport. The only ferry service is on the small 37-ft-long jaunty ex-fishing boat with an inboard diesel engine, the *Lady JJ*, owned by Troy Gellizeau (T784-432 5728, www.grenadinesconnection.com). Based in Ashton, Union Island, it does the 45-minute crossing to Hillsborough on Carriacou Monday and Thursday at 0730, and is scheduled to return at 1400, although this is sometimes delayed by the loading of cargo; one-way US$19, children (5-15 years) US$9.50, under fives free.

You must clear customs and immigration to travel between the two. From Carriacou to Union Island you do this at the Hillsborough Police Station on Main Street opposite the jetty by 1100 on the day of departure; tell them you are going on *Lady JJ*, and fill out the forms. Troy or his assistant are likely to be around to help, and will keep your passport and departure forms which will be returned once on Union Island. On arrival at Ashton on Union Island (note: only the *Lady JJ* goes to Ashton, the other ferries go to/from Clifton) you must clear in through immigration and customs at the airport, 2 miles to the west of Ashton. A minibus will be waiting to take you there (probably one of Troy's relatives) for about US$4. Again Troy or his assistant will go with you to assist with formalities.

From Union Island to Carriacou, given that the *Lady JJ* leaves at 0730, to clear out, you have to go to the airport at Clifton the day before at 1500; again explain to the immigration officer you are going on the *Lady JJ* the next morning and fill out the relevant forms, and Troy or his assistant is likely to be there to help you. The next morning, be at the Ashton jetty on time as the *Lady JJ* is very punctual going in this direction. On arrival in Carriacou, you clear in at Hillsborough Police Station, and from here there are taxis across the road and it's a short walk to the places to stay along Main Street. In the unlikely event you are not staying overnight on Carriacou, there is at least time to go to the beach for a swim or have a relaxing lunch in Hillsborough, before the Osprey Lines ferry leaves for St George's in Grenada at 1530 from the same jetty.

In both Hillsborough and Windward on Carriacou, and Ashton and Clifton on Union Island, there are water taxis that can also make this journey, usually very fast and very bumpy and expect to get a little wet; make sure life jackets are provided and someone on board has a mobile phone. Get a recommendation from the tourist office or your hotel, and meet the driver to make sure the boat is one you're happy to travel in. The critical thing is to make absolutely sure that he will assist you in clearing out and clearing in on each island; do not leave Carriacou or Union without an exit stamp in your passport.

The cost for a water taxi is (officially) US$130 per person, but if there's a group of four to six people the price will be lower. In addition, the boat clearance fees could add another US$40 or so; ensure that you know in advance how much the whole trip will cost.

Between St Vincent and Union Island
There is one fast ferry service (for 220), the *Jaden Sun* (T784-451 2192, www.jaden inc.com), on Monday, Wednesday, Friday and Sunday between Kingstown on St Vincent and Union Island via Bequia, Canouan and Mayreau. It departs from both either early morning or mid-afternoon depending on the day (check the website for schedules) and takes two hours. The full one-way fare between Kingstown and Union Island is US$40, children (2-12 years) US$20, under twos free. Fares are less for the shorter journeys. Or the leisurely and long-serving mail boat, *Barracuda* (T784-455 9835) takes 3½ hours between Kingstown and Union Island Monday, Tuesday, Thursday, Friday and Saturday via Canouan and Mayreau (but not Bequia). Departure times vary; the one-way fare between the two is US$19 per person, and again less for the shorter legs. Another passenger and cargo boat, the *Gemstar* (T784-526 1158), runs the same route and prices as the *Barracuda* Tuesday-Saturday.

Between St Vincent and Bequia
As well as the *Jaden Sun*; there's the more regular *Bequia Express*; (T784-458 3472, www.bequiaexpress.com), an efficient service that runs five times a day Monday-Friday, three times on Saturday and twice on Sunday (check the website for schedules); one-way US$9.25 per person. The *Admiral II* (T784-458 3348, www.admiraltytransport.com), offers the same service with similar schedules and prices. Sailing time is one hour but be at the jetties at least 30 minutes prior.

Between St Vincent and Mustique
The ferries above do not stop, but the dedicated Mustique ferry *Endeavour* (T784-457 1531) runs Monday, Tuesday, Thursday and Friday (and the first Wednesday of every month), takes two hours and departs Kingstown at 1400, and returns from Mustique at 0730; one-way US$9.25.

Essentials A-Z

Accident and emergency

Grenada: Police T911 or T473-439 3999.
Fire 911 or T473-440 2112. **Ambulance** T434.
Carriacou: Ambulance T774.
St Vincent: Police T999 or T784-457 1211.
Fire T911 or T784-457 1211.

Customs and duty free

Duty-free imports: 200 cigarettes or
50 cigars or 250 g tobacco, 1.5 litres wine
or spirits, 50 ml of perfume and 250 ml
of eau de toilette. Once in the islands, be
careful about accepting any wildlife-derived
object from villagers and guides. These
could include coral or shell souvenirs. If
you were to buy such items, you should
always consider the environmental and
social impact of your purchase. Attempts to
smuggle controlled products can result in
confiscation, fines and imprisonment under
the **Convention on Trade in Endangered
Species** (**CITES**) (www.cites.org).

Disabled travellers

There are few specific facilities for
disabled; for example, wheelchairs are not
accommodated on public road transport,
the towns have very uneven pavements,
and with the exception of the more modern
upmarket hotels, few accommodation
options have rooms with disabled facilities.
However, it's easy enough to get around
on an organized tour, in a rented vehicle or
boat, and local people will do their very best
to help, so being disabled should not deter
you from visiting.

Dress

Beachwear is for the beach, although it is
illegal to sunbathe naked or topless. In the
evening dress is not formal, although many
local people dress up for 'liming' (see box,
page 25) or parties. Light cotton clothing
is best for the tropical weather but pack a
sweater, cardigan or wrap for cool evenings
and some long sleeves and trousers to ward
off mosquitoes and sandflies. Do not wear
military or camouflage clothing; it is illegal.

Drugs

The Windward Island's location close
to South America makes it a direct
transportation route for cocaine and
marijuana and there is smuggling and
crimes related to drugs. Do not be tempted
to dabble in narcotics; all are illegal and the
law does not allow for 'personal possession'.
If any is found on a yacht, the government
can confiscate the vessel. Larger amounts of
marijuana or any amount of cocaine will get
you charged with trafficking and penalties
are very severe. If you are offered drugs on
the beach, in a rum shop or at a party be
warned, some visitors have been found
themselves arrested a few minutes later.

Electricity

220/240 volts, 50 cycles AC, except for Petit
St Vincent and Palm Island in the Grenadines,
which has 110 volts, 60 cycles. The standard
is British 3 rectangular pin plugs throughout
the islands. However, many hotels also
provide dual voltage with sockets for US and
European 2-pin round plugs and adaptors
are usually available on request.

Embassies and consulates

For a full list of embassies and consulates in
Grenada and St Vincent and the Grenadines
and Grenadian and St Vincentian offices
abroad, see www.embassy.goabroad.com.

Health

See your GP or travel clinic at least 6 weeks before departure for general advice on travel risks and vaccinations. Make sure you have sufficient medical travel insurance, get a dental check, know your own blood group and, if you suffer a long-term condition such as diabetes or epilepsy, obtain a **Medic Alert** bracelet (www.medicalert.org.uk). No special vaccinations are required, but a yellow fever inoculation certificate must be produced on arrival if you have arrived within 5 days of leaving an area affected with yellow fever.

Insect-borne risks

The major risks posed in the region are those caused by insect disease carriers such as mosquitoes and sandflies. The key parasitic and viral diseases are **dengue fever** and **chikungunya** (also known as chik V). Also spread by mosquitos, cases of the **Zika virus** have also been reported in in the Caribbean since early 2016. Although the risk of contracting any of these is very low, it is always a good idea to protect yourself against mosquitoes; try to wear clothes that cover arms and legs at dusk and dawn (when mosquitoes are most active) and also use effective mosquito repellent. Rooms with a/c or fans also help ward off mosquitoes at night.

Diarrhoea or intestinal upset

Some form of diarrhoea or intestinal upset may occur. The standard advice is always to wash your hands before eating and to be careful with drinking water and ice. Tap water on all the islands is generally excellent, but you're in any doubt buy bottled water. Food can also pose a problem; be wary of salads if you don't know whether they have been washed or not. Symptoms should be relatively short lived. Adults can use an anti-diarrhoeal medication to control the symptoms but only for up to 24 hrs. In addition, keep well hydrated by drinking plenty of fluids and eat bland foods. Oral rehydration sachets are a useful way to keep

well hydrated. These should always be used when treating children and the elderly.

Sun

Protect yourself adequately against the sun. Apply a high-factor sunscreen (greater than SPF15) and also make sure it screens against UVB. Prevent heat exhaustion and heatstroke by drinking enough fluids throughout the day. Symptoms of heat exhaustion and heatstroke include dizziness, tiredness and headache. Use rehydration salts mixed with water to replenish fluids and salts. If you suspect heatstroke rather than heat exhaustion, you need to cool the body down quickly (cold showers are particularly effective).

Medical facilities
Grenada

St Augustine Medical Centre, The Bocas, T473-440 6173, www.samsgrenada.com, is a small private hospital in the suburbs above St George's.

St George's General Hospital, Fort George Point, T473-440 2051, www.health.gov.gd, has a 24-hr emergency service. There are other district health centres around the island; check the website for locations.

Carriacou

Princess Royal Hospital, Belair, Hillsborough, T473-443 7400, www.health.gov.gd, has a 24-hr emergency service and critical or complicated medical cases are transferred to Grenada.

St Vincent

Milton Cato Memorial Hospital, Bentick Square, off Leeward Highway, Kingstown, T784-456 1185, accident and emergency

WARNING
Little Apple of Death

The manchineel tree (*Hippomane mancinella*) is an endangered species, but is also considered the most dangerous tree on earth, and the Spanish dubbed it *manzanilla de la muerte*, or 'little apple of death'. Resembling a small green crab apple, the fruits are the most obvious threat, and can cause hours of agony – and potentially death – with a single bite. But all parts of this tree contain strong toxins, and interaction with, and ingestion of, any part including the bark and leaves may be lethal. Even without touching the tree itself, people (and car paint) have been burned by the thick, caustic sap as rain washes it off branches overhead. You can find the manchineel especially along the beaches; do not shelter under them from the sun or when it's raining.

T784-456 1955. There are also district health centres in Chateaubelair and Georgetown; see www.health.gov.vc.

Bequia
Bequia Hospital, up the hill from Back St, Port Elizabeth, T784-458 3294.

Mustique
The island doctor, T784-488 8353, runs a clinic and dispensary offering 24-hr medical care, and critical or complicated cases are transferred to Barbados.

Canouan
Canouan Health Centre, Retreat Village, T784-458 8305.

Mayreau
There's a small clinic in the village with a nurse and a visiting doctor; better to get the ferry to one of the other islands.

Union Island
Union Island Health Centre, off the road to Ashton near the post office, Clifton, T784-458 8339.

Useful websites
www.btha.org British Travel Health Association.
www.cdc.gov US government site that gives excellent advice on travel health and details of disease outbreaks.

www.fco.gov.uk British Foreign and Commonwealth Office travel site has useful information on each country, people, climate and a list of UK embassies/consulates.
www.fitfortravel.nhs.uk A-Z of vaccine/health advice for each country.
www.travelhealth.co.uk Independent travel health site with advice on vaccination, travel insurance and health risks.
www.who.int World Health Organization, updates of disease outbreaks.

Insurance

Before departure, it is vital to take out comprehensive travel insurance. There are a wide variety of policies to choose from, so shop around. At the very least, the policy should cover medical expenses, including repatriation to your home country in the event of a medical emergency. There is no substitute for suitable precautions against petty crime, but if you do have something stolen, report the incident to the nearest police station and ensure you get a police report and case number. You will need these to make any claim from your insurance company.

> **Tip...**
> Make sure you have travel insurance as hospital bills need to be paid at the time of admittance, so keep all paperwork to make a claim.

Language

English is the official language.

LGBT travellers

Technically same-sex relationships are illegal on all these islands but it is not enforced and is largely tolerated, although public displays of affection are ill-advised.

Money

US$1 = EC$2.67; UK£1 = EC$3.50; €1 = EC$3 (Jul 2016)

Currency

The currency on Grenada and St Vincent and the Grenadines is the East Caribbean dollar, EC$ or XCD. Notes are for EC$5, 10, 20, 50 and 100. Coins come in 5, 10, 25 cents, EC$1 and 2. US dollar cash is widely accepted by businesses at the official fixed exchange rate of US$1 = EC$2.67, although most prefer to deal in East Caribbean dollars, and you will receive any change in East Caribbean dollars. Some things, such as hotel rates, air fares and sometimes activities such as diving and tours, are quoted in US dollars, but you can pay in either. On departure you can change East Caribbean dollars back into US dollars or other currencies at the foreign exchange bureaux at Grenada's Maurice Bishop International Airport or St Vincent's ET Joshua Airport.

Changing money

The easiest currencies to exchange are US dollars, UK pounds and euros, but banks also generally change Barbados and Canadian dollars, and the Swiss franc. There are ATMs and bureaux de change at Grenada's Maurice Bishop International Airport and St Vincent's ET Joshua Airport, but the smaller airports do not have these facilities. On Grenada there are plenty of banks with ATMs in St George's and the Grand Anse area, but very few in the northern part of the island. On St Vincent these can be found in Kingstown and the Villa hotel area in the south, but again there are very few in the rest of the island. On both, the few around the island in rural areas cannot be relied upon for cash; if you are travelling to the northern end of each, make sure you have enough. On the Grenadines, there are a couple of banks with ATMs on both Bequia and Union Islands, one on each for Mayreau and Canouan, but none on Mustique.

ATMs generally only dispatch notes in increments of EC$100, which are often too large for people to have change; break bigger notes when you can and save small change for items like bus fares, snacks and drinks.

Credit, debit and currency cards

Credit and debit cards are widely accepted by the larger hotels, shops and restaurants, airlines, car hire firms and tour operators. An additional levy of 5% may be charged but some businesses, so check first if paying a sizeable bill. **Visa** is the most widely accepted card, followed by **MasterCard**; **AMEX** and **Diners** far less so. Pre-paid currency cards allow you to preload money from your bank account, fixed at the day's exchange rate. They look like a credit or debit card and are issued by specialist money changing companies, such as **Travelex** and **Caxton FX**. You can top up and check your balance by phone, online and sometimes by text.

Tip...
If travelling elsewhere in the Caribbean, the East Caribbean dollar is also used in Anguilla, Antigua and Barbuda, Dominica, Montserrat, St Kitts and Nevis and St Lucia. However, Barbados has a different currency, the Barbadian or Bajan dollar, $ or BBD, which is fixed at US$1 = BDS$1.98. You will be able to exchange East Caribbean dollars to BBD at Barbados's Grantley Adams International Airport.

Opening hours

Grenada
Banks Mon-Thu 0800-1400; Fri 0800-1600.
Shops Mon-Fri 0800-1600, Sat 0800-1300, although tourist shops will be open if there is a cruise ship in port and the larger supermarkets open until 2000 and on Sun until about 1300.

St Vincent and the Grenadines
Banks Mon-Thu 0800-1300, Fri 0800-1700.
Shops Mon-Fri 0800-1600, Sat 0800-1300, although the larger supermarkets open until at least 2000 and on Sun until about 1300.

Post and courier services

DHL, www.dhl.com.vc, and **Fedex**, www.fedex.com, are in Grenada and St Vincent and the Grenadines.

Grenada
The postal service is run by the **Grenada Postal Corporation**. The main post office is at Burns Point, off the Carenage in the port area, St George's, T473-440 2526, and there are sub-post offices in the smaller towns and villages.

Carriacou
In Hillsborough the post office is next to the jetty. Post office hours are Mon-Fri 0800-1600.

St Vincent and the Grenadines
The postal service is run by **SVG POST** (St Vincent and the Grenadines Postal Corporation). The General Post Office is on Halifax St in Kingstown, T784-457 1744, and there are sub-post offices in the smaller towns, villages and islands;

Bequia, Mustique, Canouan, Mayreau, and Union Island
Post office hours are Mon-Fri 0800-1500, Sat 0800-1130.

Public holidays

Grenada
Jan 1 New Year's Day
Feb 7 Independence Day
Mar/Apr (varies) Good Friday
Mar/Apr (varies) Easter Monday
May 1 Labour Day
May/Jun (varies) Whit Monday
May/Jun (varies) Corpus Christi
Aug (1st Mon) Emancipation Day
Oct 25 Thanksgiving Day
Dec 25 Christmas Day
Dec 26 Boxing Day

St Vincent and the Grenadines
Jan 1 New Year's Day
Mar 14 National Heroes Day
Mar/Apr (varies) Good Friday
Mar/Apr (varies) Easter Monday
May 1 Labour Day
May/Jun (varies) Whit Monday
Aug 1 Emancipation Day
Oct 27 Independence Day
Dec 25 Christmas Day
Dec 26 Boxing Day

Safety

The people of these islands are, as a rule, exceptionally friendly, honest and ready to help you. Most visitors will not experience any issues and will have a safe and enjoyable stay, so there is no need to get paranoid about your safety. The general common sense rules apply to prevent petty theft: don't exhibit anything valuable and keep wallets and purses out of sight; do not leave your possessions unattended on the beach; use a hotel safe to store valuables, money and passports; lock hotel room doors as noisy fans and a/c can provide cover for sneak thieves; at night, avoid deserted areas, including the beaches, and always take taxis. Don't leave items on hotel or villa balconies when you go out. If you are driving, avoid travel outside major populated areas at night as erratic driving by others can be a problem, avoid stopping if at all possible and keep doors and windows locked. If you are staying on a yacht you should make sure it is secure, day or night.

Tax

Grenada
Hotel tax (10%) and service charge (10%) is charged by all accommodation options, usually as a single charge of 20%. Check if this has been included in quoted rates. VAT (15%) in restaurants is nearly always included in menu prices; but 10% service charge is usually added to the bill.

St Vincent and the Grenadines
Hotel tax (10%) and VAT (15%) is charged by all accommodation options. The VAT is often included in rack rates, but check exactly what is included in quoted rates as an extra 25% can be substantial. VAT (15%) in restaurants is nearly always included in menu prices; but 10% service charge is usually added to the bill.

Telephone and internet

The international code for Grenada is 473 and St Vincent and the Grenadines is 784, both followed by a 7-digit number. **Digicel**, www.digicelgroup.com, and **Flow**, www.discoverflow.co are Caribbean-wide cellular and internet providers. Local SIM cards and start-up packs are available to purchase at phone shops. In Grenada, both Digicel and Flow have shops at the Esplanade Mall at the Cruise Ship Terminal, and there are other outlets at the shopping centres in Grand Anse. In St Vincent and the Grenadines there are shops in Kingstown and the other urban areas, and even Bequia, Canouan and Union Island have small outlets.

Almost all hotels have Wi-Fi, as well as many restaurants and cafés, even beach bars.

Time

Atlantic Standard Time, 4 hrs behind GMT, 1 hr ahead of EST.

Tourist information

The tourist offices on each island are listed in the relevant chapters, in Listings under Tourist information. Good free maps for both countries are published by the tourism associations and private publishers produce ones paid for by advertisers; they can easily be found at the tourist offices and on reception desks of hotels.

Visas and immigration

To enter Grenada or St Vincent and the Grenadines all visitors must have a passport (valid for 6 months after the date of entry) and adequate unused pages (allow at least 2). Even though you may not always get asked for it, all travellers need to be able to produce a return or onward ticket, proof that they can support themselves during their stay (a credit card will suffice), and an address at which they will be staying (the hotel on your first night should be enough).

Grenada
Visas are not required for tourist visits of up to 90 days for almost all nationalities including citizens of the USA, UK, EU, most Commonwealth countries, South Africa and the Caribbean. Some Eastern European countries can apply for visas on arrival. A few nationalities including China and some in South America are permitted entry for 30 days.

St Vincent and the Grenadines
Visas are not required for tourist visits for almost all nationalities; however, the length of stay permitted varies. Citizens of the Caribbean can stay up to 6 months, UK and EU up to 90 days, other Commonwealth countries, South Africa and the USA, 30 days. Visas are required from nationals of the Dominican Republic, Jordan, Syria, Lebanon, China, Iraq, Iran and Nigeria and must be obtained through embassies in advance.

Weights and measures

Imperial.

Index

*Entries in **bold** refer to maps*

FOOTPRINT

Features

Fish Friday 73
Grenada flourishing at the Chelsea Flower Show 37
Grenada's birds 48
Grenada's five best wreck dives 80
Grenada Underwater Sculpture Park 81
Happy Island 136
Hiking La Soufrière 107
Island hopping 150
Island time 141
Ivan the Terrible 46
'Jack Iron' rum 76

Janet houses 44
Julien Fédon, revolutionary and folk hero 56
Kirani James 53
Leatherback turtles 49
Limin' 25
Little Apple of Death 154
Moonhole 128
Mustique mules 142
Natural disasters on St Vincent 98
Nutmeg 51
Spice products 78

Credits

Footprint credits

Editor: Jo Williams
Production and layout: Emma Bryers
Maps: Kevin Feeney
Colour section: Patrick Dawson

Publisher: Felicity Laughton
            Patrick Dawson
Marketing: Kirsty Holmes
Sales: Diane McEntee
Advertising and content partnerships:
Debbie Wylde

Photography credits

Front cover: AJP/Shutterstock.com
Back cover top: Pawel Kazmierczak/
Shutterstock.com
Back cover bottom: Styve Reineck/
Shutterstock.com
Inside front cover: Dosfotos/Superstock.
com, Shane P White, Sylvain Grandadam/
Superstock.com.

Colour section
Page 1: Helen Patchett.
Page 2: Styve Reineck/Shutterstock.com.
Page 4: John Miller/SuperStock.com.
Page 5: Eye Ubiquitous/SuperStock.com,
© Robert Harding Produc - www.superstock.
com, Travel Library Ltd/SuperStock.com.
Page 6: Eye Ubiquitous/SuperStock.com,
Helen Patchett, Shane P White.
Page 7: Michael DeFreitas/SuperStock.com,
Helen Patchett.
Page 8: Chris Parker/SuperStock.com.

Duotones
Page 26: alfotokunst/Shutterstock.com.
Page 86: Achim Baque/Shutterstock.com.
Page 110: Verena Matthew/Shutterstock.com.

Printed in Spain by GraphyCems

Publishing information

Footprint Grenada, St Vincent &
the Grenadines
2nd edition
© Footprint Handbooks Ltd
September 2016

ISBN: 978 1 911082 04 0
CIP DATA: A catalogue record for this book
is available from the British Library

® Footprint Handbooks and the
Footprint mark are a registered
trademark of Footprint Handbooks Ltd

Published by Footprint
6 Riverside Court
Lower Bristol Road
Bath BA2 3DZ, UK
T +44 (0)1225 469141
F +44 (0)1225 469461
footprinttravelguides.com

Distributed in the USA by
National Book Network, Inc.

Every effort has been made to ensure that
the facts in this guidebook are accurate.
However, travellers should still obtain advice
from consulates, airlines, etc about travel
and visa requirements before travelling.
The authors and publishers cannot
accept responsibility for any loss, injury
or inconvenience however caused.